OLD RUSSIAN MURALS

AND MOSAICS

BY VIKTOR LAZAREV

PHAIDON

SS. Matthew and Luke from 'The Last Judgement'. Fresco, 1408. Vladimir, Cathedral of the Dormition

OLD RUSSIAN
MURALS
& MOSAICS

FROM THE XI TO THE XVI CENTURY

BY VIKTOR LAZAREV

PHAIDON

The translation from the original Russian manuscript
has been made by BORIS RONIGER and revised by NANCY DUNN.

The Glossary and Iconographical Index
were compiled by P. B. HETHERINGTON and the
General Index by ISABEL HARIADES

MADE IN GREAT BRITAIN
TEXT AND MONOCHROME ILLUSTRATIONS PRINTED BY GEO. GIBBONS LTD · LEICESTER
COLOUR PLATES ENGRAVED AND PRINTED BY JOHN SWAIN & SON LTD · BARNET
BOUND BY A. W. BAIN & CO. LTD · LONDON

CONTENTS

FOREWORD

THE GENERAL PUBLIC is fairly well informed about Russian icon-painting, but not about ancient Russian murals, and only recently has a start been made towards publishing them in a systematic way; despite the considerable quality of early Russian mosaics and frescoes, a comprehensive work about them is still lacking. The fascination of these wall decorations lies in their monumentality, freshness and spontaneity of expression, and the simple, concise nature of their artistic methods. Although a direct and organic continuation of the Byzantine tradition, they have a specific character of their own which is deeply and unmistakably Russian. For this reason, within the general framework of medieval art and culture, they deserve their own special niche.

The mosaics and frescoes reproduced in this book are of course confined to those which either escaped the fate of over-painting or, alternatively, have had their over-painting removed. The tremendous advances made by restoration techniques during the last forty years have brought to light entirely new aspects of medieval painting, and although the works of art themselves no longer look exactly as they did at the time they were produced (usually owing to changes in the colouring), we do at least know that they are *genuine* and not forgeries or imitations. In the nineteenth century, art historians did not have the same opportunities for working with genuine material: as a rule they were confronted with works which had been ruined either by over-painting or clumsy restoration, and consequently, their prime concern was not with aesthetic considerations but with iconography. For us, however, medieval art has acquired an altogether new and exciting significance: it seems to exhibit many parallels with the creative searchings of contemporary artists and has recently been granted its rightful place among the great aesthetic manifestations of the past.

It has also become clear that within the general framework of medieval culture there existed a large number of local schools, each contributing its share to the common storehouse of art. In this respect ancient Russia was no different from other countries; on her territory too there arose a number of individual local schools. Of these the most important were the schools of Kiev, Vladimir-Suzdal', Novgorod and Moscow, and we are now able to connect with each of them not only icons but also mural decorations. Thus it has become possible for us to retrace the various artistic trends with a fair degree of accuracy.

It is a great tragedy that so many fine works of early Russian monumental painting did not survive the Second World War. Novgorod, in particular, being near the front line, suffered very badly; while the frescoes of Nereditsa and Volotovo, the Skovorodsky Monastery, and the church of Kovalyovo were destroyed in the fierce fighting. Fortunately for us, photographs had already been made of these works, and we are able to include them in the present study. They are of inestimable value, for without them our knowledge of early Russian monumental painting would be infinitely poorer.

In order to avoid undue bibliographical repetition, I have adopted the following principles: in the notes to the Text, only those books and articles are cited which refer to paintings discussed but not reproduced. Literature on the works reproduced is listed in the bibliography, which for the sake of convenience has been split up into sections corresponding to the groups of paintings analysed. Finally, in the descriptive notes, reference is made only to special monographs which either elucidate particular problems or are in some way controversial.

I should like in conclusion to thank all those who have assisted me in the preparation of this book. My efforts would not have borne fruit without the friendly advice of the restorers, L. P. Kalenichenko, the late E. S. Mamalat, O. F. Plyushch and V. V. Filatov, or that of such acknowledged experts on early Russian painting as the late Yu. N. Dmitriyev and N. E. Mnyova. I am also greatly indebted to the photographers, who have been most generous with their time and have managed, despite arduous conditions, to produce excellent results. Several of the photographs were taken by the late A. V. Lyadov, a man of exceptional talent in this field; others were taken by L. I. Kumok and V. V. Robinov. Remembering our joint efforts, and the many occasions when, balanced on somewhat flimsy scaffolding, we had to contend with lofty domes and vaults, I should like to offer them my sincere gratitude for their unfailing courage and perseverance.

―――――――――――

Numbers in square brackets throughout the text refer to the illustrations;
italic numerals refer to the figures illustrating the Descriptive Notes on pp. 225–269

―――――――――――

OLD RUSSIAN MURALS
AND MOSAICS

1. S. Demetrius, Vladimir

INTRODUCTION

THE ARTISTS AND THEIR METHODS OF WORK

IN THE HISTORY of early Russian monumental painting of the eleventh to the fifteenth centuries, three distinct periods are discernible. The first of these extends from the end of the tenth to the first third of the thirteenth century, that is, up to the time of the invasion of Rus' by the Mongols. The principal centre in the early stages of development was Kiev, capital of the powerful Kievan state, and here not only frescoes but also mosaics dating from the eleventh and twelfth centuries have been preserved. This latter genre of monumental art, very strongly Byzantine in influence, disappeared from Rus' in the later centuries, when it was completely ousted by the less expensive and increasingly popular technique of fresco.

Although Kiev was the dominant artistic force in this early period, local schools of painting—which reached their highest peak of development in the twelfth and early thirteenth centuries—also flourished in Vladimir, Novgorod and Pskov. While absorbing the artistic and cultural traditions of Kiev, these schools produced their own original solutions to the problems of monumental painting—solutions which represented a progressively radical departure from the Byzantine heritage.

The second period, which embraces the thirteenth and fourteenth centuries, was a time of great upheaval in ancient Russia, when the Tartar invasions not only caused the breaking-up of groups of artists and craftsmen but also destroyed the works of art themselves. The process of feudal segmentation of the land with the consequent dispersion of national strength was greatly intensified at this time. Novgorod and Pskov were more fortunate than other Russian towns, which had been devastated: the Tartar hordes did not reach them, and they retained their independence. For this reason all surviving fourteenth-century works of Russian monumental painting are either in Novgorod, where the celebrated Theophanes the Greek worked, or in Pskov.

The third period covers the fifteenth century. This was the time which saw the rapid emergence of Moscow as a political force, whose professed aim was to overcome the Tartars and unite under its rule the divided Russian territories. Associated with this era of national development is the work of Theophanes the Greek (*c.* 1340–*c.* 1410), who moved from Novgorod to Moscow, and of two famous Russian masters, Andrey Rublyov (*c.* 1370–*c.* 1430) and Dionisy (*c.* 1440–*c.* 1509). With the work of Dionisy we come to the end of that period of Russian art history which forms the subject of the present book.

The ancient literary sources, primarily chronicles, have preserved a considerable amount of information about ecclesiastical paintings, those who commissioned them, and occasionally, the masters who executed them, and on this basis we are able to reconstruct the creative activities of the early Russian painters who, like all medieval craftsmen, occupied a modest place in the hierarchic structures of feudal society.

Churches and monasteries in Rus' were almost invariably founded by princes or members of the higher clergy, and it was they who commissioned the works of art. This was especially true of the Kievan state and the Principality of Vladimir-Suzdal', but in the free cities of ancient Russia—Novgorod and Pskov—patrons were also found among the other ranks of society, such as the *Posadniki* (magistrates), wealthy boyars (patricians), merchant guilds, associations of local citizens (*ulichane*) and craft guilds. However, after Moscow had achieved hegemony at the end of the fourteenth century and was intensifying its efforts towards centralization of the State, this type of donor became less common and the percentage of secular and ecclesiastical aristocratic patrons again increased. These changes in the social character of the patronage to a great extent explains the more refined nature of the art of the principalities of Kiev, Vladimir-Suzdal', and Moscow, and the more popular nature of that of Novgorod and Pskov.

Like all medieval artists, the early Russian painters belonged to the artisan class. In ancient Rus' artisans of all categories were called by the same name: *remeslennik* (meaning artisan; also *remesl'nik*, *rem'stv'nik*, *remestvyanik*), or *khudozhnik* (meaning artist; also *khudozh'nik*) or *khitrets* (*khytr'ts*, *khitr'ts*) in the sense of *iskusnik*—a man of art and great skill. But the word 'master' which could be used for the least qualified craftsman as well as for architects, painters, and even military experts,[1] was the term most commonly used. When referring to the 'masters' of painting, the Russian chronicles made the following distinctions: *ikon'nik*, *ikonik*—painter of icons; *obrazopis'ts*—painter of images; *pisets*—painter; *zhivopis'ts*—painter of living things.[2] Unfortunately we have no way of knowing the precise nuances implicit in these various terms, and the fact that the fresco-painters in Rus' nearly always produced icons as well further complicates the issue.

In ancient Russia the profession of painter was endowed with great moral authority. Icon-painting was considered an activity pleasing to God (*bogougodnoye*), and the chronicles always speak with respect of the great 'masters'. The workshop was the basic cell of production, presided over by the master (*stareyshina* meaning elder, *nachal'nik* meaning chief)[3] under whom worked pupils and assistants (in the chronicles they are called the *yunoty*, i.e. the young).[4] The activity of such a workshop was closely bound up with the commissions in hand. As the making of icons required not only skill but also involved a considerable outlay on colours, particularly gold and silver, the fees charged were relatively high. The chronicler, speaking in the *Pechersky-Paterik* of the icon-painter Alimpy, stresses that he did not take up his profession for financial gain.[5] When in 1481 the celebrated Moscovite painter, Dionisy, together with three other masters, executed for the Uspensky Cathedral (Cathedral of the Dormition) the icons for the iconostasis (Deesis—in Russian *Deisus*, feasts and prophets), he was paid 100 roubles—an enormous amount for the time.[6]

Most of the painters' workshops were, it seems, attached to the courts of important principalities and to monasteries (so-called patrimonial—*votchinnoye*—handicraft), and were dependent on princes, boyars and the church hierarchy.[7] But undoubtedly in the towns there also existed free-lance artisans who carried out commissions. A workshop of this type, destroyed in 1240, was excavated by Professor M. K. Karger in the grounds of the Mikhailovski-Zlatoverkhy Monastery of Kiev.[8] Among the objects found were fourteen small clay pots with the remains of mineral colours, an almost complete set of iron tools for the processing of wood (axe, borer, plane, chisel, pick), scraps from the production of amber beads, a bronze lamp and a small silver decoration from an equestrian harness. The artisan who worked here did not restrict himself to the painting of icons but, in order to earn more money, also made amber beads and repaired various metal objects.

Since in ancient Rus', both icons and frescoes were painted by the same masters, it is of interest to describe the methods used in their respective production. In the case of icons, both the workshop and the artisans' living quarters were housed in the same building. However, when it came to executing monumental wall-paintings, the artists were naturally required to move to wherever the church happened to be. Monumental work also led to the necessity for assembling several artists from different workshops. Such associations for joint work (*arteli* or *druzhiny* as they are called by the chroniclers) were under the direction of a supreme master (*stareyshina*),[9] and undoubtedly some of these *artels* were travelling *artels*.[10] In their journeyings from one commission to another, a *druzhina* could change its composition and be directed by successive masters. As no guilds existed in Rus', the *artels* were not governed by strict regulations: the artists worked together on the basis of free contract. It is possible that, when orders for monumental paintings had been temporarily exhausted, such *artels* of travelling masters returned home to their original icon workshops, or, alternatively, set up new workshops—where they both lived and worked under the same roof—in some other district.

It would be erroneous to think that the painters of ancient Rus' were exclusively drawn from the ranks of the clerics. The chronicles show that the majority of those engaged in painting were in fact laymen, though often the monks worked side by side with them forming a single *druzhina*. For example, the monk Andrey Rublyov collaborated with the layman Theophanes the Greek in the decorations for the Cathedral of the Annunciation in Moscow, and the layman Dionisy worked at the Uspensky Cathedral, also in Moscow, together with the priest Timothy.[11]

Until comparatively recently, historians believed that nearly all the early Russian icons were made by visiting Byzantine masters, but this mistaken idea is easily refuted by the surviving icons and frescoes, the overwhelming majority of which were executed by Russian painters, and by the testimony of the chroniclers: only in five cases do they refer to Greek masters working in Rus'—and this in a time-span of more than 500 years!

The earliest reference to the inviting of Byzantine masters to work in Rus' occurs in 989 in the chronicle *Povest' Vremmennykh Let*, which records that when the Grand-prince Vladimir decided to erect the Church of the Holy Mother of God (the famous Desyatinnaya Church), he 'sent to Greece for masters'.[12] The reliability of this statement is beyond dispute. It is also certain that between 1043 and 1067 Greek mosaicists and painters (not mentioned in the chronicles) worked in the Church of S. Sophia in Kiev, collaborating with the local artists and directing the large Byzanto-Russian workshop which was intimately linked with the building of the cathedral. A later source—the *Kievo-Pechersky Paterik* (mid-thirteenth century) speaks of the activities of Greek painters in Kievan Rus', saying that 'icon-painters' were summoned from Constantinople by the Abbot Nikon for the purpose of decorating the great Uspenskaya Church (Church of the Dormition) in the Pechersky Monastery, and that they were later buried in one of the chapels there.[13] Alimpy, one of the Kievan painters, was a pupil of these visiting artists and worked with them on the mosaics for the apse of the Uspenskaya Church.[14] Since the decoration of the interior of this church was begun in 1083 under Nikon, fourth abbot of the Pechersky Monastery, Alimpy must have studied under the Greek masters during the eighties of the eleventh century. Although the accuracy of many of the statements in the *Paterik* has been called in question,[15] this particular one can to some extent be substantiated. The summoning of Greek masters to execute mosaics in the Church of the Dormition and their employment of a local master, Alimpy, is not in itself beyond the bounds of possibility and the fact that we now know with certainty that Greek masters were engaged, a little later, on the mosaics for the Church of the Archangel Michael adds to its plausibility.

It was quite usual at the end of the tenth and during the eleventh century when Russian monumental art was in its infancy, to invite Greek masters, particularly mosaicists, for the purpose of learning from them; but in the twelfth and following centuries this practice became increasingly rare. In the chronicles of Novgorod only three Greek masters are mentioned: 'the Greek Petrovits',[16] who in the year 1196 decorated the interior of the Church of the Holy Mother of God on the Gate; 'the Greek Isaiah' with his fellow-workers,[17] who in the year 1338 did frescoes for the Church of the Entry into Jerusalem; and Theophanes the Greek, who in 1378 was working in the Church of the Transfiguration.[18] Some Greek painters not mentioned in the chronicles were active also at Vladimir at the end of the twelfth century, where they co-operated with Russian assistants in the decoration of the Cathedral of S. Demetrius.

Statements in the Troitskaya and Nikonovskaya chronicles throw light on the special relationship existing between the Greek artists and the Russian masters. In 1344 the Metropolitan Theognost, a Greek from Constantinople, commissioned Greek masters to decorate his court church in Moscow.[19] In the following year, another Moscow church—the monastery church of Spas-on-Bor—was painted by order of Anastasiya, wife of the great Prince Simeon Ivanovich. This latter commission was carried out by a group of painters, presided over by Goitan, Semen and Ivan, whom the chronicler describes as: 'Russians by birth, Greeks by training'.[20] There can be little doubt that the chronicler was referring to the same Greek masters whom the Metropolitan Theognost had summoned a year earlier.

Theophanes the Greek, who migrated from Novgorod to Moscow, also had Russian pupils: in the year 1395, 'Theophanes, painter of icons, Greek philosopher', was painting in the Church of the Nativity of the Virgin in the Kremlin, together with Semen Cherny (Simeon the Black) and assisted by 'their pupils';[21] four years later he was working in the Cathedral of the Archangel Michael in the Kremlin, again together 'with his pupils';[22] and, finally, in 1405 he was engaged on paintings for the Church of the Annunciation, again in the Kremlin, where his collaborators were the elder (*starets*) Prokhor and the monk (*chernets*) Andrey Rublyov.[23] The above statements from the chronicles once again confirm that in ancient Rus' *druzhinas* for the decorating of churches were formed on the basis of voluntary co-operation between masters, who usually on joining the *druzhina* brought their pupils with them.

From these sources, we can draw the following conclusions concerning the activities of Greek painters in Rus': firstly, the instances of their coming to Rus' were rare; secondly, they usually co-operated with local masters; and lastly, they nearly always instructed young Russian artists, who then became their assistants. Whether they were bound by some agreement with the Russian civil and ecclesiastical authorities to instruct young Russian artists, we do not know. It is possible that there existed in Rus' an arrangement similar to that drawn up in 1258 in Venice where, by order of the procurators, each Greek mosaicist was obliged to take on two pupils; these were forbidden to do any work at home and had to participate in the work being done at San Marco.[24]

Needless to say, the widespread diffusion of monumental and easel painting in Rus' as early as the eleventh century meant that the vast majority of the workshops were manned by indigenous artists: both teachers and pupils were most commonly Russians, and only in very exceptional cases did they get a chance to learn from visiting Byzantine artists. From the eleventh to the fifteenth century, the *druzhinas* who painted the churches were mainly composed of Russians.

Turning now to the method of work employed by the masters of monumental painting, we must first consider the question of how many artists were needed to form an *artel'*. In the decoration of any given church, the number of persons employed naturally depended on the size of the church and the amount of time laid down by the patron for the completion of the work. Thus, for example, in S. Sophia at Kiev, owing to the vast dimensions of the cathedral, no less than eight mosaicists and a large *druzhina* of painters were employed.[25] In the small Church of S. George at Staraya Ladoga (*c.* 1167) on the other hand, two masters were sufficient to carry out the decorative scheme,[26] while at least three masters[27] were active in the Cathedral of the Nativity of the Virgin in the Snetogorsky Monastery near Pskov (1313). Due to the special circumstances involved,[28] at least eight painters worked in the church of Spas-on-Nereditsa near Novgorod (1199); they were required to complete the decoration at great speed within a month, because of the precarious political position of Prince Yaroslav Vladimirovich, the patron.[29]

The fourteenth and fifteenth centuries saw a slight increase in the number of masters, primarily because the iconostasis had become larger. The icons of the iconostasis were painted by the same masters as did the fresco-work. I. E. Grabar' writes: At the end of the fourteenth and beginning of the fifteenth century the expression *Podpisat' Tserkov'* (to paint a church) referred not only to the mural decorations but also to the painting of icons for the iconostasis. It was just at this period that the iconostasis was assuming a new importance: it was fast becoming the decorative focal-point of the church and its evolution was nearing its apogee.[30] This explains why a greater number of masters was required at this time. In the small churches built in Novgorod in the fourteenth century (Volotovo, Kovalyovo) the number of masters engaged remained small—about two or three; but in Moscow where larger churches were being erected, the numbers rapidly increased. For example, in 1344, Zachariya, Dionisy, Iosif, Nicolas, and members of their *druzhina* painted in the Church of the Archangel Michael in Moscow,[31] while in the following year the church of the Spas, also in Moscow, was frescoed by Goitan, Semen, and Ivan, assisted by their pupils and other members of the *druzhina*.[32] When in 1484, the renowned Moscovite painter, Dionisy, undertook at the request of the Reverend Iosif Volokolamsky to paint the Church of the Dormition in the Iosifo-Volokolamsky Monastery, he engaged not only his sons, Theodosy and Vladimir, to collaborate with him, but also the *starets* (monk) Paisy, and two of Iosif's nephews, Dosifey and Vassian.[33] This sharp rise in the number of masters was due not alone to the increased importance of the iconostasis but also to the changed character of the painting. In the fifteenth century, the range of subjects to be depicted was extended, and each subject comprised many figures, smaller in size than had hitherto been the case; all this not only prolonged the work, but also made it more complicated. Thus by the seventeenth century, by which time the great tradition of monumental painting had declined, it was quite normal for several dozen artists to participate on a scheme, and the work could drag on for two years or even longer.[34]

We may summarize as follows: the *druzhinas* of painters in the twelfth to thirteenth centuries were relatively small—from two to six masters, excluding pupils and assistants. In exceptional cases this number could grow to eight or more, as for example in S. Sophia of Kiev, because of its great size, and in Nereditsa, because of the precarious political position of its founder. The most common type of collaboration found was where two or three masters agreed to work together, each bringing with him his own assistants. When the work was completed, the *druzhina* either disbanded or, remaining as it was, embarked on new decorative schemes.[35]

Owing to the rigours of the Russian climate, decorative work could only be begun one year after completion of the structure, so as to allow the walls to dry out thoroughly.[36] When donors were reluctant to wait, they met with the wholly-justified resistance of the masters. Of interest in this connexion is the reaction of the painters to Evfimy, Archbishop of Novgorod, when he insisted they begin decorating the Church of John the Theologian and the refectory of the Vezhishchsky Monastery which had only just been built: 'But the painters forbade this, saying that no painting could take place for a year or more, until the building had dried out'.[37]

The decoration of churches was usually begun in the spring, not later than May, and the masters strove wherever possible to complete their work in one season. The painting could only be done effectively during the mild weather, and was generally not feasible after September. Where the church was small, the decoration could in most cases be completed in one year; but this was not always so. For example, it was not possible in the case of the Church of the Archangel Michael at Moscow, and the chronicler explains why: 'They did not finish the decoration that summer . . . because they had to paint on a very small scale'.[38] When in 1468 it was impossible to terminate the decoration of the Church of S. Nicolas-na-Ostrovke at Novgorod in one season, the chronicler explained it was because of the early onset of the cold weather: 'They could not paint it in time on account of the winter'.[39]

Mosaic-work, as compared with the art of fresco, had deeper roots in tradition. Kievan Rus' took it from the Byzantines and did not add to it anything essentially new. There is no doubt that Greek masters worked on the mosaics in Kiev, but both at S. Sophia and the Church of the Archangel Michael they engaged the local masters to help, not only in the decoration itself, but also in the production of tesserae. This is confirmed by the excavations carried out by Soviet archaeologists in Podol and in the garden of the Metropolitan at Lavra.[40] In Podol, in the stratum dating from the late eleventh to early twelfth centuries, were discovered the remains of a workshop containing furnaces lined with clay, pieces of glass alloys and tesserae. In the Metropolitan's garden, not far from the Cathedral of the Dormition, a furnace with crucibles, pots, large pieces of glass, tesserae, glass foam, etc., came to light in the stratum dating from the end of the eleventh century; also pieces of

2. Reconstructed Model of S. Sophia, Kiev

3. Interior of S. Sophia, Kiev

4. Interior of the Church of the Saviour, Nereditsa

lead—the basic ingredient of smalt; and pieces of sulphur, cobalt and iron—the colouring ingredients of smalt. If therefore, during the construction of the Cathedral of the Dormition (1073–89) a special workshop existed for on-the-spot processing of glass and the production of smalt, the same was probably true of the Desyatinnaya Church (989–996) and S. Sophia (1037–46). This arrangement marked the first step in the *rapprochement* of the Greek masters with the 'young people' of Kiev, whose help was essential for their work.

At least eight mosaicists worked in S. Sophia of Kiev, and it is easy to distinguish the hand of each. This Byzantine *artel* must have been composed not only of masters from the capital, Constantinople, but also of Byzantine provincial artists, since otherwise it would be difficult to explain certain stylistic differences in the mosaics.[41] Probably it was the mosaicists and their chief master who founded the workshop, in which Greeks and Russians worked side by side and which, in the forties and fifties of the eleventh century, was the principal nursery of art in Kiev. After completing the mosaics, this workshop turned its attention to frescoes, thereby attracting the local masters in increasing numbers.

In common with the mosaics of Byzantium, the plaster bed of the Kievan mosaics consisted of three layers. In S. Sophia, the first layer, applied directly on to the masonry, has a thickness of 15–20 mm.; the second, generally utilized for the preparatory sketch, is slightly thicker (18–25 mm.), while the third or top layer (setting bed) with the traces of the fresco painting which guided the mosaicist in his choice of colours, is 20–30 mm. thick. The total thickness of the mosaic foundation is approximately 6 cm. (In the Church of the Archangel Michael it is slightly thicker—8–10 cm.)[42] The layers of the plaster bed were composed of quartz dust, a small quantity of rock-fragments, and straw-fibres. Because the tesserae were inserted in the damp setting-bed which had previously been painted *al fresco*, the third or upper layer had to be executed in separate sections according to how much work the artist could do in one day. In the mosaics of the Church of the Archangel Michael, vertical and horizontal seams indicating the joins between the different areas of work are visible[43]; as such seams are easier to conceal in mosaic-work than in fresco they cannot always be detected.

In the mosaics of S. Sophia of Kiev, tesserae of rectangular form predominate, though some of triangular and oval form are also found. The setting was executed in a free and easy way, without excessive pedantry but also without undue haste. The practice of inserting the tesserae into the setting bed at a variety of different angles is what gives to the surface of mosaics their peculiar sparkling effect. The majority of the mosaicists were experienced masters, thoroughly versed in their job; they had a deep sense of form and knew how to convey it through subtle contrasts of colour, especially in the treatment of faces. For instance, in the setting of the face of S. Lawrence in the lower register of the apse [5], 400 cubes per sq. decimetre were used. For filling in the drapery and the background, the quantity of tesserae per sq. decimetre is considerably less; in the Virgin's robe, 123 cubes; in the gold background of the conch, 150; and so on.[44]

As Mrs. V. I. Levitskaya discovered, much smaller tesserae were employed in the mosaics of S. Sophia of Kiev than in those for the Church of the Archangel Michael also in Kiev. For example, 440 tesserae per sq. decimetre were used for the face of the apostle John in the representation of the *Eucharist* in S. Sophia [21], whereas only 262

5. S. Lawrence. Mosaic, 1043–6. Kiev, S. Sophia

cubes per sq. decimetre went into the face of the same apostle [52] in the analogous composition in the Church of the Archangel Michael though the heads in both cases were the same size—36 × 19 cm.[45]

The most striking feature of the Kievan mosaics is their colouring: the tones are deep and intense, the nuances are extraordinarily diverse and subtle. A detailed analysis of the mosaic palette at S. Sophia has revealed a total of 177 different tints; there are for instance, 21 shades of blue, 25 of gold, 9 of silver, 34 of green, 23 of yellow, 19 of red, 25 of brown, 6 of violet, 9 of grey, and so on.[46] Such an extensive range in the palette was made possible through the highly developed technique of tesserae production, and hence the craftsmen who made the tesserae were held in no less esteem than the masters who applied them to the surface, in other words the mosaicists themselves. One of the most remarkable features of the S. Sophia mosaics is the fact that the tremendous variety of shades employed does not in the least diminish the impact of the brilliant colours, but on the contrary seems to heighten their effect. This is explained by the specific quality of the smalt used, which has a very luminous and sparkling surface. The palette used in S. Sophia in Kiev demonstrates once again the fact that the quality of the colouring in mosaic-work was achieved in direct proportion to the number and diversity of tones employed. We have here a perfect

19

example of how deeply the medieval masters understood all the subtleties of colour—for them it was always one of the chief instruments of artistic expression.

Whereas in Byzantium, the art-forms of mosaic and fresco were never used together in the same building, in Kievan Rus' the two forms existed harmoniously side by side. As the Kievan state declined, the fresco gradually replaced the more costly mosaic, and finally ousted it altogether.

Up to comparatively recently, the question as to whether or not the mural paintings of ancient Russia were true frescoes, has been debated by art-historians. M. Makarenko,[47] for example, was of the opinion that in Kievan Rus' the church walls were painted on dry plaster in tempera (meaning the pigment is diluted with egg or some other binding medium). L. A. Durnovo[48] and T. Gaponenko[49] on the other hand, held the view that the painting was done *al fresco* but received its final touches on the dry ground; and the colours 'were mixed with slaked lime of the consistency of thick cream and laid out on the walls in thin layers'.[50] However, the view that the early Russian murals were true frescoes was staunchly held by Yu.N.Dmitriyev,[51] and his article shows this theory to be the correct one. Even if we concede that in some isolated cases the artist had recourse to painting on dry plaster during the final stages of his work, the painting still remained essentially a fresco. Ninety per cent of the work (except the azurite backgrounds) was done on the fresh lime plaster, which in the process of drying gave back the moisture as lime water; it was this water which, penetrating the particles of pigment, secured them to the surface. This accounts for the excellent state of preservation of the Russian murals; it also partially explains their summary and concise artistic language, devoid of unnecessary or trivial embellishments.

When deciding on the iconographical content for any given scheme of decoration, the artists had to take into account the dimensions of the church, the location of doors and windows and, naturally, any specific preferences of the donor. The Presbyter Ilarion,[52] friend and counsellor of the Grand-prince Yaroslav of Kiev, a man deeply versed in all the subtleties of medieval theology and the complex language of symbols, was responsible for the subject-matter of the paintings in S. Sophia at Kiev, where the decoration expresses an elegant and profound system of ideas. In the Cathedral of Kiev, the evangelical story unfolds from left to right in the higher register, and after completing a full circle continues in the register immediately below [6, 7; *26*]. This strict chronological sequence is not found in the churches of Novgorod and Pskov, where both donors and artists appear to have been far less rigorous in their approach to the iconographical programme. In the case of Nereditsa, one gets the impression that the painters working there never intended to have a carefully thought-out plan, and the only agreement with the donor concerned the number of Gospel scenes to be depicted and their approximate distribution on the walls and vaults of the building. Here, in contrast to S. Sophia of Kiev, the *artel'* was not at all interested in the sequence of the evangelical story, meaning that the spectator had no chance to follow the narrative in a systematic way. We find the same haphazard approach in the distribution of Gospel scenes at Snetogorsk, and also, to a lesser extent, at Mirozh [8].[53] These examples show the weakening of the inflexible Byzantine methods and the gradual growth of the *Kovrovy* (carpet) principle in fresco painting, where the walls were covered in their entirety from the floor to the keystone of the vault.

6. Schema of the Frescoes on the north wall
of the transept. Kiev, S. Sophia.

7. Schema of the Frescoes on the south-wall
of the transept. Kiev, S. Sophia.

Once agreement had been reached with the donors regarding the iconographical content of the decoration, the masters could then set to work.

In the decoration of churches, it was usual to begin with the upper parts and the apse, after which the central and western parts were tackled. This is confirmed by a story in the Ipat'yevskaya chronicle of 1288, which relates how the decoration of the Church of S. George at Lyuboml' was interrupted by the death of Prince Vladimir Vasil'kovich, patron of the church: 'They began by decorating the three apses and the drum, but the work was not finished because illness [of Prince Vladimir] prevented it . . .'.[54]

The great strength of the early Russian painters lay in the fact that they always thought of the frescoes in direct relation to the architecture of the building, the frescoes being in their eyes an integral part of the wall surface; hence their system of decoration followed the architectonic structure.[55]

Since the images were distributed on the walls in a series of friezes running one above the other, the painters had first to calculate the number of friezes which would fit, and then taking into account the general iconographical scheme prescribed for the church, decide how many Gospel scenes each frieze should contain. The decoration of the pendentives, the dome and the drum did not present similar difficulties, as they were reserved for the more traditional subjects and each composition was exactly suited to its appointed place—the *Ascension* or *Pantocrator* in the dome, figures of prophets or apostles in the drum, figures of the evangelists in the pendentives. The question of the decoration of the

21

8. Interior of the Spaso-Preobrazhensky Cathedral in the Mirozhsky Monastery, Pskov. Middle of the 12th century

arches and vaults was also relatively easy to decide since these can be conveniently divided into two equal sections. It was therefore the compositions for the walls which presented the greatest problems, particularly as the factor of door and window openings had to be taken into account. These openings, already an intrinsic part of the structure, could not be ignored, though in some cases agreement regarding the location of the windows could be reached in advance between the architect and the head (*stareishina*) of the *druzhina*. For example, in the Church of S. George at Staraya Ladoga, the low window of the diaconicon—on which is depicted the monumental representation of S. George and the Dragon [84]—has been left out, whereas the corresponding window of the prothesis exists. From this we may deduce that the composition was of special importance to the founder and was provided for in the architectural plan of the church.[56]

Unlike mosaic, whose plaster bed was composed of three different layers, fresco was painted on a ground of two coats (or *Levkas*, to use the Russian term).[57] The undercoat, applied directly to the wall, served as a foundation and was two or even three centimetres thick, whereas the top coat was only a few millimetres thick. As far as the basic ingredients were concerned, both layers were similar in composition, but greater care went into the preparation of the material for the upper layer and finer particles were used in it. Among the lime plasters used by the early Russian painters, we can distinguish two types: (1) lime with an admixture of pounded brick; (2) lime with sand and an organic filler. (This filler could be either flax, hemp or straw cut up in small pieces, or sometimes even charcoal.) Ground containing pounded brick, which has a delicate pink or yellowish tinge, is found only in fresco-work of the eleventh–twelfth centuries (e.g. in the Nikolo-Dvorischensky Cathedral and the Church of S. Clement at Staraya Ladoga); but even at this period it was rarely employed and later dropped out of use completely. In composition and appearance, this ground is similar to the construction mortar (*Tsemyanka*) used at the time, in which the addition of brick powder to the mortar gave it a particular toughness and increased its resistance to the action of water. The second ground we mentioned, that containing the organic filler, became much more widely used. In order to render it more robust, a bread broth was occasionally added, which explains the presence of grains of corn in some grounds dating from the eleventh–twelfth centuries.[58] The introduction of organic ingredients into the mortar not only increased the binding properties of individual particles of ground, but also rendered it more porous and delayed the process of drying. As far as material and methods of preparation were concerned, both types of ground were very similar to the mortar employed in the actual building-work; in this way the entire project—from the basic construction to its subsequent adornment with frescoes—acquired a deep inner logic and unity.

It is well known that in the great frescoes of the Italian Renaissance a careful sketch of the future composition, outlined first in charcoal and then elaborated in ochre and red colour, was made on the first layer of ground or *arriccio*. These preliminary sketches, which have survived in great number, are called *sinopie*.[59] They sprang from the need for a more careful preparation of the fresco itself, and Cavallini was probably the first artist to utilize them in a systematic way. From the end of the thirteenth century onwards, mural painting was moving towards realism, and a careful modulation of light and shade was required in order to produce its three-dimensional appearance.[60] This new approach made fresco painting a much more protracted and difficult affair, and a thoroughly

8. Frescoes in the north-west tower of S. Sophia, Kiev. About 1120-5

prepared sketch was needed. When this had been applied to the *arriccio*, the artist then proceeded to cover it with the second coat, or *intonaco* as it is called. Since it was essential for the *intonaco* to remain damp during the actual painting, it could only be laid on in comparatively small sections corresponding to the amount of work the artist could accomplish in one day—hence the visible evidence of joins or seams, so characteristic of fresco-work. In the case of the Italian Renaissance fresco, with its emphasis on three-dimensional form, complex buildings in perspective and precise characterization, the preliminary sketch on the *arriccio* was an essential requirement without which it would have been impossible to execute even a small section of fresco during the brief time before the *intonaco* hardened. We know for instance that Masaccio painted the *Expulsion from Paradise* in the Brancacci Chapel in four days,[61] while Michelangelo spent seven days on the painting of one figure—the *Delphica*—in the Sistine Chapel.[62] It was from the example of the Byzantine mosaic, where similar drawings were usually made on the second layer of ground (the plaster bed of these mosaics, as we have seen, consisted of three layers), that the Italian adopted this method of working from a precise sketch on the *arriccio*.[63]

In the early Russian frescoes, however, the technique employed was entirely different: here, too, the ground consisted of two layers, but without any preparatory drawing on the first layer. The only preliminary markings, done with the help of cords, were those defining the basic vertical and horizontal lines of the different registers; the actual creation of the fresco took place on the surface layer, which as with the Italian technique, could only be applied in sections. But in contrast to the Italian method, the early Russian frescoes had no preparatory sketch on the first layer of ground; they came into being solely

23

and entirely on the second layer, and in very short periods of time, since the damp plaster was laid out in much larger sections than in the Italian frescoes.[64] In the course of a single day, the painter had to level out the surface of the second layer, mark vertical and horizontal lines for the frame, outline the preliminary sketch with his brush and complete it *al fresco* before the ground had time to dry. All this required a very experienced hand, accurate visual estimation, and a summary treatment of form. The painters were forced by the limitations of their technique into employing a concise artistic language and using traditionally tried and trusted methods which enabled them to work speedily and accurately.

The artist tried, where possible, to complete his composition in one day, so as to bring the seam to the edge of the frame where it would be least noticeable; this is apparent in such frescoes as *Jesus among the Doctors* [*62*] and *The Descent of the Holy Ghost* [109] at Snetogorsk.[65] Where compositions were comparatively large, it was necessary to work especially quickly. In his investigations carried out in the Church of the Transfiguration in Nereditsa, Yu. N. Dmitriyev found that the representation of the *Baptism* [102] on the south wall was painted on a single section of ground measuring just over nine square metres; another, slightly smaller, composition, the *Nativity*, was likewise done on a single section, six and a half metres square. Again in the same church, the figures of the Fathers of the Church in the upper register of the main apse were the work of two masters: one painted the south side, the other the north. Initially, the ground was prepared for just nine figures in the centre; of these the first master painted four, and the master who worked on the north side painted five. The total area of the section was approximately 14 sq. m., each figure measuring 1·50 m. in height. The masters fixed in advance the extent of the section, and defined its limits by means of *grafya* (i.e. lines scratched on the damp plaster) which are still clearly visible. When the nine figures of the Church Fathers were completed, two figures still remained to be done on each side of the upper register, and these were executed separately. These valuable observations made by Yu. N. Dmitriyev[66] show that the early Russian fresco painters accomplished far more work—from 6 to 9 sq. m.—per day (or in exceptional cases two days) than did the Italians, a fact which is further confirmed by an analysis of the fresco *S. George and the Dragon* [84], 5 sq. m. in size and painted on a single section of ground.[67] If we remember that the preliminary sketch was made on this same (second) layer of the ground and was executed in liquid colour (yellow, brown or green) with fluent and rapid strokes, it is clear that the whole working process must have required meticulous and highly efficient organization. Furthermore, the sketch generally did no more than indicate the broad outlines of the composition and a few of its more important details such as the facial features, the line of the drapery folds, etc. Frequently the painters deviated from the sketch, altering details or modifying anything that was not to their satisfaction. Sometimes in order to improve the effectiveness of the guide lines, these were grooved into the damp ground (*grafya*). However, these *grafyas* [e.g. 69], which made it possible to continue work on the fresco even after the surface had been covered by the first coat of paint, were used comparatively seldom by the early Russian painters, as a rule only for defining the circular outline of the nimbus.[68]

After drafting the sketch, the master set to work on the fresco.[69] First he covered both the nimbus and the face with yellow ochre, and over this applied a greyish-green colour which in the later stages remained untouched in the areas of half-shadow. On this basic combination of colours, the lighter and convex parts were then painted, usually in two separate stages: first in a pale yellow, put on either in patches or in broad strokes; then in a lime white almost completely covering the original light parts. Work on the eyes, nose and so on was also done in two stages: first a reddish-brown pigment was applied, and later a dark green, near to black. The same reddish-brown colour was used for the shadows round the contours of the face, below the cheeks and around the beard. The draperies were executed in a similar fashion; white fabrics have an underlying greenish tone as they were painted by applying, in two stages, broad white strips which leave uncovered the basic tone for half-shadows; the deeper shadows are filled in with red.

10. Head of Prophet. Fresco, about 1167. Staraya Ladoga, S. George

This method of painting, which with few changes continued to be used in the frescoes of the fourteenth–fifteenth centuries,[70] required that the artist should construct his forms logically and economically. Gradually the light areas are built up, culminating in fine white colour. In later murals of the fourteenth–fifteenth centuries only the handling changes: the principle of the construction of the form remains the same. The areas of greatest light which formed an ornamental pattern of lines in the paintings of the twelfth century [e.g. 10] are treated in a different way, more freely and picturesquely; the highlights are rendered by vigorous strokes and nervous little lines (*dvizhki*), thus losing their former abstract character [e.g. 145].

There is no longer any doubt that the colours used by the early Russian painters were primarily natural colours (so-called *zemlyanyye* meaning 'from the earth').[71] For example, Dionisy, who decorated the Cathedral of the Nativity of the Virgin in the Ferapontov Monastery, employed in the making of his colours pebbles (*gal'ka*) which were collected from the banks of local rivers and the shores of the Bodayevsky Lake.[72] The colours most frequently used were ochre of various shades, umber, cinnabar (natural or artificial), glauconite (*Prazelen'*), verdigris (*yar'medyanka*), mountain blue (*gornaya sin'*), green (with chrome and iron oxide). Unfortunately, in the overwhelming majority of early

25

11. Apostles,
from 'The Last Judgement'.
Fresco, about 1195.
Vladimir, S. Demetrius

Russian frescoes, the original colours have not survived; the plaster or lime whitewash which covered them for so long damaged the surface paint, causing the loss of the pupils of the eyes, the blackening of the highlights of the cheeks, and so on. In most cases, after cleaning, the colours in the frescoes begin to fade. This process of discolouration is a universal phenomenon in medieval painting, and very difficult to combat. We must therefore bear in mind that the colours of the early Russian frescoes were rather different in their pristine state—brighter, fresher, more intense. This is especially true of the blue used in the backgrounds, for the azurite generally comes away with the removal of the over-painting and the background is left showing a dark indigo tone.[73] It is essential to remember this point when studying the paintings of the eleventh–fifteenth centuries.

We have now to consider another very important question connected with the activity of the early Russian painters, viz. the models on which they based their frescoes; and here the old literary sources provide us with some very interesting material.

26

Like their fellow-artists in Byzantium and medieval Europe,[74] the early Russian painters undoubtedly made extensive use of models (in the West such a model was called an *exemplum*). For example, when the young Prince Vladimir (later Grand-prince Vladimir Monomakh) decided, after his miraculous cure, to build at Rostov a church on the lines of the Church of the Dormition in the Pechersky Monastery of Kiev, he had the Kievan church carefully measured, and the plan of its scheme of decoration reproduced on parchment, faithfully recording the exact position of the various compositions in the cycle of Feasts (' . . . and the sequence of the feasts and their location were written on parchment . . .').[75] This case was certainly not unique, and we have good reason to believe that every decorative ensemble was based on some model or other, a theory which is further confirmed by the letter which Epifany sent to Kirill of Tver' about 1415. In his letter, Epifany, describing the working methods of the great Theophanes the Greek, emphasizes the fact that unlike the Russian painters, he did not look at other models, but invented his own original designs. 'When he sketched or painted all this, no one ever saw him looking at model drawings, as some of our painters do, who, in embarrassment, are always looking [at them], glancing here and there, and who look more at models than paint with colours. But he paints a fresco with his hands, constantly walking to and fro, talking with visitors and pondering wise and lofty thoughts in his mind. . . .'[76]

We do not know what the early Russian model drawings of the eleventh to the fifteenth centuries looked like, since none has been preserved. Later originals, *podlinniki* (i.e. collection of models for various compositions) dating from the sixteenth–seventeenth centuries do exist, but they typify a new phase of development, when models played an incomparably bigger role eventually exerting a negative influence on the painter to the extent, sometimes, of producing purely mechanical copying. In the period with which we are concerned, the attitude to the model was different—much freer and more creative. The model served in the first place as a guide to the iconography of the subject; it also assisted the artist in the layout of his composition and the disposition of the figures. But as far as detail and aesthetic interpretation were concerned, the master exercised his own ingenuity. All the early Russian paintings prove this: they offer an amazing variety of solutions, although the themes remain the same.

Apparently the early Russian models were very similar to the 'Book of Models from Wolfenbüttel'[77] and the 'Sketchbook of Villard de Honnecourt',[78] and must have been outline drawings of compositional schemes for the various biblical scenes, giving the appropriate gestures for different types of figure, whether evangelists, apostles or prophets, and reproducing important details. These drawings were generally stitched together in the form of exercise books, but could also be drawn on parchment scrolls. Of particular interest is the scroll from Vercelli, dating from the mid-thirteenth century, which in a careful pen drawing reproduces the decoration in the Church of S. Eusebio.[79] A few lines added in verse states that this sketch was made to serve as an *exemplum* for future decorations. Frescoes from the north and south walls of the central nave are shown on the parchment as two parallel strips, in which the different scenes are given in sequence, by the faces of their upper frames turning towards each other. This *rotulus* recalls a passage in the *Pechersky Paterik* which relates how, after the deaths of the Byzantine masters who had frescoed the Church of the Dormition in the Pechersky Monastery, there remained in

12. Church of the Nativity at the Cemetery, Novgorod

the vestry 'their *svity* . . . and their books (*knigi*)'.[80] The word *svity* was generally, but wrongly, interpreted as referring to some kind of clothing.[81] In reality, *svity* are parchment scrolls* used here as an *exemplum* during the execution of the mosaics. The *knigi*† were either illustrated manuscripts whose miniatures served as models, or were sketches, for the same purpose, stitched together in book form. The statement in the *Pechersky Paterik* gives support to the theory that in ancient Rus', as in western Europe at the same period, the models were collected together either in the form of scrolls or codices, but probably in the vast majority of cases they consisted of outline drawings bound together in copy-book form.

In Romanesque frescoes, when transferring a small *exemplum* to the wall, the painters sometimes marked the second layer of ground with auxiliary geometrical lines before the actual frescoing was begun.[82] Traces of such lines have been discovered in the paintings of the Benedictine Abbey of Nonnberg in Salzburg, the Church of S. Savin in Poitou, and in many other Romanesque paintings of the twelfth century. These lines form either acute-angled triangles or circles made with compasses. With the help of such geometrical designs the human figure was constructed on the surface. It is only natural that a method of this kind tended to produce abstract representations, since an organic form was being forced

svitok is the Russian for scroll – Tr.
†*knigi* is the Russian for book – Tr.

28

into a geometrical shape. This method was not practised in early Russian painting, or at least no trace of such lines has yet been discovered in the frescoes. This partially explains the less abstract, more informal and freer style of the early Russian painting, in whose art the abstract elements are infused with a vital feeling of reality, which gives to them their attractive spontaneity and vigour. In the images of the early Russian master we will not find the psychological insight and refinement which distinguishes the icons and murals of his contemporary Greek fellow-artists; what we do find is an inner strength and immediacy of expression which is completely absent from the more formal and canonical art of Byzantium. The early Russian painter speaks his own artistic language, a language so vital that it retains, even to our own day, the full force of its emotional impact.

13. Church of the Saviour, Nereditsa. 1198

29

14. Head of the Pantocrator. Detail of mosaic, 1043–6. Kiev, S. Sophia

Chapter I

KIEVAN RUS'

THE HISTORY of early Russian monumental painting begins in the age of Vladimir Svyatoslavovich, grand-prince of Kiev (978–1015). It was he, who having consolidated the political and military successes of his predecessors, made of Kievan Rus' one of the largest and most important states in Europe. In 988 after his marriage to Anna, sister of the Byzantine Emperor Basil the Second, Vladimir was converted to Christianity, an event which prepared the way for strong Byzantine cultural influence in Rus'. Henceforth Greeks and Russians shared the same religion, a fact which the patriarchs of Constantinople did not fail to exploit in an attempt to govern the Russian Church and through it to influence the secular authorities. This peculiar situation was the source of many conflicts which reflect the Russian people's struggle for ecclesiastical autonomy. Nevertheless, the ecclesiastical channels were destined to remain the principal source of Byzantine influence in Rus'.

After his conversion, Vladimir summoned Greek masters to Kiev for the construction and decoration between 989 and 996 of the stone Church of the Virgin. The structure, crowned by domes and having an obscured cross plan with three naves and a narthex, was known as the Desyatinnaya Church (*desyatina* meaning one-tenth) because Vladimir set aside for its maintenance one-tenth of the income of the principality. The interior of the church, which collapsed in 1240, was elaborately decorated with marble, slate, porphyry, mosaic and frescoes. In the dome was shown the half-length figure of Christ Pantocrator, and in the apse the Virgin in the Orans or praying position.[83] As regards iconography, the decorative scheme seems to have followed the standard Constantinoplian pattern. The few fresco fragments found in excavations do not permit us to deduce the origins of the master who worked in this church, but an examination of the best-preserved fragment—the upper part of the face of a young saint—reveals in the large eyes, sharp shadows and heavy lines the presence of archaic elements. However this is insufficient evidence for attributing the entire decoration of the Desyatinnaya Church to masters from Thessalonica, as did N. P. Sychyov.[84]

During the reign of Yaroslav (1019–54), grand-prince of Kiev and son of Vladimir, many fine religious buildings were erected in Kievan Rus'. In 1037, on the site which marked his decisive victory over the Pechenegs a year earlier, Yaroslav began the construction of S. Sophia. This, then, was a cathedral founded to commemorate the crushing of one of the nomadic tribes who represented a grave threat to the stability of Kievan Rus', but it also had another significance in the life of the people. The chronicler calls it the *Mitropol'ya*,[85] that is to say, the Cathedral of the Metropolitan, which meant that the church was destined to be used by the Metropolitan himself for all religious functions. It was just at this time that the seat of the Metropolitan was transferred from Pereyaslavl' to Kiev, and the new Metropolitan appointed by Constantinople, the Greek Theopempt, arrived to take up his duties. S. Sophia thus became the principal church in Kiev; the throne or cathedra of the Metropolitan was installed in the central apse; henceforth not only the highest dignitaries of the Church were ordained and consecrated within its hallowed walls but finally the enthronement of the grand-prince of Kiev was also solemnized here.

Although construction work was begun in 1037, the interior of S. Sophia was not ready for decoration until 1042. The mosaics [16–27; *1–8*] must have been executed between 1043 and 1046, the year in which the first consecration of the cathedral took place.[86] This period also saw the creation of the frescoes for the central nave, transept and gallery [28–30, 36–38; *9–11,17–19,21*]. The frescoes in the side-naves [31–35,39,44,49; *12–16,20,22–25*] may date from a little later though they must certainly have been completed by 1061 or 1067 when the cathedral was consecrated for the second time. Finally, the frescoes in both towers [40–43, 47, 48, 50; *28–33*], in the Baptistry [*39*], and in the outer gallery [*34–38*] are still later in date, as these sections of the building were not constructed until the first quarter of the twelfth century.

The cathedral of S. Sophia is an enormous multi-domed building, having an obscured cross plan with five naves and an open gallery of three sides of its interior. (In the first quarter of the twelfth century an external gallery which included the two towers at the angles was also added.) The original area of the cathedral measured *c.* 486 m. Owing to the extensive internal gallery, the sides of the church appear much lower in height than the central part, the latter standing out not only by virtue of its greater height but also because of its better illumination [2]. For this reason, the mosaics are concentrated in the main apse and in the area under the central dome. They adorn the conch and walls of the apse, the vault and wall of the bema, the central dome, its drum, and the arches and pendentives supporting the dome, thus drawing the eye to those parts of the cathedral where the sacred ceremonies were being performed. Dominating the altar, the iconostasis and the ambo (situated in the centre of the crossing under the dome), the mosaics contributed in some measure towards heightening the impact of the three basic acts of the liturgy. When following the latter, the gaze was inevitably drawn to contemplation of the mosaics.

Although in S. Sophia the most conspicuous points were reserved for the mosaics, in quantity it is the frescoes—adorning the central and side naves, the transept and the gallery—which predominate. This arrangement of the frescoes enabled the architect to guide the circulation of people within the church. In the side naves the frescoes are distributed in such a way that the spectator is encouraged to move from west to east, that is, from the entrance gallery to the apses. Entirely different, on the other hand, is the arrangement of the frescoes in the central cross: here they are superimposed in three tiers (the upper tier covers the vaults

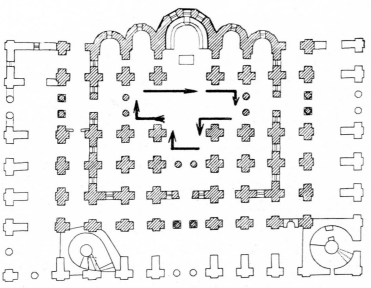

15. Plan of the Cathedral of S. Sophia, Kiev

16. The Virgin of the Annunciation.
Mosaic, 1043–6. Kiev, S. Sophia

17. The Virgin, from 'The Deesis'. Mosaic, 1043–6. Kiev, S. Sophia

of the arms of the cross; the middle tier, the semicircles over the arches of the gallery which has three bays; the lower tier, the wall over the ground floor arches, which also has three bays [6, 7; *26*]). Within the frame of each tier, the evangelical story unfolds in a clockwise direction [15], so that the spectator has to circulate three times around the area under the dome in order to take in all the Gospel scenes. This arrangement of the frescoes, calculated to make the spectator move in a circle, is radically different from that which we find in the basilica-type church, where the mosaics or frescoes appear as linear compositions over the arches of the central nave, thus encouraging the onlooker to move in a straight line from the entrance in the west wall to the altar.

The principle of the circular arrangement of the frescoes is not difficult to comprehend: it derives logically from the central-domed plan and from the nature of the liturgical action which took place round the ambo situated in the centre of the square under the dome. The spectator will fully appreciate the architectural beauties of S. Sophia of Kiev

34

18. John the Baptist, from 'The Deesis'. Mosaic, 1043–6. Kiev, S. Sophia

if he moves in the space leading from one branch of the central cross to another; only then will he perceive all the magnificent perspectives contained in this interior. By moving from the central nave to the side naves, and thence returning from their semi-obscurity to the brilliantly illuminated area under the central dome, he can thoroughly appreciate the originality of the architectural conception of S. Sophia of Kiev, with its wealth of form, light and shadow.

This cathedral is undoubtedly the greatest of the religious buildings of ancient Rus', not only on account of its vast size but in the complexity of its planning. It shares, however, one important feature with all other Russian churches, that is the obscured cross plan with the crossing surmounted by a dome, and for this reason the early Russian system of church painting was based on the same principle, i.e. the circular arrangement of the frescoes around the central square under the dome. It should, however, be stressed that nowhere is the principle so rigorously followed as in S. Sophia; in other churches, especially in

35

19. Christ the Pantocrator. Mosaic, 1043–6. Kiev, S. Sophia

those of Novgorod and Pskov, deviations from the strict chronological sequence of the Gospel story occur. From this point of view the decoration of S. Sophia is exceptional for its deep inner logic; in fact, without the advice of highly-cultivated members of the clergy it could never have been created.

Pride of place among the mosaics is occupied by the enormous figure of the Virgin in the conch of the apse [20] and the half-length figure of Christ in the dome [14, 19]. The Virgin is shown full length in the attitude of praying (*Orans*) with uplifted arms. As

20. The Virgin Orans.
Mosaic, 1043-6. Kiev, S. Sophia

37

21. The Apostles, from 'The Eucharist'. Mosaic, 1043–6. Kiev, S. Sophia

representative of the Church Militant, she dominates the cathedral together with the Pantocrator before whom as mediatrix she intercedes for the human race. Situated at the highest point in the building, Christ, the head of the Church Triumphant reigns supreme in space, His powerful half-length figure seen in an aureole of diagonal rays of sunlight which penetrate the windows of the drum. The book which He holds in His left hand is to remind us of the terrible Day of Judgement when, according to the apocalyptic prophesies, it will be opened. Enclosed within a medallion, Christ is surrounded by a retinue of four archangels in festive attire covered with pearls; only one of these, much damaged, now remains [1]. Lower down, between the windows of the drum, the apostles, the propagators of Christ's teaching were shown; only the half-figure of S. Paul remains [2]. On the pendentives appeared the seated figures of the evangelists; the figure of S. Mark is the only one still intact [3]. Their position on the pillars supporting the dome was not fortuitous since in medieval theology they were regarded as the four pillars of the teaching of the Gospels.

Above the triumphal arch we see the *Deesis*—three medallions containing the half-length figures of Christ, the Virgin [17] and John the Baptist [18]. This is an allusion to the approaching Day of Judgement; the Virgin and John the Baptist are depicted with arms

38

22. The Eucharist. Mosaic, 1043–6. Kiev, S. Sophia

raised towards Christ as they intercede for the *gens christiana*. Above the eastern and western arches, between the evangelists, there are medallions containing half-length figures of the Virgin and of Christ, the latter portrayed in the guise of a priest [4]—a rare iconographical feature. The pillars of both sides of the triumphal arch are decorated by figures of the Virgin and the Archangel Gabriel who announces to her the birth of a Son— the future Saviour of the world [16].

In the middle register of the apse is the great monumental composition of the *Eucharist* [21–24]. In it we see the ciborium above the altar and the angels bearing rhipidia (liturgical fans) standing next to Christ, who is depicted twice. He is engaged in administering the Holy Sacrament to the apostles approaching Him from the right and the left. This composition is intimately related to the fundamental sacramental act in the liturgy in the course of which, according to the teaching of the Christian Church, bread and wine are miraculously changed into the body and blood of Jesus Christ. The frieze containing the *Eucharist* is flanked by figures of the High Priests, Aaron and Melchisedek (not preserved), who were regarded as the Old Testament prototypes of the priestly dignity of Christ.* This theme was further developed in the lost mosaics of the bema which portrayed the Old

*See the Epistle of Paul the Apostle to the Hebrews, v, 4–10. [Tr.]

23. Angel, from 'The Eucharist'. Mosaic, 1043–6. Kiev, S. Sophia

40

24. The Apostle Paul, from 'The Eucharist'. Mosaic, 1043–6. Kiev, S. Sophia

Testament kings and prophets, regarded as the biblical prototypes of Christ the King and Christ the Priest. In the keystone of the vault of the bema, was probably represented the *Etimasia* which symbolized Christ in Glory after the Resurrection, and Christ as Judge in the Second Coming.[87]

The lower part of the apse is occupied by a frieze with two archdeacons and eight saints (the lower half of the figures is lost), which is one of the most impressive parts of the whole ensemble [25, 26; *6–8*]. Finally, the arches supporting the dome are decorated by medallions with half-length figures of the Forty Martyrs of Sebaste [only fifteen medallions remain, e.g. *27, 5*]. The aim of the various saints portrayed in the apse would seem to be that of redirecting our thoughts to earth after contemplation of heavenly matters (as symbolized by the celestial world in the dome and vault). Earth was the platform of their heroic deeds, and as the consolidators and organizers of the Church Militant they were purposely placed in the lower registers. In this way, the decorative scheme of the cathedral is subordinated to a strict hierarchic principle.

The mosaic decoration of S. Sophia has its logical continuation in the fresco-paintings which, in the nineteenth century, ignominiously disappeared under a layer of oil-colours. Their uncovering was begun in 1936, but owing to the tremendous area involved and the very bad state of preservation, the work is still going on today.

In respect of subject matter the mosaics of S. Sophia follow exactly the standard system of Constantinople. (Only two images were dictated by local interests in Kiev: the figure of

25. Order of Saints. Mosaic, 1043–6. Kiev, S. Sophia

26. Basil the Great, from the 'Order of Saints'. Mosaic, 1043–6. Kiev, S. Sophia

43

27. Nicolas, Martyr of Sebaste.
Mosaic, 1043–6.
Kiev, S. Sophia

Pope Clement, whose relics were deeply venerated in Kievan Rus', and the image of Christ the Priest, which diverges from the orthodox canon.) The frescoes on the other hand, are far less conventional. They reveal a much greater degree of freedom both in the choice of subject and in the manner of their arrangement on the walls and vaults of the church. In the first place, this freer approach influenced the Gospel cycle which shows several major deviations from the system of 'Feasts' accepted by the Byzantine Church.

The cycle of the Gospel story began on the vault of the northern arm of the central cross and, unfolding clockwise, was continued in the vaults of the southern and western arms, finally descending to the two lower registers, and, within the limits of each, again describing a full circle. On the three great vaults, the following scenes which have not

44

survived were probably shown: the *Nativity*, *The Presentation in the Temple*, *The Baptism of Christ*, *The Transfiguration*, *The Resurrection of Lazarus*, and *Christ's Entry into Jerusalem*. From the vaults the Gospel story moved to the upper register of the walls (lunettes above the three bays of the arches of the gallery). Here, in a poor state of preservation, are the scenes from Christ's Passion: *Christ before Caiphas*, *The Denial of Peter* [28; 9], *The Crucifixion* and *The Descent from the Cross* or *Entombment* (which has not survived). The spectator saw the continuation of the story in the lower register (i.e., the walls above the three bays of the first-floor arches), where scenes from another cycle are depicted: *The Resurrection*, *The Holy Women at the Sepulchre*, *The Descent into Limbo*, *Christ appearing to the Holy Women*, *The Incredulity of Thomas*, and *Christ appearing to the Eleven Apostles* [29]. This last episode, comparatively rare in the iconography of the time, was taken from the Gospel of S. Matthew (xxviii, 16–20), and the reason for its inclusion at S. Sophia was that it clearly illustrated the words of the Risen Christ to the apostles: 'Go ye therefore, and teach all nations, baptizing them . . .' Undoubtedly it is an allusion to the recent conversion of Rus' to Christianity and the consolidation of Christian belief in the young nation. A further allusion to the conversion of Rus' is provided by the scene of *The Descent of the Holy Ghost* [11] which concludes the Gospel cycle. The apostles, having miraculously acquired the faculty to speak in diverse tongues, spread the Christian teaching through all the countries of the world, including Rus' where, according to the oldest chronicle *Povest' Vremennykh Let*, the apostle Andrew preached.[88] In this way the Gospel cycle, as portrayed in S. Sophia at Kiev, laid emphasis on the three basic dogmas of Christian teaching; the Sacrifice of the Cross, the Resurrection, and the teaching and missionary role of the apostles.

From the evidence of the mosaics in the apse and the representation of Christ the Priest above the eastern arch under the dome, it is clear that an enormous significance was attached to the mystery of the Eucharist, and we find the same theme once more reiterated in the series of frescoes for the gallery where the Eucharistic sacrifice and its Old Testament prototypes form the main theme.[89]

On the southern and northern walls of the gallery two Gospel scenes, whose symbolism is directly related to the sacrament of the Eucharist, are shown facing one another: *The Last Supper* at which Christ instituted this sacrament, and *The Wedding at Cana* [10] when he changed the water into wine. Since it is known that the medieval theologians drew a close parallel between the miraculous occurrence at Cana and the Eucharistic transformation of wine into Christ's blood, the placing of these scenes close to one another assumes an added significance. One other scene, now almost totally lost, originally accompanied them—*The Miracle of the Loaves and Fishes;* painted beneath *The Last Supper*, this subject had a close symbolic connexion with the Eucharist, the loaves being regarded as foreshadowing the sacred bread. In a similar way, it is easy to explain the presence of the four Old Testament scenes also in the gallery. *The Sacrifice of Isaac* and the *Hospitality of Abraham* were generally considered in the Middle Ages to be the Old Testament prototypes of the Eucharistic sacrifice; the two other scenes of *Three Angels appearing to Abraham* and the *Three Hebrew Children in the Fiery Furnace* were allusions to Christ as one of the three Divine Persons, and as God who took on Himself the sufferings of mankind in order to atone for sin, and who rose again after His death.

45

28. The Apostle Peter, from 'The Denial of Peter'. Fresco, 1043–6. Kiev, S. Sophia

46

The collocation in the gallery of the scenes relating to the Sacrifice on the Cross and the Sacrament of the Eucharist was not just accidental. It is known that in Byzantium when the emperor and empress attended service in their court churches, they sat in the gallery, and there received Communion. Similarly, in Kievan Rus', the gallery was reserved for the family of the grand-prince, who during the receiving of Communion could contemplate the allusions to the mystery of the Eucharist contained in the nearby scenes from the Old and New Testaments. Thus an intimate relationship was established between the decoration and the religious rites being performed before the grand-prince and his family.

In S. Sophia a very special place was given to the group portrait of Yaroslav's family [30, 36; 27]. As recent research has shown,[90] this was situated on the western wall of the central nave and on the adjoining southern and northern walls. The reconstruction of this

29. Group of Apostles, from 'The Apparition of Christ to the Eleven'. Fresco, 1043–6. Kiev, S. Sophia

47

30. Son of Prince Yaroslav. Fresco, about 1045. Kiev, S. Sophia

unique eleventh-century portrait has been aided by a surviving copy of it made in 1651 by the Dutch artist Abraham van Westervelt. On the western wall Christ was shown enthroned, approached on His right by the grand-prince Yaroslav and his eldest son, the former bearing a maquette of the cathedral, and on His left by the grand-princess Irene and her eldest daughter. Four other daughters bearing candles were portrayed on the southern wall, while on the northern wall were the figures of four younger sons. Both the grand-prince and princess wore crowns of the Byzantine type. Yaroslav, referred to in a graffito from the year 1054 as *tsar*,[91] is here depicted as a worthy rival to the Byzantine emperor. Also significant in this group portrait is the inclusion of his daughters, Elizabeth, Anna and Anastasia, who were shortly to become the respective Queens of Norway, France and Hungary.

This family portrait must have been painted in 1045, before any of Yaroslav's daughters was yet married, otherwise Elizabeth, Anna and Anastasia would have been shown wearing crowns. At any rate the frescoes of the central crossing were completed by May 11, 1046, the date of the first consecration of the cathedral.

There is good reason to believe that the choice of themes for the frescoes in the side naves originated in a programme devised by Yaroslav and his advisers, but the carrying out of the programme could have persisted right up to the second consecration of S. Sophia which took place on November 4, 1061 or 1067.

The prothesis was dedicated to the apostles Peter and Paul. Scenes from the life of S. Peter adorned the apse. Of these only four scenes in a very damaged state survive as well as some insignificant fragments of a fifth. (So far only one episode has been deciphered, that of *S. Peter's Delivery from Prison*.) The apse of the diaconicon contained scenes from the proto-evangelical cycle [31–35; *12*], and the reason for this unusual siting of them was that Yaroslav, in dedicating the diaconicon to Joachim and Anna, wished to commemorate his mother Anna, who had died in 1011, and his wife Irene, who on entering a religious order had taken the name of Anna. The death of Irene which took place on

31. Mary and Elizabeth. Detail of fresco in the diaconicon, 1046–61/7. Kiev, S. Sophia

49

32. The Annunciation to Anna. Fresco in the diaconicon, 1046–61/7. Kiev, S. Sophia

33. The Annunciation at the Well. Fresco in the diaconicon, 1046–61/7. Kiev, S. Sophia

34. The Presentation of Mary in the Temple. Fresco in the diaconicon, 1046–61/7. Kiev, S. Sophia

35. The Presentation by Mary of the Temple Veil to the Priest. Fresco in the diaconicon, 1046–61/7. Kiev, S. Sophia

36. Daughter of Prince Yaroslav.
Fresco, about 1045. Kiev, S. Sophia

February 10, 1050, provides us with circumstantial evidence for determining the precise date of these diaconicon frescoes.

The subjects of the paintings in the two most lateral naves are even more closely linked with Yaroslav's personal life. The northern nave is dedicated to S. George, the patron of the grand-prince whose Christian name was Yury (George). The handsome figure of the martyred saint adorns the conch of the apse, while on the vault six episodes from his life were shown, of which only one, *The Interrogation of S. George by Diocletian*, is fully preserved. A further scene from this cycle of the saint's life, *The Flagellation of S. George*, was recently uncovered on the northern wall. The outer nave on the right honours the name of the archangel Michael, revered in Rus' as the patron of princes and warriors. His half-length figure fills the apsidal conch, while on the vaults are shown six scenes commemorating the exploits of archangels: *Jacob wrestling with the Angel; The Overthrow of Satan; Gabriel appearing to Zacharias; The Archangel appearing to Balaam; The Archangel appearing to Joshua;* and one other scene now lost.

Our examination of the iconographical scheme of S. Sophia of Kiev would not be complete without a mention of the single figures [37–39; *14–23*], which are placed either round the apertures of the arches or else adorn the arches and cruciform pillars. Their distribution does not follow any logical pattern—they alternate in a haphazard way with bands of decorative motifs and crosses. Since the massive pillars of S. Sophia are cruciform in section, each of them provided the fresco-painter with twelve vertical surfaces which were ideal for the representation of standing saints—a fact which partially explains the abundance of such figures in the cathedral. Compared with these images of individual saints, literally overwhelming the spectator by their numbers, the scenes from the Gospel and the Old Testament occupy in the total scheme of decoration a relatively modest place. On entering the cathedral, the spectator is confronted on all sides with a host of saints, who with their grave and penetrating gaze seem to pursue him relentlessly and fill him with a sense of his own helplessness.[92]

37. Unknown Saint. Fresco, 1043–6. Kiev, S. Sophia

Hitherto, the frescoes in the two towers of S. Sophia have generally been studied in direct relation to the overall decorative ensemble of the cathedral, but recent architectural research has revealed that the south-west tower was erected contemporaneously with the outer gallery and the superstructure of the inner one[93]—most probably during the reign of

53

38. S. Nicolas. Fresco, 1043–6. Kiev, S. Sophia

39. The Prophet Elijah. Fresco, 1046–61/7. Kiev, S. Sophia

40. The Palace of Kathisma with the Galleries. Fresco in the south-west tower, 1113–25. Kiev, S. Sophia

Vladimir Monomakh (1113–25). The north-west tower was erected a little later, following on the frescoing of the pillars and flying buttresses of the outer gallery. These conclusions arrived at by the architectural historians are confirmed by an analysis of the paintings in both towers, where the style of the frescoes, the work of several teams of painters, is very different from that which prevailed in Yaroslav's time.

One of the themes illustrated in the paintings of the south-west tower is undoubtedly borrowed from Byzantium and possibly expresses Vladimir Monomakh's great love for the Greek world (his mother was the daughter of the Byzantine emperor, Constantine X Ducas, and one of his own daughters married Leo, son of Romanus IV Diogenes). On the walls of the tower are depicted the various sporting activities of the Hippodrome at Constantinople. On the right, dominating the east side of the arena is the Kathisma Palace [40, 41; 28] from which the emperor and his retinue watched the games and contests; the emperor is shown sitting in the imperial box while his suite have taken their places in the open galleries. There is also a high wall built of massive stones; this is pierced by two windows through which the emperor's bodyguards are peering. Below stretched the arena with two quadrigas (only their outlines are preserved). To the left of the palace we see the place set aside for the competitors (known as the carceres); the tympani of the porticos are

56

decorated with discs bearing half-moons which were regarded as talismans by the charioteers at the start of the race. From the carceres the chariots, representing the factions of the Blues, the Whites, the Greens and the Reds, emerge with their drivers standing erect in them. To the right of the palace could be seen a wild-horse hunt and dancing mimes and musicians. We may well ask why episodes from the life of the Constantinople Hippodrome should have found a place in the decoration of the towers of Kiev Cathedral, and the answer is that such scenes symbolized the triumph of the Basileus who claimed to be a direct successor to the Roman emperors.[94]

In such a centralized state as was Byzantium, it was not so much the charioteers and gladiators who gained kudos from their triumphs, no matter how brilliant, as the emperor himself who always presided at the Hippodrome: he was considered the principal victor and was hailed as 'Ever victorious'. These scenes were therefore a symbol of triumphant imperial power, and, understandably, they occupy

41. Spectators at the Hippodrome of Constantinople. Fresco in the south-west tower, 1113–25. Kiev, S. Sophia

a very important place in Byzantine art (in consular diptychs, the marble base of the obelisk of Theodosius, several paintings in the imperial palaces no longer preserved but described by contemporaries). Kiev borrowed these subjects from Byzantium and very skilfully adapted them to glorifying the power of her own grand-princes. When the Kievan princes mounted the stairs to the gallery and saw the various arena scenes, the association uppermost in their minds was not the power of the Byzantine emperors but rather the concept of political power as such.

Not that all the paintings in the south-west tower are concerned with the activities of the Hippodrome at Constantinople; on the contrary, a considerable if not the greater part of them are devoted to hunting scenes—another variant of the 'triumph' motif. It is well known that Byzantine artists frequently commemorated with their brush the valiant hunting exploits of the emperors.[95] Thus for instance Nicetas Choniates tells us that Andronicus Comnenus ordered his palace to be decorated with pictures of his valorous deeds 'with bow, sword, and at the Hippodrome'.[96] In the famous 'Precepts of Vladimir Monomakh', a great deal of attention is given to the hunt. Vladimir tells his sons how in the dense forests near Chernigov he bound with his own hands thirty wild horses, how aurochs twice attacked him, how deer butted him and elks trampled him, how a wild boar

57

wrenched his sword from his hip, how a bear bit his knee, how a savage beast jumped at him and brought him and his horse to the ground.[97] References to princely hunts appear continually in the chronicles.[98] These hunts, which were one of the chief pastimes of feudal nobility, lasted for several days, sometimes even weeks. It is not surprising that in the *Slovo o Polku Igoreve*, out of a total of two thousand eight hundred and fifty-three words, no less than sixty-one hunting terms are found.

An attentive study of the paintings in the south-west tower shows that nearly all the beasts portrayed belong to the northern fauna. We see the hunting of wild boars and squirrels with dogs, the hunting of wild horses (*tarpany*) with cheetahs and also with the lasso [*31*]. In a niche and on the walls there are scenes of a fox running, a wild boar being pursued [*29*][99] and a hunter on horseback being attacked by a wolf.

Just as many hunting exploits are to be found on the walls and vaults of the north-west tower, among them a rider tussling with a bear [*9*, *42*], a hound in pursuit of a deer; also portrayed are different species of hunting birds such as falcons, gerfalcons and hawks in collars. These birds are skilfully inserted into medallions, one of which contains a

42. Mounted warrior fighting a bear. Fresco in the north-west tower, about 1120–5. Kiev, S. Sophia

complete scene of a hawk attacking a hare. N. V. Charlemagne, who made a special study of the various species of animal depicted on the walls and vaults of both towers, came to the conclusion that the majority of these belonged to the local fauna. In his opinion the empty spaces where the frescoes have completely disappeared, probably contained scenes of the hunting of aurochs, elks and beavers, as well as the trapping in nets of swans, geese, ducks and cranes.[100]

Unfortunately the surviving frescoes in both towers are not only very badly preserved but also very fragmentary. The existence of numerous gaps, which originally contained more complex compositions makes it impossible to trace a meaningful connexion between the surviving pieces. Scenes from court life were apparently also portrayed in the north tower. Against an architectural background, we see the seated emperor with his body-guard [33] and the empress standing with ladies of the court; also a representation of the emperor on horseback. But the precise significance of these scenes, and in what way the fragments are linked, remains uncertain.[101] The presence of nimbuses around the heads of the principal personages suggests that the artists were describing scenes from Byzantine, rather than Kievan, court life.

43. Warrior fighting a masked man. Fresco in the north-west tower, about 1120–5. Kiev, S. Sophia

We have deliberately examined in great detail the iconographical content of S. Sophia of Kiev. The decoration, taken as a whole, is a unique ensemble in eleventh-century art. Nearly all the essential elements for piecing it together are there, and what has been lost can be imaginatively reconstructed with a reasonable degree of probability, enabling us to form an idea of the entire scheme—amazing in its wealth of images and in its complexity.

Though the chronicles do not mention the summoning of Greek masters by Yaroslav, there can be no doubt that they participated in the building and especially in the decoration of the Cathedral of S. Sophia. But the participation of local artists is no less certain, since otherwise it would be hard to explain the presence in the Kievan decorations of many features not usually found in purely Byzantine monuments; one of these is the bold use of mosaic as well as fresco in the one building, a combination generally avoided by the Byzantines.

A characteristic of Byzantine sacred buildings is the combination of mosaics with walls faced in marble. As a rule the mosaics were reserved for the upper part of the interior—domes, vaults, conchs, squinches—while the walls were covered with marble, strong and monolithic, presenting a brilliant polished surface to the eye. This surface, contrasting with the picturesque glimmer of the mosaic tesserae, served to emphasize still more the peculiar beauty of the mosaics.[102] Such a contrast is absent from S. Sophia of Kiev, where the walls right down to the floor are covered in frescoes conveying a totally different texture to that of marble—uneven, porous, with only the barest sheen, like that on an egg-shell. Though the frescoes are placed in tiers one above the other, the symmetry of the arrangement is frequently disregarded; the levels of the borders do not always coincide, the figures often alternate with ornamental bands, the pillars embracing the apertures of the arches are fitted into the scheme of decoration in a variety of different ways. All this deviates from the strict and rigorous principles of Byzantine tectonics.

The purely ornamental elements in the S. Sophia frescoes are also non-Byzantine in character,[103] and since they occupy a very important place in the general decorative scheme, they must be regarded as a specifically Russian contribution. They undoubtedly reflect the influence of Russian folk art with its primordial taste for pattern. This wealth of ornamentation gave to S. Sophia of Kiev, both internally and externally, an essentially indigenous stamp, considerably tempering the austere character of the religious images imported from Byzantium.

Local stylistic traits are also clearly discernible in the mosaics with which the decoration of the interior was begun. Next in order of execution came the frescoes of the central cross, the work of a mixed Byzanto-Russian workshop which later, assimilating an increasing number of local masters, embarked on the painting of the side naves and the interior gallery. We are now able to recognize the hand of no less than eight mosaicists, among whom the most eminent was the author of the figures of the saints on the south side of the apse [25, 26; 6, 7]. He was apparently the chief master, and there is every reason for connecting him with the school of Constantinople. He has the gift of sharp individual characterization, his drawing is highly expressive, with ease he creates the most subtle effects of colour. The other mosaicists work in a different manner, from which we may conclude that the team of Greek artists who came to Kiev was also composed of provincial masters who brought with them different artistic traditions. These traditions are clearly manifest in the composition of the *Eucharist* [21–24] where the apostles approaching Christ are portrayed in stiff almost identical poses, their thick-set figures with massive limbs drawn in sharp heavy lines. The same heavy lines are also used in the faces with their strong features and lack of individuality. There is little subtlety in the transitions from light to shadow, and because there is no indication of a horizontal ground plane, the figures give the impression of floating in air. The execution of the composition is exaggeratedly two-dimensional. Equally archaic are the representations of the Pantocrator [14, 19], the Virgin Orans [20] and S. Mark the Evangelist [3]. In their general approach, the mosaics of S. Sophia at Kiev are very different from the art of Constantinople with its sense of grouping, its fine colour harmonies, its efforts to suggest a third dimension. The nearest stylistic affinities to the mosaics of Kiev are found in the mosaics of Hosios Lukas, dating from the beginning of the eleventh century. Both reveal pronounced archaic trends. In Kiev

44. Archangel. Fresco, 1046–61/7. Kiev, S. Sophia

these trends were largely conditioned by the fact that Russian monumental art was then in its infancy and naturally archaic, so that local artists participating in the creation of the mosaics were bound to be closer in spirit to the provincial Greek masters than to the chief master from Constantinople. The truth of this is borne out by the evidence of the mosaics done by Kievan masters, such as the images of two of the martyrs of Sebaste: Nicholas [27] and Aetius. In them the archaic tendency is clearly expressed in the flatter forms, the heavier lines, and the stiff countenances devoid of personality.

Owing to their bad state of preservation, it is difficult to judge the style of the frescoes. It seems that work on the mosaic decoration was prematurely interrupted (on the western arch under the dome the medallions with the half-length figures of the Martyrs of Sebaste are not in mosaic but fresco)—perhaps due to the sudden departure for home of the Greek mosaicists. But certainly some of the Greek masters remained and continued to collaborate with the local artists, and from this Byzanto-Russian workshop came all the frescoes which decorate S. Sophia. The team of painters working on these frescoes must have been very large, otherwise it would be hard to explain the many differences in the manner of painting.

The frescoes for the central crossing, very monumental and finished not later than May 1046, the year of the first consecration of the cathedral, form the earliest group [28–30, 36–38; *17, 19, 21*]. Many-figured compositions, compact and impressive in scale, fit very nicely into their allotted space. As a rule they are orientated in the plane of the wall, and often have a definite central axis on either side of which the parts are equally distributed. The large imposing figures are placed in a row and the architectural background is always

61

45. The Centurion Cornelius from 'The Apostle Peter with the Centurion Cornelius'. Fresco, 1046–61/7. Kiev, S. Sophia

46. A Hebrew Youth. Fresco, 1043–6. Kiev, S. Sophia

47. Musician. Fresco in the north-west tower, about 1120–5. Kiev, S. Sophia

on a plane parallel to the surface plane. This treatment lends to the Gospel story a majestic epic quality. Similarly treated are the representations of the single saints which adorn in vast numbers the walls and pillars of the central cross. Firmly anchored on their feet, these saints are distinguished by their monumental scale and the grave and steady gaze of their robust countenances. The rather summary treatment accorded to these faces is a far cry from the detailed linear elaboration of form characteristic of the painting of the mature twelfth century; they are rounded rather than elongated; the lines defining the brows, eyes, nose and mouth are pleasing because of their expressive simplicity and clarity; the planes of forehead and cheeks are not broken up, but presented as uninterrupted, generally fairly strongly-lit, surfaces. The modelling of the faces is achieved through the use of dense and heavy green shadows. In these stylistic features there is an echo of the Roman portrait-painting of the late Empire. It is no mere coincidence that some of the faces recall the portraits of Fayum for, in fact, representations of male and female martyrs occurred very frequently in the martyria of Palestine,[104] from whence they passed into church painting at a later date and so kept alive the traditions of antiquity.

By the sixties of the eleventh century, when the second consecration of the cathedral took place, the painting of the side-naves and the interior gallery must have been completed. Dating from the twelfth century are the frescoes which adorn the outer gallery, the towers and the baptistry. These were primarily the work of Russian artists, as is evidenced not only by the Slavonic inscriptions but also the style which is flatter and more linear in character. The frescoes for the towers come into a category of their own; their archaism and abundance of oriental motifs is astonishing. The artists responsible were obviously very familiar with oriental silverware and patterned silks, from which they copied the exotic motifs of griffons [50; *30, 32*], leopards, camels [48] and other animals. Another curious feature is that the beasts of their own native fauna give the impression they had been taken from a Sassanian plate or a precious Byzantine fabric. Once again we see how complex are the sources of artistic culture in Kievan Rus'.

Apart from a single fresco-fragment [*40*] dating from the late thirties of the eleventh century[105] and belonging to the Cathedral of the Transfiguration of the Saviour (Spasso-Preobrazhensky Cathedral) at Chernigov, all the remaining works of monumental painting in Kievan Rus' belong much later—in the twelfth century. This was the time when, besides the Kievan court, other centres of culture began rapidly to develop, among which the monasteries were to play an important role. The chief of these monasteries was Pechersky. Founded about the middle of the eleventh century, it enjoyed the intellectual support of the first Russian Metropolitan, Ilarion, and to it gravitated all who were opposed to the 'Constantinople party', a faction which demanded unconditional obedience to the Greek clergy. The priors and monks of the Pechersky Monastery did their utmost to establish closer relations with Slav countries and with Athos, in order that Russians might come in contact with Greeks, Serbs and Bulgars. Through these channels the models of Greek provincial and Slavonic art made their way into Kievan Rus', though, we should add, the cultural connexions of the monastery were not restricted to Athos alone— its Statutes were in fact received from Constantinople, from the Monastery of the Studion. It was also from Constantinople that the artists were invited who, between 1083 and 1089, decorated the great Church of the Dormition, the principal church of the Pechersky Monastery (cf. pp. 27, 29, 72). As the statement of Archdeacon Paul of Aleppo shows,[106] the system of decoration employed in this church followed the tradition of Constantinople and was very similar to that adopted for S. Sophia of Kiev (e.g. the Virgin in the Orans position and the *Eucharist* in the apse, the *Pantocrator* in the dome). Unfortunately nothing from this church has survived, and hence we are unable to comment on the style.

48. Camel with driver.
Fresco in the north-west tower,
about 1120–5. Kiev, S. Sophia

49. Seraph. Fresco, 1046–61/7. Kiev, S. Sophia

50. Griffon. Fresco in the south-west tower, 1113–25. Kiev, S. Sophia

Until recently, a source of much discussion has been the question of the date of another Kievan mosaic ensemble, of which only some scattered fragments remain. This ensemble was commonly thought to have adorned the Church of the Archangel Michael founded in 1108 by Svyatopolk (Michael), Grand-prince of Kiev, but this view was strongly contested by M. K. Karger who maintained that it belonged to the Church of S. Demetrius in the Dimitriyevsky Monastery, founded by the Grand-prince Isyaslav (Dmitry) Yaroslavich, and finished not later than 1062. This church was subsequently confused with the Church of the Archangel Michael.[107] However, the plan of the Church of S. Demetrius (whose foundations were excavated by A. S. Annenkov in 1838) was recently discovered by Yu. S.

51. The Eucharist. Mosaic, about 1108. Kiev, Church of the Archangel Michael

Aseyev,[108] and clearly shows that under no circumstances can this church be identified with that of the Archangel Michael. Thus M. K. Karger's theory is refuted, and the surviving fragments of mosaic can safely be attributed to the Church of the Archangel Michael. According to the testimony of Paul of Aleppo,[109] the decoration of the central apse in the Church of the Archangel Michael differed only slightly from that adopted in the apses of S. Sophia of Kiev and the Church of the Dormition in the Pechersky Monastery. In the conch was represented the Virgin Orans, below which was a register containing the *Eucharist* and lower still a frieze with figures of saints. In common with S. Sophia of Kiev, the mosaics were combined with frescoes. From this splendid decorative ensemble only part of the apsidal mosaics has survived, plus several fragments of frescoes. The mosaics show the *Eucharist* [51–54, 57]; the figures of Demetrius of Thessalonica [56] and the archdeacon Stephen [55] which adorned the inner sides of the pillars in the apse; the figure of the apostle Thaddeus (in this church four apostles were portrayed on either side of the *Eucharist*); the frescoes show the *Annunciation, Zacharias*, fragments of saints [41] and some excellent ornamental motifs. After the demolition of the Church of the Archangel Michael these mosaics and frescoes were transferred to one of the upper chapels in S. Sophia in Kiev, and the mosaic with the figure of Demetrius of Thessalonica was given to the Tret'yakov Gallery in Moscow.

A comparison between the composition of the *Eucharist* in S. Sophia of Kiev and the same theme in the Church of the Archangel Michael reveals a greater degree of freedom in the structure of the latter. In S. Sophia the apostles approaching Christ are depicted in very similar attitudes, and are placed almost equidistant from one another, thus producing a composition of a solemn and measured character. In the mosaic in the Church of S. Michael, on the other hand, the figures of the apostles, more elegantly and less rigidly portrayed, form loose and pleasing groups. The artists are not afraid to place figures behind one another instead of side by side at regular intervals, and show a taste for intersections and asymmetric arrangements. The attitudes and gestures effectively express the reactions of the apostles to the most solemn moment in the rite: Andrew, dignified, contains his emotion while Simon, turning towards Philip, openly registers his amazement; Bartholomew, arms upraised, is deep in prayer, while Paul, leaning forward is about to drop to his knees. In the treatment of the faces, these mosaicists do not exaggerate the eyes (as did the mosaicists of S. Sophia), but aim at a harmonious balance in which no one feature is allowed to predominate. By varying the arrangement and shade of the hair, the colour of the skin, the shape of the eyes, the line of the nose, the contour of the face, the artists gave to each of the apostles a distinctive personality.

Many art historians, puzzled by the excessive elongation of the figures in these mosaics, have been tempted to attribute this feature to a lack of experience on the part of the artists who created them. In reality, however, this elongation serves a definite artistic purpose. In the Church of S. Michael, the frieze with the *Eucharist* was located very high up and, in addition, covered a highly concave surface. Owing to the laws of perspective, the figures would consequently have appeared sharply foreshortened to the spectator's eye had not the mosaicists deliberately lengthened them (with the exception of Christ and the angels, who were given normal proportions since they appeared in the centre where the wall of the apse was least concave). By this means the artists made allowances for optical distortions, and thereby revealed their familiarity with traditions going back to antique art.

The mosaics of the Church of the Archangel Michael, like those of S. Sophia, are remarkable for the exceptional beauty of their deep rich colours, among which a whole series of greens, ranging from emerald to muted dark green predominate. The extensive use of gold in the folds of the chitons and cloaks lends to the draperies an air of pageantry. White, pink, grey and red tesserae are utilized in the faces. Dark greys and olive-greys were widely used for the shading. Hair is either light grey, white, dark grey or dark brown. Especially effective, however, is the gamut of colours used in the draperies, striking in the subtlety of its nuances: white and grey merge imperceptibly into emerald green, brownish-red, violet, steel blue, and delicate pink—forming a remarkably iridescent colour range, controlled with great virtuosity by the Byzantine masters. Each colour is treated not as a separate entity but in intimate relationship with its neighbours with which it combines to form an indivisible whole. Each drapery is a finished symphony of colour, but from the harmonious juxtaposition of all the draperies together there arises a new synthesis, an even more perfect unity. In this respect the mosaics of the Church of the Archangel Michael occupy a distinctive and honourable place in the history of medieval monumental painting.

If one compares the mosaics of the Church of the Archangel Michael with those of S. Sophia, the perceptive eye will at once detect in the former a greater fervour in the application of linear principles. The lines which cover the draperies with an almost web-like tracery have acquired an elegant calligraphical character. Not only do they follow the

69

52. The Apostles, from 'The Eucharist'. Mosaic, about 1108. Kiev, Church of the Archangel Michael

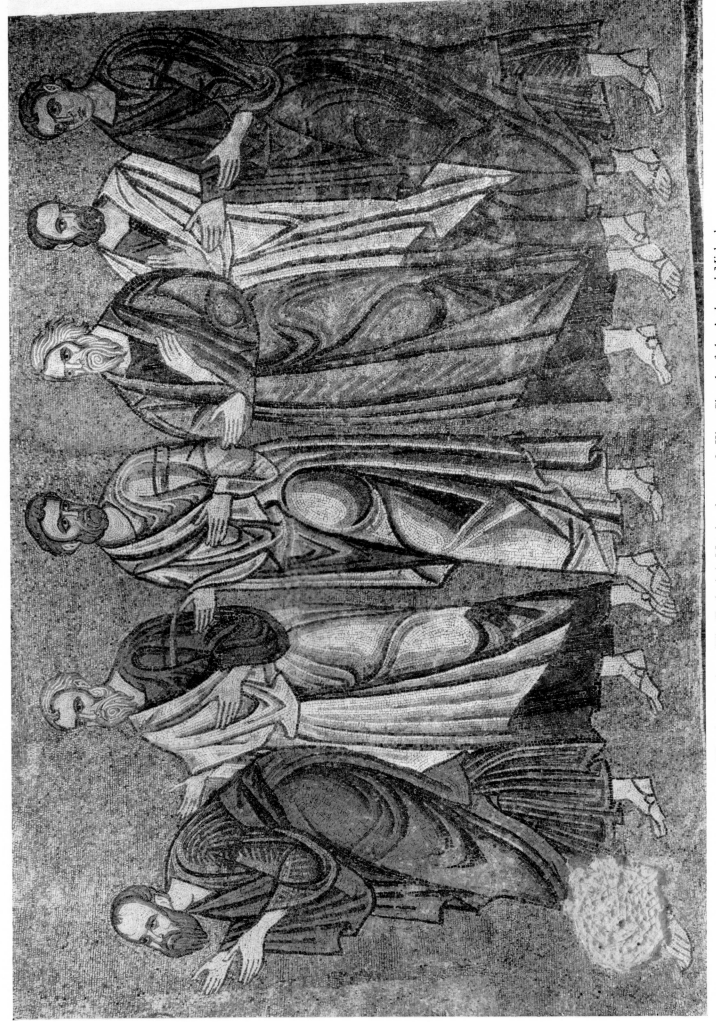

53. The Apostles, from 'The Eucharist'. Mosaic, about 1108. Kiev, Church of the Archangel Michael

54. Head of Angel, from 'The Eucharist'. Mosaic, about 1108. Kiev, Church of the Archangel Michael

rhythmic movement of the form, they also have an intrinsic ornamental significance. The mosaicists no longer adopt the large smooth planes so much favoured by the masters of S. Sophia, but instead divide up the planes with lines, sometimes breaking them, sometimes forcing them to wind, sometimes placing them in parallel rows. This new approach points to the influence of miniature-painting, which first established the basic principles of the linear-calligraphical style. Although the mosaics of the Church of the Archangel Michael definitely gravitate towards the monumental painting of the twelfth century, they nevertheless contain several persistent Hellenistic elements. The presence of this Hellenistic heritage brings them close to the famous mosaics of Daphni, which out of all the works of eleventh century monumental decoration is the one which most closely approximates to the great works of antiquity. In style the mosaics of the Church of the Archangel Michael mark a transitional phase between, on the one hand, the mosaics of Nea Moni (1042–56), those of the narthex of the Church of the Dormition at Nicea (1065–67) and the cycle at Daphni (second half of the eleventh century); and on the other the mosaics of the southern gallery of S. Sophia of Constantinople (1118–22) and those in the Gelati Monastery (c. 1130).

Since a period of seventeen years was all that divided the completion of the great Church of the Dormition from the building of the Church of the Archangel Michael, the artists who created the latter's mosaics could easily have come from the ranks of craftsmen who worked on the Pechersky Monastery. This theory becomes even more credible in the light of the evidence of the *Pechersky Paterik*, which states that the Greek masters from Constantinople who built and decorated the Church of the Dormition did not return home but remained in Kiev, where they died and were buried under the name of 'the twelve brethren'.[110] D. V. Ainalov was therefore right to connect the mosaics of the Church of S. Michael with the Constantinople school.[111] As was the case in S. Sophia of Kiev, these Greek masters were undoubtedly assisted by the indigenous artists who, however, in this case contrary to what Galassi thought, did not play a substantial role.[112] Otherwise, it would be difficult to explain the errors occurring in the Slavonic inscription over the mosaic of the *Eucharist* (here the word *Zaveta*—Testament—is repeated twice!).[113] A mistake of this

55. Archdeacon Stephen. Detail of mosaic, about 1108. Kiev, Church of the Archangel Michael

kind could only be made by someone unacquainted with the Slavonic language. As usual, several craftsmen participated in the mosaics for the Church of the Archangel Michael. The part of the composition which is most truly 'Greek' is the central part with the figures of Christ and the angels, whereas in the treatment of the apostles' robes (particularly Andrew's) a certain negligence is evident in the drawing, denoting less experienced hands. Much larger pieces of tesserae are employed for the figures and the faces than were used in S. Sophia and there are also differences in the colours used in both schemes; the principal emphasis in the Church of S. Michael being on shades of emerald green. All this proves that the workshop of mosaicists who decorated the Church of the Dormition and the Church of the Archangel Michael was in no way connected with the workshop responsible for the decorations in S. Sophia, also that the masters of the Church of the Archangel Michael followed different and later artistic traditions.

The mosaics in the Church of S. Michael were the last to be executed on Russian soil. This branch of art, indivisibly connected with the heyday of the political and economic power of the Kievan state, was so costly that in the succeeding period it was omitted altogether from the decoration of sacred buildings. The rulers of the small principalities could not afford to use mosaic in the decoration of their churches, but a curious reminder of the art is found in the gilded backgrounds of some fresco fragments found among the ruins of the church built in 1197 by Prince Ryurik Rostislavovich.[114] Eager to impress the public with the splendour of his church, Ryurik Rostislavovich, though unable to use mosaic, remembered the technique—probably associated in his mind with the age of the 'great' Yaroslav—and as a substitute for the glittering splendour of the tesserae had gold backgrounds introduced into the paintings.

Not mosaic but fresco was the art form destined to live on and to enjoy great development in ancient Rus'. In the Cathedral of S. Sophia it already played an extremely important role, covering vast areas of the walls and vaults. In the subsequent period it was increasingly used, and through this medium the emerging national traits found rapid embodiment. The influence of the artistic heritage of Constantinople, so extensive in the age of Vladimir and Yaroslav, was by the twelfth century gradually losing its hold and under the impact of local traditions underwent a radical change. The refined picturesqueness of mosaic work gave way to a linear treatment of form—the artists preferring the graphic means of expression. The range of colours was reduced, thus producing effects of greater brilliance and saturation; the tender half tones gradually disappeared. What the images lost in elegance and refinement they gained in power and spontaneity. Along this path early Russian monumental painting developed its own artistic language, enriched by a variety of individual contributions from the various local schools.

Regrettably, the surviving examples of twelfth-century Kievan monumental painting are all either in a very poor state of preservation or not yet cleaned. To the first category belong the frescoes of the Church of S. Michael in the borough of Ostersk (the Virgin Orans between the archangels Michael and Gabriel, the *Eucharist* and figures of saints in the apse, executed between 1098 and 1125),[115] as also the twelfth-century frescoes from the baptistry of the church of the Dormition in the Monastery of Yelets in Chernigov (fragments of the *Baptism*, figures of saints, and the Old Testament subject of the *Three Hebrew in the Furnace*). To the second category belong the frescoes of the Monastery

ΑΓ ΔΗ · ΔΗΜΗΤΡΙΟϹ

56. S. Demetrius of Thessalonica.
Mosaic, about 1108.
Kiev, Church of the
Archangel Michael

57. Head of Christ. Detail from 'The Eucharist'. Mosaic, about 1108. Kiev, Church of the Archangel Michael

of S. Cyril, dating from the 'seventies or later, and the frescoes of the Church of the Arch-angel Michael in the Vydubitsky Monastery, probably dating from 1199. Among these the most important is the large ensemble of frescoes in the Monastery of S. Cyril, which are urgently in need of careful restoration.[116] These paintings are notable not only for the complexity of their iconography (the Virgin Orans, the *Eucharist*, figures of saints in the apse, scenes from the Gospels on vaults and walls, scenes from the life of S. Cyril and S. Athanasius of Alexandria in the diaconicon, the *Last Judgement* on the western wall, many saints, especially warrior saints on the pillars), but also for their affinities with southern Slav works. A connexion with the Balkans is further suggested by the presence of large numbers of saints of Balkan origin, such as Cyril, Methodius, Clement of Bulgaria, John of Macedonia, Joseph of Thessalonica and others. It would be premature to pronounce any judgements on the style of these frescoes in the Monastery of S. Cyril until they have been thoroughly cleaned and restored, but even at this stage it is evident that they were painted

76

by local masters, not only on account of the Slavonic inscriptions but also because of the rather archaic style, which has close affinities with the style of Romanesque painting.[117]

Kievan Rus', which bore the full brunt of the nomadic onslaught paid a high price for it and exhausted herself in a prolonged and wearisome struggle for survival. By the end of the eleventh century the process of feudal disintegration had already begun. This process was particularly intense in the southern principalities, in Pereyaslavl', Chernigov and Kiev. Obliged to rely increasingly on their own resources, these principalities were unable to resist the pressure exerted on them from all sides by the Polovtsy (Cumans). In that remarkable poetical work entitled *Slovo o Polku Igoreve*, Southern Rus' has left to us a bitter lament on her fall. Unable to resist the pressures from without, Kievan Rus' finally collapsed at the end of the twelfth century. However, her great cultural traditions lived on in the works of the architects and painters of Novgorod and Vladimir-Suzdal', and were carried to the western principalities and to Pskov. Everywhere they served as a basis for the development of local schools which flourished widely in the twelfth and early thirteenth centuries. And though fine art in ancient Rus' was never to recapture the monumental quality which was the hallmark of Kievan art in the tenth–eleventh centuries, it developed in later ages a greater diversity of forms. Thanks to the growth of the centrifugal forces, the cultural legacy of Kiev had a chance to reach out to the bulk of the Russian people. Fertilized by contact with the living art of the masses, it acquired even more vivid and vital traditional elements. With the consolidation of the small feudal principalities, many local schools arose with their own masters who proved worthy rivals to the architects and painters who arrived from Kiev. Russian art in the period between the twelfth and fourteenth centuries moved in the direction of decentralization; making full use of the Kievan tradition, it became not only more varied in its manifestations but also more deeply rooted in the Russian soil.

58. S. Artemius. Fresco, about 1189. Vladimir, Cathedral of the Dormition

Chapter II

THE RUS' OF VLADIMIR-SUZDAL'

AFTER KIEVAN RUS' it was the lands of Rostov-Suzdal', on the upper Volga, which emerged as the second cradle of Russian sovereignty and civilization. In them the spirit of Great-Russia was forged and national aspirations proved strongest and most steadfast.

The princes of Kiev had for a long time shown interest in the Rostov lands. They had tried to exercise political influence over them and annexe them to their own territories. Vsevolod, son of Yaroslav, had already succeeded in uniting Rostov, Suzdal', and the area adjoining the Volga with Pereyaslavl'-of-the-South. From time to time Vladimir Monomakh, who had founded the town of Vladimir-on-the-Klyazma, used to ride over these lands, and his son Yury Dolgoruky (c. 1090–1157), after settling in Suzdal', embarked on an energetic programme of building new towns (Pereyaslavl'-Zalesky, Yur'yev-Pol'sky, Dmitrov, Moscow, Zvenigorod, etc.) So, gradually, the Zales'ye saw the birth of new urban centres, with their artisan population engaged in commerce. These town-dwellers were a force to be reckoned with in the twelfth century: the 'Autocrat' Andrey Bogolyubsky (1111–74) depended on their support during his political struggles, and the powerful Vsevelod-the-Big-Nest (1154–1212) was also obliged to treat them with deference. And if the towns of Vladimir-Suzdal' appeared to be only isolated landmarks among the vast tracks of forest-land and farming settlements, their role in the cultural development of the region was nevertheless of the utmost importance. For in them were concentrated the craftsmen without whom no building of any significance could have been erected, let alone decorated.

During the early stages of development, the Rostov-Suzdal' lands drew to a large extent on the artistic heritage of Kievan Rus'. But as the political and cultural importance of Kiev waned, the independence of the principality of Vladimir-Suzdal' correspondingly grew. Whereas Yury Dolgoruky still tried to hold on to the Kievan throne, his son, Andrey Bogolyubsky, completely abandoned the idea and firmly established himself in Vladimir which he built up to rival Kiev, Rostov, and Suzdal'. He extended and enlarged the town, filling it with 'merchants, craftsmen, and artisans of every kind'. In 1158, under the auspices of the Cathedral of the Dormition, also erected by Andrey Bogolyubsky, the systematic writing of the Vladimir chronicles was begun. The most notable feature of these chronicles is their great range: their assessment of historical events embraces the whole of Russia. In them the power of the prince of Vladimir is treated as an all-Russian power, and the town of Vladimir as the new centre of all-Russia. This same concept of the unity of the Russian people is expressed in a remarkable literary work written in Vladimir and entitled *The Service of the Intercession (Pokrov) of the Virgin*. Here the Virgin is regarded not merely as the patroness of the sovereign-city of Vladimir and its prince, but as the protectress of all its citizens and of the 'Russian' lands in the broad sense. The struggle against 'the darkness of our disunity', that is, against the feudal disintegration of Rus', was the *leitmotiv* of this cult of the Intercession of the Virgin. Thus the anonymous clerical writer of Vladimir re-echoes ideas and aspirations very similar to those expressed by the brilliant author of *Slovo o Polku Igoreve*.

If we leave aside the fragment of the *Last Judgement*, formerly in the cathedral in Pereyaslavl'-Zalesky dating from the late fifties of the twelfth century[118] and now preserved in the Moscow History Museum, the frescoes on the original north façade of the Cathedral of the Dormition in Vladimir must be regarded as the earliest achievement of monumental painting in the principality of Vladimir-Suzdal' (1158–61). When this church was rebuilt by Vsevolod between 1185 and 1189 the north wall became the inner wall of the northern nave. Between the little columns of the arcading several standing figures of prophets and two peacocks and an ornament which framed a window [59] were discovered. While these poorly preserved frescoes show the hand of an experienced master, confident in the use of his brush, of even greater interest to us is the fact that they offer conclusive proof that the exterior walls of Andrey Bogolyubsky's Cathedral of the Dormition were adorned with paintings. Since the columns of the arcading were originally gilded, these figures of prophets, holding unfurled scrolls in their hands, were formerly displayed in a gold setting. It is highly improbable that this rich polychrome painting would have been the only one of its kind on Vladimir-Suzdal' soil. Apparently the custom of painting the exteriors of churches with frescoes was widespread in old Rus', and the almost complete absence of such painted exteriors today can only be attributed to the loss and destruction of so many monuments. Of course we are not referring here to the painting of the whole exterior, as was later practised in Roumania, but only to the painting of the arcading friezes, niches above entrances, and the pillars of open galleries. Thus, for example, in S. Sophia at Kiev, the pillars of the exterior gallery were decorated in fresco, and on the inner sides of the arches half-length figures of martyrs were shown; it is also possible that frescoes existed in the niches above the arcade of this same gallery.[119] This external decoration meant, of course, that the church façades had a much more attractive and less austere appearance than they have today.

After the murder of Andrey Bogolyubsky, his brother Vsevolod-the-Big-Nest ascended the grand-princely throne of Vladimir in 1176 and consolidated the all-Russian authority of the Vladimir dynasty by energetically expanding the borders of his territory. Not without reason is he referred to by the Vladimir chronicler as 'great' and 'Sire'; the chronicles even propound the theory that the tsar is like to men only in his terrestial substance—'in power he is like unto God'. This theory, borrowed from Byzantium, was propagated in an attempt to surround the power of Vsevolod, who called himself 'Grand-prince', with an aura of purely Byzantine greatness and glamour.

We know that Vsevolod spent his youth in Constantinople, where between the years 1162 and 1169 he was in exile with his mother, a Byzantine princess.[120] She was the step-mother of Andrey Bogolyubsky but a strained relationship between them had forced her to depart with her sons to distant 'Tsar'grad'. It was during these years that the young Vsevolod learnt to appreciate the beauty of Greek art and civilization, and his enthusiasm was shared by other members of his family: his son, Constantine, spoke excellent Greek, and in Vladimir, his brother Michael founded a school run by Greek and Russian monks and also a library containing over a thousand Greek manuscripts.[121] It is obvious that in this grand-princely milieu the great artistic creations of Byzantium met with a lively appreciation, and it is not difficult to see why Greek artists were invited to paint the churches which Vsevolod was erecting.

Between 1185 and 1189 Vsevolod completely rebuilt the Cathedral of the Dormition—originally founded by Andrey Bogolyubsky but later damaged by fire—and saw to its redecoration. Unfortunately, only a few fragments have survived which do not permit any valid conclusions to be drawn about the origins of the artists. The fragments comprise the severely damaged figures of the prophet Habakkuk, an unidentified saint behind the iconostasis (by its northern and southern edges), and the figures of S. Artemius [58] and S. Avraamy [42] which decorate the arch in the southwest corner of the cathedral. The two latter figures were accompanied by ancient Greek inscriptions, renovated during the restorations of 1888–91 but since lost.[122] The figures of Artemius and Avraamy, painted inside the small ornamental arches, reveal in their execution an assured hand and notable skill. Because of extensive damage to the upper coat of paint, it is very difficult to determine the nationality of the master who worked here: he was either a Greek, or else a local artist who had received a thorough Greek training.

59. Prophet. Fresco, about 1161. Vladimir, Cathedral of the Dormition

The frescoes of the Cathedral of S. Demetrius, built by Vsevolod between 1194 and 1197 [60–68] provide us with an easier task. There is no doubt that a master from Constantinople took part in the painting of this church and that, in creating a remarkable decorative ensemble, he was assisted by Russian artists. Of the former extensive decoration only the frescoes on the large and small vaults under the gallery have survived; twice restored in former times, these works were again cleaned in 1918 by the members of the All-Russia Restoration Committee.

The theme illustrated in these surviving frescoes is that of the *Last Judgement*. On the large vault the twelve apostles are shown seated, with angels standing behind them; on the small vault we see two scenes—*Paradise*, depicting the Virgin enthroned, an angel, Abraham, Isaac, and James, and the *Entry of the Righteous into Paradise*, where the apostle Peter heads the procession and two trumpeting angels bring up the rear. The

81

60. Apostles and Angels, from 'The Last Judgement'. Fresco, about 1195. Vladimir, S. Demetrius

paintings are primarily the work of a Greek master, but there is no doubt that he was helped by Russian artists.

The twelve apostles and the right-hand group of angels on the southern slope of the large vault were painted by the Greek master and reveal the touch of an outstanding artist [60–63]. He portrayed the apostles in relaxed attitudes as if quietly discoursing among themselves. They gaze in different directions, the body following easily the movement of the head, while the draperies fall in a complex pattern of folds forming a series of varied linear harmonies. This skilful arrangement of folds brings instantly to mind the motifs of Hellenistic sculpture. The draperies elegantly envelop the figures, following the contours of the handsome well-proportioned physiques; the gestures are rendered with grace and ease; particularly rhythmic are the inclined positions of the heads, adding vigour to a composition which has nothing stiff or static about it. Instead of lining up the foreground figures in a row, the Greek master working in the Cathedral of the Dormition has created a varied group full of rhythmic movement. Each of the apostles has his own individuality; under the veneer of traditional iconographic canon, individual traits break through so that the faces assume a remarkable life-like quality. In these figures a subtle inner force

61. Head of the Apostle Philip, from 'The Last Judgement'. Fresco, about 1195. Vladimir, S. Demetrius

62. The Apostle Matthew, from 'The Last Judgement'. Fresco,
about 1195. Vladimir, S. Demetrius

and a splendid physical exterior are blended together in a manner worthy of classical antiquity.

The mastery with which the figures of the apostles and the right-hand group of angels on the southern slope have been executed is truly remarkable. The colouring too is particularly fine, though naturally not a little of the pristine freshness and brightness has been lost. The colours which predominate are pale blue and green, steel-blue intermingled with light brown, purple, reddish-brown and greenish-yellow. In the treatment of the draperies, iridescent colours are widely used, of which the combination of green and violet is the most effective. The faces which, as we have noted, are such a significant feature of the composition have been treated with special delicacy and artistry. The brush-strokes model the forms sometimes by means of broad patches diminishing to nothingness, sometimes by clearly defined narrow strips (for example around the nostrils or below the eyes), and sometimes by sharp dabs of the brush, applied with exceptional confidence and forcefulness. These lush white highlights, placed on the greenish flesh tints, mould the forms, add relief to them and draw them out from the surface plane; they are handled with unusual skill. Unlike the Italian artists of the fourteenth century, this master does not construct his forms by means of light and shade, but by modelling with colours. His technique is absolutely uniform—he draws with his brush and everything is determined by its movement.

In the Cathedral of S. Demetrius one can distinguish quite clearly between the work of the visiting Greek artist and that carried out by his Russian apprentices and assistants. Apart from the figures of the twelve apostles, the master in charge also executed the right-hand group of angels on the southern slope of the large vault. These angels are endowed

63–64. Heads of Angels from 'The Last Judgement'. Fresco, about 1195. Vladimir, S. Demetrius.
Left: From the south side of the vault. *Right:* From the north side of the vault.

with such liveliness and such a spiritual quality that their equal can scarcely be found among the entire painting of the twelfth century. The artist powerfully moulds the forms with the aid of lush highlights, nor is he afraid to use asymmetry as a means to attaining greater emotional force. On the other hand the angels in the left-hand group of which the four extreme heads are in a poor state, present a rather different appearance; by comparison they look solid and thickset, and psychologically speaking, dull and prosaic. The drawing of the faces and particularly of the hands is more primitive in character, the facial features are more robust, the gentle moulding by colour has given place to a more emphatic treatment of form. All this strongly suggests that the left-hand group is the work of the master's closest assistant, who would have been recruited from among the local artists of Vladimir.

The third artist to contribute to the painting of the large vault was the author of the figures of the angels on the northern slope [64]. Stylistically he is close to the second master, but his work lacks the same quality. The faces of his angels are even more fleshy, his lines heavier, his draughtsmanship less assured, and in his treatment of flesh he prefers even tones to sharp highlights. His timidity in the use of highlights on the flesh tints means that they do not so much mould the form as lightly hint at it—from serving a definite purpose they have become an ineffectual stylistic convention. One gets the strong impression here of a pupil just embarking on his career; these are the first tentative steps. But it is precisely this fact which makes his innovations even more significant. The oval of the face has lost the exaggerated refinement and delicacy which those of the best angels on the southern slope possess; it has acquired a more down-to-earth, more rotund character. The nose has become more pronounced, the eye-recesses smaller, the eyebrows straighter. The Greek-type face has in fact been replaced by a Slav one—in other words, a face observed from life.

In the decoration of the small vault, where the old Slavonic inscriptions occur, it is quite evident that the Greek artist had no part, but in the scene of the *Entry of the Righteous into Paradise*, the hand of the author of the left-hand group of angels on the southern slope of the large vault is easily recognizable. The same somewhat puffy faces with their strong features and the same disposition of highlights [65, 69] are found again here. In the treatment of the stern face of S. Peter, one is struck by the same tendency towards stylization, while the figures of the two trumpeting angels [67], for all their expressiveness, fall far short both in draughtsmanship and painting of the best figures of the angels of the southern slope of the large vault, the work of the Greek master.

It is not so easy to arrive at conclusions about the paintings of the southern slope of the small vault, since the left-hand section has greatly deteriorated with time and the right-hand one has suffered from past restorations. The figures of the Virgin and the angel beside her [66], set amid the profuse vegetation of the Paradise Garden [70], are rendered somewhat lifelessly and betray none of the brilliance we have come to associate with the main artist. The drawing is somewhat cramped, the highlights are not always accurately placed, and there is a greater simplicity in the drapery folds. The figures of the three patriarchs and the souls of the righteous—symbolized by infants—suggest an even more inexperienced hand. Clearly in both these instances we are dealing with the work of the master's pupils, though we cannot identify them with any of the painters who assisted him on the frescoes of the large vault.

Thus, in the paintings of the large and small vaults, we can distinguish the hands of several artists—one Greek and three or four Russians working under his tutelage. Of the latter the most gifted was the author of the left-hand group of angels and of the *Entry of*

65. The Entry of the Righteous into Paradise. Fresco, about 1195. Vladimir, S. Demetrius

66. Virgin and Angel in the Garden of Paradise. Fresco, about 1195. Vladimir, S. Demetrius

the Righteous into Paradise. Enlisting the co-operation of local artists, the Byzantine master entrusted them with the less vital parts of the work; in this way he speeded up the execution, while at the same time shaping the indigenous talent to his own style of painting— inasmuch as joint work on one and the same composition naturally led the younger artist to follow the example of the more experienced master.

The decoration of the Cathedral of S. Demetrius not only provides an excellent example of how Russian and Greek artists worked together, but it also throws light on the way in which the Russian painters adapted the existing Byzantine heritage to their own need for self-expression. By modifying the rigid laws of Byzantine art, the Russians strove to achieve a more natural and less conventionalized art. They did not hesitate to introduce rich vegetation into church painting (which made their Paradise so attractive), they clothed the women in the *Entry of the Righteous into Paradise* in Slavonic dress, and they stamped a national imprint on the faces of the angels. Thus traditional modes of representation gradually assumed a new look in which purely Russian elements came increasingly to the fore.

Two more fragments of church painting have survived in the old Vladimir-Suzdal' principality. The first of these is in the Church of Boris and Gleb in Kideksha, not far

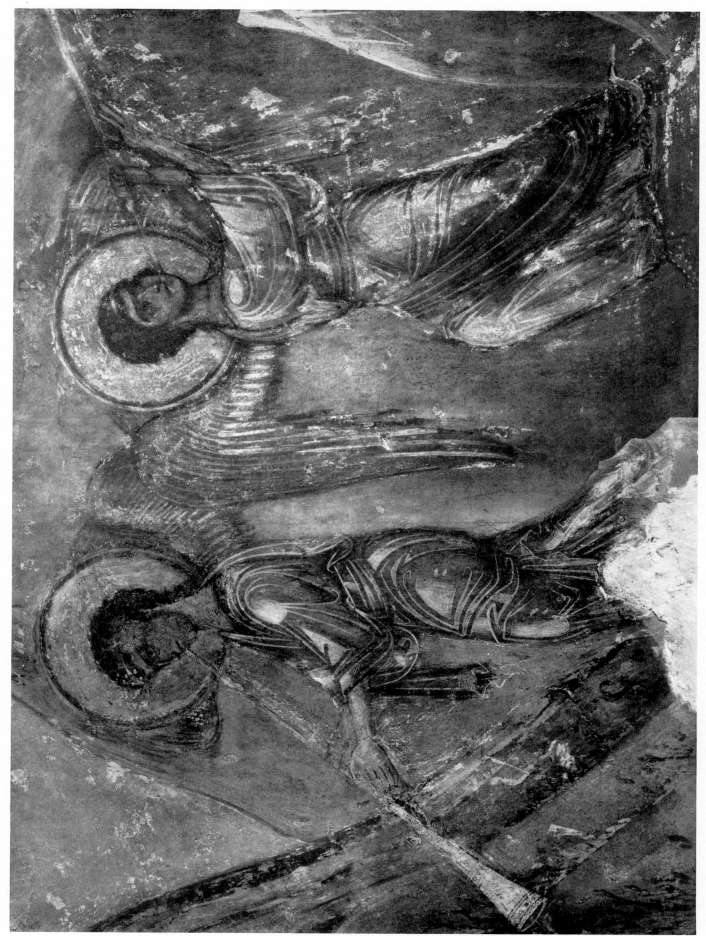

67. Trumpeting Angels from 'The Entry of the Righteous into Paradise'. Fresco, about 1195. Vladimir, S. Demetrius

68. Pious Women, from 'The Entry of the Righteous into Paradise'. Fresco, about 1195. Vladimir, S. Demetrius

69. Unknown Saint. Fresco, 1233. Suzdal', Cathedral

from Suzdal',[123] where a much damaged fresco was discovered in a niche above the tomb of Maria, widow of Prince Boris (Yury Dolgoruky's son); this depicted the martyr Maria and S. Helena, the namesakes of Prince Boris's widow and of Yury Dolgoruky's second wife. The figures are placed in a setting of trees and sacred birds, and the work with its heavy forms, graceless silhouettes, maroon-red draperies and dark olive-green vegetation sharply stands out against the neutral white background. In addition to this fragment, the remains of other compositions (*The Denial of Peter*, *The Three Hebrew Children in the Fiery*

Furnace, and *The Dormition*) were also discovered. Above the gallery, trees and birds from a representation of the *Garden of Eden* still survive, and, finally, cleaning revealed two figures on horseback and trowels decorated with seven-branched candlesticks and trees. What distinguishes these fragments which date from the eighties of the twelfth century is their considerably archaic style. In the opinion of N. P. Sychyov, the artists who worked here belonged to the Chernigov school, but owing to the very poor state of the surviving pieces this conclusion is still open to doubt. One thing, however, we can affirm with certainty: Greek artists had no hand in the decoration of the Church of Boris and Gleb.

The second scheme consists of frescoes dating from 1233 in the diaconicon of the Suzdal' Cathedral [69].[124] Originally, the apse of the diaconicon was richly ornamented. On the northern and southern pilasters of the apse, two finely executed heads of elderly saints, grave and ascetic in countenance, came to light during cleaning; they are part of full-length figures inserted within ornamental arches. The rigid precise draughtsmanship, the muted treatment of ochrish tones in the lighter areas, the absence of sharp contrasts of light and shade so favoured by Novgorodian artists—all contribute to the air of strained sobriety in the faces. There is no Russian work of the late twelfth–early thirteenth centuries which bears any close stylistic resemblance to this manner of painting. Since these frescoes for Suzdal' Cathedral came under the general decorative programme undertaken by Cyril, Bishop of Rostov, in the churches of Rostov, Suzdal', and Yur'yev-Pol'sky, they may confidently be attributed to local artists from Rostov or Suzdal'.

The fearful onslaught of the Tartars brought the great flowering of early Russian culture which had taken place in the twelfth and first quarter of the thirteenth century to an abrupt end; from 1223 onwards the Russian lands were systematically sacked and plundered by the invading hordes. With the exception of Novgorod, most towns came under Tartar domination. These events marked the beginning of a dark era in Russian history. The population were forced to take sanctuary in the impenetrable woods, out of reach of the Tartar cavalry. The principalities became more and more deeply split; cultural contacts with Byzantium and the Balkans were almost completely severed; the level of national morals and customs declined; the standard of education fell, religious piety waxed as the feeling of doom grew. Skilled craftsmen were in short supply, resources were lacking, and gone was the stability essential for the creation of grandiose monuments. Under these conditions, monumental painting and sculpture, starved of patronage, suffered an almost total eclipse.

The fourteenth century saw the political ascendancy of Tver' and Moscow, and these towns consciously adopted the culture of the principality of Vladimir-Suzdal'. The Moscow princes regarded themselves as the direct successors to the grand-princely power of Vladimir, and it is significant that until 1432 they were invested with their title of 'Grand-prince' beneath the ancient vaults of the Cathedral of the Dormition in Vladimir. When they began to build stone churches it was to the Vladimir-Suzdal' 'white-stone' architecture that they turned for models. But it was not only the Moscow architects who kept this heritage alive—the great Russian artist, Andrey Rublyov was in many ways a product of the same tradition; in 1408 he was given the task of restoring the ancient frescoes in the Cathedral of the Dormition, and contact with them acted as a stimulus to his creative genius. Finally, the Pskovian and Italian architects who were engaged to build the Cathedral of the Dormition in the Moscow Kremlin were advised by the Grand-prince Ivan III to make a preliminary excursion to Vladimir in order to study its architectural monuments. This advice was prompted by the awareness that the greatest and most lasting Russian monuments of the twelfth century had been created on Vladimir soil, in an age when Rus', before being crushed by the Tartar yoke, was independent and powerful under the rule of the Vladimir princes.

70. Detail from 'The Garden of Paradise'. Fresco, about 1195. Vladimir, S. Demetrius

Chapter III

NOVGOROD AND PSKOV

B Y THE FULL WATERS of the river Volkhov stood Novgorod, one of the most ancient cities of all Russia. Due to its strategic geographical position it had already in the tenth century become a great trading and manufacturing centre for eastern Europe. The bogs and impenetrable marshlands surrounding it saved it from the Tartars —the tidal-wave of the Mongol invasion halting on the borders of its domains. During those perilous times when the Russian people experienced the full weight of Mongol oppression, Novgorod held on to its independence and native culture. In the thirteenth and fourteenth centuries it became a bastion against Swedish and German encroachments. This city was the outpost of the culture of Old Russia and the guardian of her best traditions, and, later, Moscow was to draw deeply on its artistic heritage.

The history of free Novgorod, this oldest of Russian republics, recalls in many ways that of the Western communities. Owing to the rapid development of trade and industry in the town, the artisan classes soon became strong, and indeed before long grew into a redoubtable force commanding consideration even from the mighty Novgorodian boyars. The part they played in the political life and defence of the town led the chroniclers to refer to them more and more frequently by the respectful terms of 'sirs', alongside that of 'people'. Together with the peasants, the artisans acted as skirmishers in the town's uprisings. Using their own resources they constructed churches in the name of their patrons and gave banquets which were attended by all the members of their artisan guild. From their midst the heresy of the Strigol'niks arose (*c.* 1375) which was directed against the feudal hierarchy of the Church. A sober, down-to-earth outlook typified these Novgorodian artisans. Their attitude to religious dogma was a flexible one; their preference was for a more lively, realistic art, in much the same spirit as those entertaining historiated initials of the fourteenth-century Novgorod manuscripts, with their humorous scenes from everyday-life showing quarrelling fishermen, drunkards, bathers, musicians and mountebanks. Under the influence of the artisans' taste, popular and realistic elements gradually seeped into the official religious art of Novgorod and undermined its traditional orthodoxy.

But, strong as were the artisan classes in Novgorod, it was not they who shaped the destiny of the town, for the real power was concentrated in the hands of two other groups —the rich boyars with their vast estates, and the prosperous merchants who formed themselves into trade associations either on a family, or simply company, basis. It was in fact these groups which were to commandeer the key administrative posts and the most profitable economic positions; behind the scenes, they controlled the Council of Citizens (*veche*) through the Council of Lords; they put into office civil authorities (*posadniki* and *tysyatskii*) from their own ranks and carried out a systematic policy to further their own vested interests. It was they who in the second half of the twelfth century reduced the role of the princes to that of virtual figureheads; they who spurred on the inhabitants to the

93

71. S. Helena. Fresco, second half of 11th century. Novgorod, S. Sophia

energetic colonizing of the north; they who gave such a tremendous power and impetus to feudal ownership. By the fifteenth century however, the Novgorod boyars had degenerated into an overt oligarchy whose separatist anti-national policies were brought to an end in 1478 by the annexation of Novgorod to Moscow.

It was between the eleventh and fourteenth centuries that the most noteworthy Old Russian mural paintings were created on Novgorod soil. They have their own particular style—simple, informal and expressive, and reveal national characteristics in a much more marked way than did the mosaics and frescoes of the Kievan school where the inherited link with Byzantine art is present to a much greater degree.

At the end of the tenth century and during the first half of the eleventh, Novgorod was a dependency of Kiev and within the orbit of her cultural influence. But when in 1054, shortly before his death, the Grand-prince Yaroslav of Kiev decided to divide up his lands there was no mention of Novgorod in his will—an obvious sign that he no longer regarded her as a Kievan dependency, and officially recognized her independent status. As far as its political structure went, the principality of Novgorod in the eleventh century differed little from the other Russian principalities. The princes still retained the right to own land, to appoint and dismiss civil authorities and to administer justice. As with Kiev, power over the populace was in the hands of whoever ruled the heart of the city, that is to say the Detinets (Kremlin). From the second quarter of the twelfth century, when Novgorod became a republic ruled by the Council of Citizens, the situation underwent a radical change. Step by step the boyars decisively curtailed the power of the princes, with the result that these were transformed into nothing more than the hired military defenders of the city. They were obliged to settle outside the confines of the town, in a place called Gorodishche, near which the largest of the royal monasteries sprang up: first, the Yur'yev Monastery, and a little later the Monastery of the Saviour on the Nereditsa. Henceforth, the boyars became part-masters of the Detinets; their interests were represented by the *posadnik* and by the Archbishop of Novgorod. Thus in the history of the town began a new chapter, inseparable from the growth of democratic trends, and it is to this period (second half of the twelfth to the end of the fourteenth century) that the greatest number of Novgorod mural paintings belong.

The earliest example of Novgorod wall-decoration is the fragment, unique in style, which has survived in the southern gallery of the Cathedral of S. Sophia in Novgorod, a church which was built between 1045 and 1050, but remained for the most part unpainted until 1108. Prior to this, the decoration was apparently confined to images of saints on the

94

pillars fulfilling the function of monumental icons, yet stylistically independent. To them belong the fragment in the southern gallery depicting S. Constantine and S. Helen full-length [71]. In the faces of these saints there is no attempt whatsoever at modelling; the elegant graphically precise lines are drawn by a sure and experienced hand thoroughly conversant with all the finesses of calligraphy; the pale, tenuous colours (the most common are sky-blue, flake-white and pinkish-orange) are captivating in their transparent quality and peculiar luminosity. The style of this fragment is so unusual that it is difficult to find any close analogy to it among the monuments of East-Christian and Byzantine painting.

Of the paintings of 1108 (when according

72. The Prophet Daniel. Fresco, 1108. Novgorod, S. Sophia

73. King Solomon. Fresco, 1108. Novgorod, S. Sophia

to the First Novgorod Chronicle, the fresco-decoration of S. Sophia was begun), there have survived seven figures of prophets in the drum [72, 73], figures of SS. Anatole, Karp, Polycarpus of Smyrna and Germanus, the Patriarch of Constantinople, in the apertures above the passages leading from the main apse to the lateral ones, and some insignificant fragments which had been knocked from the walls during the barbarous restorations of 1893[125] and which were afterwards found under the new floor. From the account which has been handed down to us of these restorations, we can form an idea of the general layout of the paintings. In the apse were depicted the Virgin Orans,

95

74. The Wife of Job, from 'Job on the Dung-Hill'. Fresco, soon after 1113. Novgorod, Nikolo-Dvorishchensky Cathedral

75. Unknown Saint. Fresco, 1125. Novgorod, Cathedral in the Antoniyev Monastery

The Eucharist and the Order of Saints; at the sides of the triumphal arch, *The Annunciation;* on the arches, half-length figures of saints in medallions; on the vaults, scenes from the New Testament; on the walls, full and half-length figures of saints in rectangular frames. If to all this we add the Pantocrator surrounded by four archangels in the dome,[126] we have here an iconographical scheme quite similar to those of the Kievan churches.

Although in the course of the 1893 restorations, the majority of frescoes were either over-painted or retouched, those which have survived provide us with enough evidence for judging their style. In particular, we are struck by the marked archaism of the prophets, bearing scrolls with Slavonic inscriptions: strong and thick-set, they stand in stiff, frontal poses; their draperies fall in straight and weighty folds, the hems forming harsh horizontal lines; noticeably solid are the extremities—huge, stumpy feet, broad hands with thick stubby fingers; the stern oriental-type faces are notable for their large eyes which seem to hypnotize the onlooker. This severe type of monumental art bears a close stylistic affinity to the more archaic group of mosaics and frescoes in S. Sophia of Kiev. Were it not for the evidence of the First Novgorod Chronicle and the paleography of the inscriptions (both indicating the twelfth century), the frescoes in the drum of the Cathedral of S. Sophia in Novgorod could easily be mistaken for works of the eleventh century, so closely are they linked to the early traditions. At any rate, these paintings provide ample evidence for dismissing the later and scarcely reliable evidence of the Third Novgorod Chronicle which claims that the artists of S. Sophia of Novgorod were 'icon-painters from Tsar'grad' (the Russian word for Constantinople).[127]

Two other examples of early twelfth-century art in Novgorod—the paintings from the Nikolo-Dvorishchensky Cathedral and the cathedral in the Antoniyev Monastery—show that at this period a great variety of stylistic trends were being followed in Novgorod, a phenomenon which may have been connected with the activities of different workshops, some of which may even have been of foreign importation.

The fresco-fragments from the Nikolo-Dvorishchensky Cathedral, built in 1113 and attached to the residential palace of the princes, date from the second decade of the twelfth century. In the south-west lower part of the church remains of a monumental composition of the *Last Judgement* were discovered, as well as *Job on the Dung-hill*, a scene rarely met with; and in the central part below, figures of the bishops were found. The stately figure of Job's wife with her thin, stern face [74] is a relic of Kievan traditions, and indeed it is quite possible that we are dealing here with the work of a visiting master from Kiev, or of a Novgorodian artist who had passed through a Kievan school. It is clear, at any rate, that this art associated with the princely court is not at all like the archaic paintings of 1108 to be found in the Cathedral of S. Sophia.

The paintings in the Cathedral of the Nativity of the Virgin in the Antoniyev Monastery, completed according to the First Novgorod Chronicle in 1125, were the product of quite a different school [75–76; *43–44*]. Between 1923 and 1947, a number of frescoes were uncovered in the apse and tower of this cathedral: figures and heads of saints, medallions with half-length figures of bishops, the remains of the *Presentation* in the prothesis, two scenes from the life of S. John the Baptist in the diaconicon (*The Beheading of John the Baptist, The Presentation of the Baptist's head to Herod*), and fragments from *The Adoration of the Magi* and *The Dormition* on the walls. All the frescoes have been damaged

76. Youth, from 'The Discovery of the Head of John the Baptist'. Fresco, 1125. Novgorod, Cathedral in the Antoniyev Monastery

97

by holes made when they were subsequently covered over with a fresh layer of plaster. Large heads with thick fleshy features testify to the un-Byzantine character of these images, and the way in which they are painted is not Byzantine either. The faces are outlined with energetic reddish-brown lines; over the ochrish flesh-tones are placed green shadows and reddish touches—the latter having darkened with time stand out like dark stains. The handling is broad and free, virtually devoid of any graphic stylization (with the possible exception of one face—that of a bearded old man in the central apse). The rather sober and solemn colour scheme is limited to cold tones among which priority is given to grey. In its general approach and feeling, this severe art can be related to the monuments of Romanesque art, in particular the paintings of S. Croce in Gerusalemme in Rome (1144) and the miniatures of the Reichenau and Ratisbon schools, and such a connexion is not surprising in view of the vigorous cultural contacts between Novgorod and the West. Moreover, in the *Zhitiyo* (biography) of the founder of the Antoniyev Monastery, we learn that he came from Rome.[128] On his arrival in Novgorod, Antony (1067–1147) knew no Russian and understood only Greek and Latin.[129] 'The Tale of Antony the Roman' relates how a barrel which he cast into the sea miraculously drifted ashore at Novgorod, and how inside it were discovered, besides gold and silver, ecclesiastical vessels of foreign workmanship, 'the inscriptions on the vessels are written in the Roman tongue'. F. I. Buslayev[130] has already referred to the *Zhitiyo* as possibly providing additional evidence of the influence of Western art on Novgorod. In Novgorod one could undoubtedly find examples of Romanesque art, as for instance, the famous bronze doors of 'Korsun' in the Cathedral of S. Sophia, enamels from Limoges, etc. Neither can we exclude the possibility that Romanesque fresco-painters were active in Novgorod; working alongside the masters of the Novgorod school they may well have co-operated in the frescoes for the Antoniyev Monastery Cathedral, which today represent the most 'Romanesque' of the Novgorodian paintings.

The recently-cleaned frescoes in the tower of the Cathedral of S. George in the Yur'yev Monastery (figures of bishops, S. George, and the half-length figure of Odigitria between the windows of the drum), belong to the first half of the twelfth century. While it is unlikely that these badly-damaged frescoes can be contemporary with the building of the cathedral in 1119, they were certainly completed not later than the middle of the twelfth century. In the resolute, manly, heavy-featured faces, one already finds so much that is essentially Novgorodian that these frescoes must be ascribed to local masters. Among the pure tones, the most common are golden-yellow, green and light blue, while the hair of the old men has a bluish tint.

There is no uniform style to be found among the Novgorod frescoes of the first half of the twelfth century. It is clear that a number of different workshops were active at this time, some of whom may have come from other towns. For instance, the fragments in the Nikolo-Dvorishchensky Cathedral strongly indicate that courtly taste looked towards the brilliant art of Kiev, while the frescoes of the dome and of apertures near the main apse in the Cathedral of S. Sophia, as also the frescoes in the Cathedral of the Nativity of the Virgin in the Antoniyev Monastery point to quite different artists, connected with more archaic traditions, especially the Romanesque. Parallel with these trends, an independent local school was developing (the eleventh-century fragment in the southern gallery of the

77. Women weeping,
from 'The Dormition'.
Fresco, middle of 12th century.
Pskov, Cathedral of the Transfiguration
in the Mirozhsky Monastery

Cathedral of S. Sophia, the paintings in the tower of the Cathedral of S. George), which was to play a dominant role from the second half of the twelfth century onwards. It is significant that in none of the above-mentioned works do we come across Greek inscriptions, as was the case in the monuments of Kiev and Vladimir.

Before turning to the Novgorod paintings of the second half of the twelfth century, we must pause to consider a monument of interest in Pskov: the frescoes for the Cathedral of the Transfiguration of the Saviour in the Mirozhsky Monastery [77–83; *45, 46*]. These paintings, still not completely revealed by cleaning, date from about the middle of the twelfth century (not later than 1156) and were commissioned by Niphont, Bishop of Novgorod—a Greek by birth whose persistently Graecophil policy led him into conflict with the people of both Novgorod and Kiev.[131] Pskov was, in the twelfth century, one of the satellite towns of Novgorod, subject to it in administrative and ecclesiastical matters. Impatient with this state of affairs, Pskov succeeded in 1348 in achieving complete independence by the terms of the treaty of Bolotovo and became a political centre with the same rights as Novgorod-the-Great. The full flowering of the Pskovian school of painting took place during the fourteenth and fifteenth centuries, but there is every indication that as early as the twelfth and thirteenth centuries she was already developing her own local

99

78. The Archangel Gabriel. Fresco, middle of 12th century.
Pskov, Cathedral of the Transfiguration in the Mirozhsky Monastery

traditions. Not only the Pskov icons of the thirteenth century demonstrate this, but also the frescoes of the Cathedral of the Mirozhsky Monastery which are altogether unlike other contemporary Pskovian paintings. Although Greek artists, summoned by Niphont, participated in the execution of these frescoes, the paintings nevertheless contain stylistic traits which can be ascribed only to works of purely Pskovian creation.

The decorative system follows the scheme of Byzantine churches—not those in Constantinople itself but those in the provinces. In the conch of the apse we see the *Deesis*, which occupies this place only in the monuments of the East-Christian world. Above the *Deesis* there is a depiction of *Etimasia*. The apse is decorated with the traditional *Eucharist* (in two versions) and with frontal standing figures of bishops and deacons, placed in two registers [8]. On the vault of the bema is shown *The Transfiguration*, and on the chancel-arch, flanking a medallion of Christ-Emmanuel, are the figures of Melchisedek and Aaron. On the frontal sides of the altar pillars are *The Annunciation*, and the Virgin standing with a scroll in her hand, and *Christ Enthroned*. On the pendentives we see the evangelists between whom are placed two images of the Holy Face and the half-length figures of Joachim (?) and Anna (?). In the summits of the arches supporting the dome are the half-length figures of Emmanuel, Mary and an archangel with a rod (the half-length figure of the southern arch has been lost), while on the curves of these same arches appear the Righteous of the Old Testament. In the drum, sixteen prophets are depicted. In the dome we do not find the usual twelfth-century half-length portrayal of the Pantocrator but instead *The Ascension* (Christ seated on a rainbow, surrounded by eight angels, the twelve apostles and two angels flanking John the Baptist and Mary)—a relic of older traditions. The vaults and walls are completely covered with frescoes arranged in superimposed friezes (their number ranges from three to five), and as there are no vertical divisions, the scenes which occupy these friezes flow directly into one another. The narration of the New Testament does not begin at the northern arm of the crossing (as in S. Sophia of Kiev) but in the southern arm, with the result that the sequence unfolds from right to left. Moreover, the pictures on the upper part of the walls, that is to say, in the lunettes under the vaults, participate in the same cycle of scenes as the ones on the vaults: *The Presentation* (eastern slope of southern vault), *Baptism* (lunette of the southern wall), *Raising of*

79. The Miraculous Draught of Fishes. Fresco, middle of 12th century. Pskov, Cathedral of the Transfiguration in the Mirozhsky Monastery

80. Head of the Archangel Gabriel.
Fresco, middle of 12th century.
Pskov, Cathedral of the Transfiguration
in the Mirozhsky Monastery

Lazarus (western slope of southern vault), *Entry into Jerusalem* (southern slope of western vault), *Last Supper* (lunette of western wall), *Washing of the Feet* (northern slope of western vault), *Crucifixion* (western slope of northern vault), *Mourning over the Dead Christ* (lunette of northern wall), and the *Descent into Hell* (eastern slope of northern vault). The story then loses its chronological sequence. The frescoes in the two lower registers do not adhere to a logical and consistent plan either. Thus for instance, underneath the *Presentation* we have the *Incredulity of S. Thomas* and *The Nativity;* under *The Baptism, The Miraculous Draught of Fishes, The Apparition of Christ to the Eleven*, and other episodes; under *The Raising of Lazarus, The Agony in the Garden* and various miracle scenes; under *The Last Supper, The Descent of the Holy Ghost;* under *The Crucifixion, The Kiss of Judas, The Denial of Peter* and some miracle scenes; under the *Mourning over the Dead Christ*, scenes from *The Judgement of Christ;* under *The Descent into Hell, Christ appearing to the Holy Women* and *The Dormition.* In the last series of frescoes on the eastern side, one can read the paintings vertically (from top to bottom), but on all the other walls the chronological sequence is utterly confused. Furthermore, the episodes of the miracles are dragged into

102

81. Mary, from 'The Annunciation'.
Fresco, middle of the 12th century.
Pskov, Cathedral of the Transfiguration
in the Mirozhsky Monastery

the friezes in the most arbitrary way, so that one is forced to conclude that their sole purpose was to fill up any empty spaces that remained. These observations are indicative firstly, of a weakening of those architectonic principles which so firmly governed the Byzantine mosaic ensembles, and secondly, of the growth of the 'carpet' trend in church decoration, where the paintings were spread over the entire wall from the floor to the apex of the vault.

In the prothesis and the diaconicon of the Cathedral of the Transfiguration of the Saviour are half-length figures of the Baptist and the archangel Michael, together with scenes from the life of the Precursor and exploits of the archangels. (The first of these cycles is very damaged, the second is better preserved permitting the identification of a whole series of episodes: *Jacob's Ladder, Jacob wrestling with the Angel, The Expulsion from the Garden of Eden, Abraham's Sacrifice, The Hospitality of Abraham*, etc.)

Of considerable interest are the paintings in two small chapels by the western wall, cornering on the northern and southern walls. Before the later structural additions, both these chapels were originally lower than the four main arms of the cross, and consequently

103

their paintings were on a much smaller scale. In the north-western chapel, seventeen episodes from the life of S. Peter appear, while in the south-western chapel a no less detailed account of the life of Joachim, Anna and the Virgin is related in sixteen episodes. Unfortunately, like most of the frescoes in this church, neither of these cycles has yet been cleaned, which deprives us of the possibility of judging their iconography and style.

The paintings of the cathedral are rounded off by a series of figures, in severe frontal poses, of martyrs, stylites, warriors and numerous saints covering the lower register of the walls; unfortunately they are the worst preserved of all since during the stormy spring floods the River Velikaya habitually overflows into the lower part of the building.

When the cleaning of the paintings in the cathedral of the Mirozhsky Monastery is completed, we shall have a unique ensemble of mid-twelfth century Russian frescoes—especially in view of the loss of the Nereditsa church—but even on the basis of what has already been done, we can form some idea of the style. This is notable above all for its marked linear stylization; the figures and the faces [78–80] are delineated with heavy lines, which intersect and divide the draperies, the areas of exposed flesh and faces, as well as hillocks and trees. The figures are almost totally lacking in any form of modelling, and are subject to the plane of the wall [79; 45, 46]; here the graphic element is so marked that even the highlights on the faces have been rendered with narrow, precise strokes of the brush. Where the Novgorodian masters prefer broad dabs, the authors of the Mirozhsky paintings rely on lines which they handle with great skill. As a result of this extremely powerful linear stylization, the frescoes possess a certain aridness, though one cannot deny them an austere dignity. Various compositions (as for instance, *The Appearance of Christ to the Holy Women* [82]) in their conciseness, sometimes recall purely heraldic modes of representation.

82. The Appearance of Christ to the Holy Women. Fresco, middle of 12th century.
Pskov, Cathedral of the Transfiguration in the Mirozhsky Monastery.

83. Christ and the Samaritan Woman.
Fresco, middle of 12th century.
Pskov, Cathedral of
the Transfiguration
in the Mirozhsky Monastery

It would be premature at this stage to draw any decisive conclusions about the number of masters who were attached to this commission, though it seems almost certain that the *artel'* was directed by a visiting Greek master—the Greek inscriptions, the Byzantine iconography, the stylistic similarities with the frescoes in the Church of S. Pantaleon in Nerezi (1164) all point that way. That this master did not, however, bring to Pskov the traditions of Constantinople itself, but rather those which prevailed in the eastern provinces of the Byzantine Empire is strongly suggested by the treatment of the friezes as a continuous uninterrupted narrative, as also the presence of a whole series of archaic survivals in the iconography (*The Ascension* in the dome, *Deesis* in the conch of the main apse, the many scenes of miracles and healings). Local painters from Pskov must have helped this Greek master; it was they who tried to render the religious images less forbidding and to enrich the emotional content. The portrayal of grief in all its manifestations obviously interested them (cf. the daughters of Jerusalem in the scene of *The Dormition*, [77]; Mary and the angels in *The Crucifixion* scene, etc.), but they never lapse into exaggerated emotionalism or those ecstatic forms of expression so beloved of Gothic masters. Their story is told on a calm epic note avoiding over-dramatization, and their majestic manly art falls entirely within the stylistic framework of the twelfth century.

One element in particular, perhaps not immediately noticeable, testifies to the participation of Pskovian artists in these Mirozhsky frescoes, viz. the rich linear treatment of the draperies, clearly derived from the gold hatching of icons [82]. An analogous treatment of folds is found in the frescoes of the Snetogorsky Monastery (1313), and in a series of early Pskovian icons (the *Deesis* in the Russian Museum, S. Nicholas in the Tret'yakov Gallery, etc.). As a substitute for gold, which was too costly, the Pskovians generally adopted a rich yellow pigment, which enabled them to resort to delicate parallel hatchings

84. S. George and the Dragon. Fresco, about 1167. Staraya Ladoga, S. George

to enhance the draperies; this practice, unusual for Byzantine frescoes, is found extensively in the Mirozhsky paintings, on which visiting Greek artists and local masters worked simultaneously.

Since the next example of monumental art in Pskov—the frescoes for the Cathedral of the Nativity of the Virgin in the Snetogorsky Monastery—is dated as late as 1313, let us now return to the Novgorod school, which in the second half of the twelfth century experienced a period of rich and vigorous development.

In the light of new research, the frescoes of the Church of S. George in Staraya Ladoga (the northern *prigorod* or suburb of Novgorod) may be considered as the earliest ensemble falling within the period with which we are concerned. The paintings were completed about 1167, soon after the siege by the Swedes, who unable to take the fortress retreated to the Ladoga Lake. There, on May 28, 1164, at the mouth of the river Voronaya, they were overtaken by the Novgorod army under Prince Svyatoslav Rostislavich and the Posadnik Zakhariya, and thoroughly routed.[132] It was, presumably, in honour of this victory that the Church of S. George was erected a year later, and dedicated to the saint whom the people of Rus' revered as the patron of warriors and a faithful ally in time of war. In these circumstances, the portrayal of *S. George and the Dragon* [84] on the wall of the diaconicon (a unique siting for this particular subject) becomes understandable as an undoubted allusion to the Novgorodian victory over the Swedes.

The frescoes which have survived from the Church of S. George are only fragmentary [84–91; *47, 48, 51, 52*]. In the apse are the remains of *The Communion of the Apostles* two figures of saints (S. John Chrysostom and S. Basil the Great), and two medallions with half-length figures of John the Almsgiver and another unidentified saint. In the prothesis, a half-length portrayal of the archangel Gabriel [89], and a scene from the proto-evangelical cycle (*The Refusal of Joachim's Offering* [*51*]) have survived; in the diaconicon are preserved a half-length figure of the archangel Michael, and the already noted large monumental composition of *S. George and the Dragon* [84], together with a frieze of three medallions enclosing half-length portrayals of bishops (the central one depicts S. Anthimus). In a better state are the frescoes of the dome and drum where *The Ascension* [86–88] and the figures of eight prophets [10, 85, 90, 91] are shown. A large composition of *The Last Judgement* occupies its traditional place on the western wall and adjoining vaults [*47, 48*]. Of the cycle depicting the Feasts which used to decorate the vaults and walls, only a fragment from *The Baptism* has survived on the southern wall. From amongst the formerly numerous portraits of saints, only those of S. Gleb (?) [*52*], the prophet Daniel, a half-length portrayal of S. Nicholas, an unknown martyr (S. Sebastian?) and the martyr Mary have survived.

In this church, the frescoes were arranged in three main registers, which included scenes from the New Testament and the life of S. George, as well as full-length figures of the prophets. There were also two narrow registers with half-length figures of saints painted in medallions framed by rich ornamentation, which occupied the lower levels of the walls and also stretched between the middle and upper registers. Finally the plinth part of the walls was covered by painted panelling in imitation of marble facing. The combination of the three wide and two narrow registers made for a nice flexible rhythm and helped to banish monotony from the overall presentation. By this means architectonic

85. Unknown Prophet. Fresco, about 1167.
Staraya Ladoga, S. George

principles were respected. The frescoes did not cover the walls like one vast uninterrupted tapestry, as in the cathedral of the Mirozhsky Monastery and the church of Nereditsa, but formed a well-proportioned and orderly system, wherein we are forcibly reminded of the monumental painting of the eleventh century. In the decoration of this small church, we get an attractive arrangement of planes as a result of which the interior does not give the same over-burdened impression as do the churches of the Eastern-Christian world.

In the paintings of the Church of S. George, the images of the saints are stamped with a great sternness, bordering on severity; indeed some [10, 85, 89] have a near-fanatical expression, while others appear almost belligerent. The majority are presented in motionless frontal poses, very similar to icon images. All these prophets, martyrs and saints transfix the spectator with their gaze as if hypnotizing him with their large eyes. They seem to possess a mysterious transcendental power calculated to instil a feeling of awe in the mind of the believer.

The masters who worked in this church were highly skilled in the layout of their compositions on the wall-surface: their frescoes are conceived in relation to the wall and not as a superimposed adornment. For them the wall and the painting together form an intrinsic unified whole. Particularly significant in this respect is the composition of *S. George and the Dragon* [84] which covers the curved wall of the diaconicon. The mounted figure of S. George is placed in the centre, in other words on the flattest part of the wall, where there can be no perspective distortion and where it is easiest to extend it horizontally. To the side, where the wall has a pronounced curve, a vertical-type building is shown, which would not suffer greatly from foreshortening, and towards this building is directed the sharply ascending line of a hill. This line plays quite an important role in the composition, linking the central part with the lateral part so that both can be viewed, despite the curve in the wall-surface, as one optical whole. Doubtless, a corresponding line, but this time directed diagonally towards the left, outlined a hill (now lost) on the northern side of the diaconicon, behind which must have stood a building more or less similar to the one depicted on the right. Here, too, the artists would have allowed for the distortion

86 and 87. Angels, from 'The Ascension'. Frescoes, about 1167. Staraya Ladoga, S. George

88. Apostles, from 'The Ascension'. Fresco, about 1167. Staraya Ladoga, S. George

89. The Archangel Gabriel.
Fresco, about 1167.
Staraya Ladoga, S. George

due to perspective. Thus, by careful calculation, a unified artistic impression was produced, which could only be achieved by strict adherence to the specific laws of monumental painting.

Subjecting their frescoes to the plane of the wall, the authors of the Staraya Ladoga paintings make line the prime vehicle for their artistic expression. It is line which plays the leading role throughout—in the structure of the forms, the delineation of the silhouettes, the treatment of faces, and in the ornamentation. The drapery is divided into narrow flat folds, which at times fall straight, at times form sharp angles, zigzag, wind into knots or expand diagonally, at times curve into flowing parabolas. In the treatment of these draperies, one senses a playful abandonment to the vagaries of purely ornamental draughts-manship—they are the work of an outstanding draughtsman, who not only knows how to reveal the structure or rather the rhythm of the drapery, but also how to exploit with a truly sophisticated and elegant touch the purely ornamental aspect of the folds.

The same virtuosity is apparent in the outlines of the figures, as for instance the particularly expressive silhouette of S. George on the prancing horse [84]. Only a master who thoroughly appreciated the beauty of the sparing yet flexible line could achieve such a simple yet meaningful artistic effect. In general, fresco-painters preferred broken, angular lines, using for this purpose cloaks whose ends flow out or drape downwards and which deliberately have sharp-angled forms [85, 88].

But it is probably in the treatment of the faces that the use of the ornamental line shows itself to greatest advantage. Lush highlights and dabs have given way to an ornamental type of lighting, represented by a series of bright lines which weave capriciously across the greenish-yellow flesh tints [10, 85, 89, 91]. It is with the aid of such white lines that the forehead, the nose and all its contours, the eye-recesses, the cheek-bones, the chin and the neck are fashioned, conveying the impression of a surface divided into small isolated compartments. Treated in a somewhat different manner are the more youthful faces [90], where the lighted areas are brought out in a much softer way through greater emphasis on shading than on lines; in this way the modelling of the faces acquires a more picturesque character and the harsh transitions from light to shadow are considerably attenuated. The face of King Solomon is treated almost completely in white (as in the series of figures in Nereditsa), with the result that the ornamental elements reveal themselves not in the bright but in the shaded areas, a feature which does not disturb the fundamental principles of ornamental art. Here, one could say, to use an analogy from the field of photography, that the negative has been replaced by the positive.

It is only natural that artists with such an inordinate interest in the potentialities of line should have been drawn towards an ornamental type of art. This is precisely the case in the decoration of the Church of S. George. Ornamentation is resorted to wherever there is the slightest pretext for it, and there is an intimate bond between the white tracery of the ornamental structures and the highly stylized areas of light on the faces. This, indeed, is a manifestation of something which was greatly esteemed by the people of Old Russia, namely 'pattern' (*uzoroch'ye*).

The mural paintings of the Church of S. George, small in size, were the work of two artists—a chief master and one assistant. Although several scholars (Diehl, Schweinfurth, Talbot Rice)[133] have favoured the attribution of these frescoes to Byzantine masters, there is abundant evidence for ascribing them to local Novgorodian artists: for instance, the Slavonic inscriptions and characteristic 'Novgorodisms' (the substitution of 'ch' for 'ts', etc.); the extensive use of ornament bearing close affinities to Slav book ornamentation with its complex interweaving of stripes; the portrayal among the saints of John the Almsgiver and the martyr Gleb, who were particularly popular in Novgorod; and finally the many points in common with the iconography and style of the frescoes in the Mirozhsky Monastery, and those in the churches of Arkazhi and Nereditsa. All these decorative ensembles of the second half of the twelfth century combine to form quite a coherent stylistic group which could for convenience' sake be called the North-Russian, or more

90. King Solomon. Fresco, about 1167. Staraya Ladoga, S. George

91. King David. Fresco, about 1167. Staraya Ladoga, S. George

92. Unknown Saint. Fresco, about 1189.
Arkazhi, Church of the Annunciation

accurately, the Pskov-Novgorod group. At the same time we do not wish to deny the obvious links between the Staraya Ladoga frescoes and those of purely Greek creation, in particular with the paintings of the Church of S. Pantaleon in Nerezi (1164). Amongst the Novgorod murals of the twelfth century, the ones in Staraya Ladoga are the most Graecophil, as witnessed by the sternness and austerity of the images and also the marked refinement of form. These paintings belong in fact to the 'Byzantinizing' trend in Novgorodian art, which also produced a whole series of magnificent icons (the *Ustyugh Annunciation*, the *Holy Face*, *S. George*, etc.). There are good reasons for believing that this trend was connected with the court of the prince, but with the weakening of his position it soon faded out, gradually absorbed by the flood of new images and forms which sprang up from local and popular sources.

Among the Novgorod paintings dating from the end of the twelfth century, the earliest are the frescoes of the Church of the Dormition (now called the Annunciation) near the village of Arkazhi, three kilometres south of the city. Since the church was consecrated by

Gavriil, Archbishop of Novgorod, on June 4, 1189,[134] the frescoes [92, 93; *53*] must also have been completed about that time. They were for a long time concealed under whitewash and overpainting, but in 1930 the task of uncovering them was started. In the diaconicon are scenes from the life of S. John the Baptist, and also figures of saints; in the prothesis, a proto-evangelical cycle derived from apocryphal sources; in the arches leading from the central to the side apses, saints and warrior-saints; in the central apse, figures of bishops and an archdeacon. All are painted in that same free and bold manner which the Novgorodians liked so much. Particularly expressive are the resolute, strong faces, full of irrepressible energy [92]. The highlights are brought out either through a gentle heightening of the light areas [93], or by sharp lines, which in places (forehead, cheek-bones, nose, neck) are so intensely stylized as to create a complex filigree pattern. This sort of stylized treatment of highlights which generally confers on the faces an expression of extraordinary force and psychological strength, was a favourite device of the Novgorodian fresco-painters, and also highly characteristic of them is the range of colours

93. Head of a Youth. Fresco, about 1189.
Arkazhi, Church of the Annunciation

used, based on clear and bright tones (golden-ochre, sky-blue, light-green and pink). The faces are painted mostly in pure ochre with touches of pale green in the shadows.

The fresco depicting the half-length figures of the Deesis, found in 1948 on the wall of the Martiriyevskaya Parvis in the Cathedral of S. Sophia in Novgorod [54], also dates from the late twelfth century. Yu. N. Dmitriyev[135] was inclined to attribute it to the year 1144, when the Bishop Niphont ordered the paintings for the chapels of the cathedral.[136] But the problem is not quite so simple, since this particular fresco formed part of a funerary monument (under it stood a tomb) and its creation was determined by the devotion of the repose of the soul. One cannot therefore regard it as an intrinsic part of the paintings of the Martiriyevskaya Parvis. No doubt it was painted at the express wish of the deceased or of his nearest relatives, as was customary in the Middle Ages (see also the recently discovered mosaics and frescoes in the Church of the Chora—Kariye Camii—placed above tombs).[137]

In this tomb fresco, Christ is represented with the Virgin, the archangel Michael and the apostle Peter on His left [54], while on His right are John the Baptist, the archangel Gabriel and the apostle Paul. This depiction of the half-length figures of Deesis is a direct imitation of the icons usually shown on the architrave above the royal gates of the altar-barrier,[138] and the composition was used by the artist for the purposes of the cult of the repose of the soul—the saints interceding with Christ for the deceased. The purely Novgorod types of faces with their heavy, thick features, and the energetic manner of painting indicate that this was the work of local artists.

One of the greatest losses to art during the Second World War was the destruction of the Church of the Saviour-on-the-Nereditsa, not far from Novgorod. The paintings in this church [94–108; 55–61], completed in 1199,[139] represented one of the best preserved medieval fresco-ensembles in Europe. However, their claim to fame lay not alone in this, but also in the rare completeness of their subject matter, so that in their entirety they offered an almost comprehensive picture of the system of twelfth-century church painting.

The art of the Nereditsa church is an austere art, revealing in its ideas one of the severest currents of Christian thought in Russia. Here, there is no joyful acceptance of the world as in the reliefs of the Vladimir-Suzdal' churches, and the fifteenth-century icons; on the contrary, the dominant feeling is one of fear in the face of the mysterious omnipotence of God and the torments to be endured in the life beyond the grave. Significant in this respect is the fact that the huge representation of *The Last Judgement*, in which all the various tortures of Hell are illustrated in detail, occupies the principal place among the paintings. Wherever the spectator turned his gaze—towards the vaults, the conch, the dome or the lunettes—armies of saints glared at him in an intimidating way; compared with these mighty and firmly-anchored figures whose jet-black eyes shone so penetratingly, man was reminded of his own puniness and insignificance. The emotional impact of this art was so great that even the modern viewer falls under its spell and can appreciate what the people of Novgorod must have felt in the twelfth century, when, somewhat apprehensively, they entered the church erected by their prince and were reminded, as they gazed in trepidation upon *The Last Judgement* scene, of the destiny of mortal existence and the punishment meted out to sin.

The frescoes in this church are noteworthy for their great monumentality. The figures are presented in stiff, frontal poses [94]; if they move at all, their tread is heavy; if

94. SS. Lazarus, James and Phocas. Fresco, 1199. Nereditsa, Church of the Saviour

they stand motionless, they seem riveted to the spot. The compositions fall into separate, self-contained units [101–102]; usually there is a nice balance between their various elements, and intercrossings and intersections are avoided. The images unfurl along the wall, governed by a stately rhythm. Because the faces of the protagonists are in most cases turned towards the spectator, the Gospel scenes unfold themselves in slow motion and acquire an air of timelessness. The ponderous figures with their large heads and thick-set limbs serve to emphasize even more the monumentality of this art—one which is solemn and majestic, virile and resolute.

As we have already mentioned, the spiritual ideas embodied in the Nereditsa frescoes are severe; yet at the same time they have been made to stretch as far as the limits of realism would permit in those times. Some of the saints' faces, for instance, are quite astonishing in their expressiveness and true-to-life aspect. A marked peasant strength emanates from

117

95. S. Lazarus. Fresco, 1199. Nereditsa, Church of the Saviour

96. S. Matthew. Fresco, 1199. Nereditsa, Church of the Saviour

97. Elijah. Fresco, 1199. Nereditsa, Church of the Saviour

the heads of the prophets, the evangelists Luke and Matthew [96, 59], the prophet Elijah [97], various female saints [100], martyrs, and particularly the saints in the apse [94, 95, 99; 58, 60]. S. Nicholas Thaumaturgus, S. Dometian, S. Blaise, S. Gregory of Nazianzus, S. Phocas, S. Lazarus—all these have an unforgettable expressiveness and vitality which breaks through the superficial veneer of Byzantine convention. Sharp and resolute, they are unmistakably Novgorodian; executed in a bold and vigorous manner, enhanced by the contrast between the green of the shadows and the white of the highlights,

98. 'The Ancient of Days'. Fresco, 1199. Nereditsa, Church of the Saviour

they represent one of the highest peaks in the development of Novgorodian monumental painting in the twelfth century.

In the church of Nereditsa, the frescoes began almost at floor level and covered the entire walls and vaults. They were placed in registers one above the other, but the composition of each register differed. These registers are not at all symmetrical; medallions arbitrarily intrude within the margins; compositions with many figures alternate with single images; the vertical dividing lines between adjoining registers frequently do not coincide; rectangles containing the various scenes and figures do not adhere to a standard format; compositions boldly curve round corners and flow across onto the adjoining flat surfaces. All this conspires to make the frescoes look like some gigantic multi-coloured carpet which completely enwraps the walls and vaults. Yellow, light and dark blue, reddish-brown, white and green are the predominant tones, forming a dense and somewhat mottled effect.

121

99. S. Gregory of Nazianzus. Fresco, 1199. Nereditsa, Church of the Saviour

100. S. Barbara. Fresco, 1199. Nereditsa, Church of the Saviour

The system of decoration followed here differs fundamentally from the Byzantine practice wherein strict architectonic principles were of supreme account. In Greek churches, the upper parts of the interior (vaults, lunettes, pendentives, squinches, cupola) were usually reserved for mosaics, while the walls were faced with marble; furthermore, the entire decoration was subordinated to the dictates of the architecture. Mosaics and frescoes were presented within a strict framework, forcing the viewer to observe them as individual pictures retaining vivid echoes of Hellenistic art. In the Nereditsa, however, the system was built on an entirely different basis: the paintings formed a complete uninterrupted surface, reaching from the floor right up to the summits of the vaults and the cupola. In this way the interior lost its sectional character and acquired an air of impressive massiveness similar to that found in Asia Minor, Caucasian and Romanesque decorative schemes, and for which there is no analogy in purely Constantinopolitan art. This affinity of the Nereditsa frescoes with Eastern and Romanesque monuments is further confirmed by their iconography, which retains, as V. K. Myasoyedov has shown, many archaic survivals.

In the main apse is depicted the Virgin Orans, with a medallion on her breast showing the half-length figure of Christ (the so-called *Znameniye*). She is approached on both sides by figures, much smaller in size, of holy men and women led by SS. Boris and Gleb.[140] Beneath the Orans are three friezes with the traditional Eucharist and figures of bishops. Below the main apse, in a niche above the elevated chair of the bishop, Christ is shown in the guise of a priest [55]—the same iconographical type already encountered in the mosaics of S. Sophia of Kiev. To the left of Christ there is a medallion of John the Baptist, and to the right a medallion of Mary (incorrectly referred to in the inscription as Martha).[141] In the left arcosolium the prophet Elijah is seen being fed by a raven [97], while the right arcosolium shows Bishop Peter of Alexandria who, according to legend, did not dare to sit on the 'high chair' because he saw 'the light of heaven and the presence of a divine power' upon it.[142] The portrayal of the prophet Elijah in the main apse is symbolic, for his feeding by the raven was generally regarded as a biblical prototype of the Eucharist in the New Testament.

Above the Virgin Orans is the Empty Throne (*Etimasia*), while the Ancient of Days is shown in the apex of the altar vault [98]. This depiction of Christ as an old man, grey with age, was very closely connected with the dogma of the indivisibility of the Trinity; Christ was portrayed as 'The Creator' of the Old Testament, thus stressing the eternal union which existed between Father and Son.

The prothesis is decorated with the half-figure of the Virgin (of the *Znameniye* type) before whom are two inclining figures. This refers to the well-known Syrian legend of the supplication of S. Alexius (the 'Man of God') before the image 'not made by human hands' of the Virgin in Edessa. Lining the walls are figures of bishops, and on the vaults scenes from the life of Joachim and Anna, a particularly popular theme in Rus'.

The half-figure of John the Baptist fills the conch of the diaconicon while the vaults show scenes from his life; the apse on the other hand is decorated with figures of female saints whose inclusion here is not fortuitous since deaconesses were permitted to enter the diaconicon though not the prothesis. Of these female saints, Ripsimiya is the most interesting; although she had entered early into the menology of the saints of the Eastern

101 and 102. The Presentation of the Virgin and the Presentation in the Temple; The Baptism.
Frescoes, 1199. Nereditsa, Church of the Saviour

125

103. The Crucifixion. Fresco, 1199. Nereditsa, Church of the Saviour

Church, she was particularly revered in the Caucasus. Another female saint closely connected with the Caucasus (S. Nina) may also have been depicted in the Nereditsa church; Sh. Yas. Amiranashvili thought she might be the unidentified woman represented in the Orans attitude.[143]

Contrary to the practice of the Kievan churches, the *Ascension* and not the *Pantocrator* is shown in the cupola of the Nereditsa; in it we see Christ seated on a rainbow, surrounded by six angels, while lower down the figures of the apostles are found. Gesticulating vigorously they point to the miraculous occurrence, at the same time showing their awareness that they must now assume the spiritual leadership of the world (the inscription 'Let all the races of the world applaud' seems to echo their words); among the apostles stands the Virgin flanked on either side by an angel. Lining the walls of the drum are the prophets, serene and plunged in reverie. This comprehensive composition in the dome is a survival of an iconographical theme from the early Byzantine monuments, which by the eleventh century had been superseded in the Byzantine world by the representation of the half-length figure of the Pantocrator; the earlier version continued to persist in the outposts of the Byzantine empire (particularly in Asia Minor), and also in the Caucasus, the Romanesque West and Rus'.

The pendentives of the Nereditsa church contain the traditional images of the four seated evangelists [96, 106; *59*], between whom are placed representations of Joachim and Anna, and two images of the 'Holy Face' [*56*]. On the transversal arches are medallions with half-length figures of the martyrs of Sebaste. Of particular interest are the large half-length figures of the archangels Raphael, Uriel and Selaphiel in the northern, southern, and western lunettes: these archangels, together with Michael and Gabriel, painted according to custom on the eastern vault, and the cherubim in the lunette of the eastern wall of the prothesis, constitute a complex 'angelic hierarchy' which was most probably included here at the express wish of the church's founder, Prince Yaroslav Vladimirovich. We have already seen that angels were regarded in Rus' as the patrons of heroic warriors and, more especially, of princes—hence the important role allocated to them in the Nereditsa church erected by the Grand-prince.

The remainder of the church is decorated with biblical scenes, of which those from the New Testament are mainly concentrated in the transept—*The Nativity*, *Presentation* [101], *Baptism* [102], *Transfiguration*, *Crucifixion* [103] and a series of scenes from the Passion—while the Old Testament scenes—*Sacrifice of Isaac*, *Hospitality of Abraham*,

126

etc.—are placed in the western nave. These compositions, crowded with figures, alternate quite arbitrarily with the multitudinous rows of saints, among whom the martyrs and warrior-saints appear nearest to the altar, while the female saints are placed farthest away. In the west nave, the father of Alexander Nevsky, Yaroslav Vsevolodovich, is shown offering the model of the church to Christ enthroned [108; *57*]; this fresco, as Yu. N. Dmitriyev[144] has shown, was a later addition, datable about 1246 when the exterior frescoes on the façade were also completed (*The Dormition* flanked by the figures of Vladimir and Ol'ga and the portrait of S. Nicholas. *The Transfiguration* on the other hand was executed simultaneously with the frescoes of 1199).

Perhaps the most fascinating part of the Nereditsa paintings was the great scene of the *Last Judgement* on the western wall under the gallery and on the adjoining southern and northern walls of the nave. Together with all the traditional elements, this scene also included a series of figures and episodes which were not at all customary. Hell, for instance, is represented as follows: Satan sits astride a wild beast holding Judas in his hands; the personification of 'earth' rides on a ferocious monster which is chewing a human being [105]; the 'sea', personified by a woman mounted on a dragon vomits up the dead; the various torments of Hell are represented by darkly-framed boxes bearing such inscriptions as 'Impenetrable Darkness', 'Pitch', 'Hoar Frost', 'Gnashing of Teeth', and so on. Particularly noteworthy is the little scene, not devoid of humour, of the rich man [104] who

104 and 105. Rich Man in Hell; The Personification of 'Earth'.
Frescoes from 'The Last Judgement', 1199. Nereditsa, Church of the Saviour

106. S. John. Fresco, 1199.
Nereditsa, Church of the Saviour

amidst the flames beseeches Abraham, on whose bosom the poor man Lazarus rests, to ease his sufferings. Pointing to his tongue he cries out: 'Father Abraham, have mercy on me and send down Lazarus that he may dip the tip of his finger in water and cool my thirst, for I am tormented by these flames'. In answer, Satan offers him a vessel of fire saying 'Rich friend, drink of some burning flame'.

The iconography of the Nereditsa paintings is, as we have noted, not related to the monuments of Constantinople but to those of the East. The majority of the New Testament scenes are derived from ancient Syrian sources, on which the Caucasian masters, too, drew deeply. Also worthy of note is the presence of saints and apochryphal motifs popular in the East (as for example the Syrian legend of the *Supplication of S. Alexius* before the miraculous image of the Virgin in Edessa), to which may also be added the motifs of Romanesque origin (the procession of the saints in the conch of the apse). The iconographical types met with in the Nereditsa church do not give the impression of having been adopted from their original source (i.e. Constantinople), but rather suggest a more

107. Sleeping Disciples, from 'The Agony in the Garden'. Fresco, 1199. Nereditsa, Church of the Saviour

roundabout route, i.e. the Eastern Provinces; the archaic stylistic forms bear witness to this. Despite the rich diversity of these paintings, they reveal many points in common with the monuments of Asia Minor and the Caucasus, although it would be wrong to conclude that the fresco-painters invited to work in the Nereditsa church were directly influenced by the masters of Asia Minor and Georgia. Their art was one of the many off-shoots of that rich Eastern-Christian artistic culture which had spread its roots deep into the far-flung territories of the Byzantine Empire, both East and West. This art was more readily appreciated by the young nations of the Caucasus, ancient Rus' and the Romanesque West than was the refined culture of Constantinople which, precisely because of its extreme sophistication, often remained a treasure-house beyond the understanding of the Barbarian world.

The fact that between eight and ten masters worked on these frescoes can probably be explained by the urgency to complete the work. Though the hands of the various masters can on the whole be quite easily identified, there is at times a problem in trying to classify the styles accurately because, not infrequently, the artists deliberately changed their brush-work to deal with effects of distance between the frescoes and the onlooker. For example, in the upper frescoes, the contrasts of light and shade are more sharply defined and the faces are covered with a uniform green colour onto which a yellowish light is thickly and broadly imposed, while on the lower frescoes the highlights are superimposed on an ochre base, in places heightened by narrow white strokes, and the paint is less thickly applied.

Viewed as a whole, the distinguishing feature of the Nereditsa frescoes is their great picturesqueness. They are executed in a bold and lively manner at times almost bordering on carelessness. The masters who worked here were in complete command of the fresco technique which they enriched with innovations of their own, and with their new decisive way of using colour. In order to appreciate the value of Novgorod's contribution to the monumental art of the Middle Ages, one must see for oneself with what skill eye-brows, eye-lashes and nostrils are worked in black, with what virtuosity the jet black pupils are painted over the bluish base of the whites of the eyes, with what delicacy of touch white, green or bluish hues are blended in the grey hair, and how cleverly by means of yellow, red, blue and black brush strokes, variety is introduced into the other shades of hair.

Although the Nereditsa church was a princely foundation, in its decorative scheme there is no trace of those characteristics which were generally so highly valued by the upper stratas of feudal society, such as a deep spiritual quality and complex abstract symbolism. It is in fact thoroughly down-to-earth, and the full-blooded images denote an unusually forceful 'folk-art' element. These features—all the more striking in the case of a court commission—suggest that the court of the prince was at this period coming under the influence of the celebrated Novgorod artisans who were beginning to play an increasingly vital role in the life of the city.

While the decoration of the Church of S. George at Staraya Ladoga differs in its more Graecophil character from that of the Church of the Annunciation at Arkazhi and the Church of the Saviour-on-the-Nereditsa, there is nevertheless justification for grouping all these works into one stylistic category with specific Novgorodian traits, thus proving the existence in Novgorod in the second half of the twelfth century of an independent school

108. Prince Yaroslav Vsevolodovich.
Fresco, about 1246.
Nereditsa, Church of the Saviour

of fresco-painters who freely adapted from abroad Byzantine, East-Christian and Roman-esque elements. The attempt by a number of art historians to attribute these decorative ensembles to visiting Greek masters is untenable;[145] there can be no doubt that local artists supported by strong local traditions worked in these churches.

Novgorod may have escaped direct domination by the Tartars, but it could not remain altogether indifferent to the terrible events taking place in the rest of Rus'. Reports of the Tartar atrocities scared even its courageous citizens and in the thirteenth century the building of churches virtually ceased. One of the first churches to be built during that century was the Church of S. Nicholas on Lipna, erected in 1292 and painted about two years later.[146] Badly damaged by German artillery, this church has now been fully restored, although the frescoes which in 1877 were overpainted have, in essentials, been lost. Among the best preserved was one of the frescoes in the eastern part of the building which, as far

109. The Descent of the Holy Ghost and Figures of Saints. Fresco, 1313.
Cathedral of the Birth of the Virgin in the Snetogorsky Monastery

as can be judged from the fragments cleaned in 1930 and 1946, showed remarkably archaic traits. It clearly displays a weakening of Byzantine influence and its replacement by strong native characteristics (Russian-type faces, thickset figures with large heads, generalized geometrical lines, brilliant colours). The thirteenth century, during which the cultural links between Novgorod and Byzantium were almost completely severed, saw the consolidation of folk art as the basis for future Novgorodian art, and this extremely important process explains to a great extent the further development of painting in the city.

The next ensemble of frescoes in order of chronology is that in the Cathedral of the Nativity of the Virgin in the Monastery of Snetogorsk [109–114; 62], situated some kilometres to the north of Pskov, on the high bank of the river Velikaya. The church was erected in the years 1310–11[147] and painted in 1313.[148] The frescoes were executed by local Pskovian masters who worked in a manner rather similar to that of the artists of Novgorod, though at the same time retaining their own individual stamp. The frescoes of Pskov, like her icons, are characterized by a candid and naïve patriarchality, in which the popular note is strong and the artistic language betrays a spontaneity and impulsiveness often bordering on expressionism.

Excluding the west wall of the nave which is filled with a monumental composition of the Last Judgement, the frescoes in the remainder of the cathedral of the Snetogorsk Monastery are arranged in three superimposed registers. The lowest is devoted either to full-face figures of saints or compositions illustrating the life of the Virgin; the middle and upper registers include scenes from the lives of Joachim, Anna, Mary and Christ. Forming a kind of fourth register in the general scheme of decoration are the frescoes in the vaults which portray the 'Feasts'. The presence of scenes from the proto-evangelical cycle[149] can be explained by the fact that the church of Snetogorsk was consecrated to the Virgin, and for the same reason the whole northern wall of the northern arm of the church is

110. Angel bearing an Apostle on a Cloud. Fresco, 1313. Cathedral of the Birth of the Virgin in the Snetogorsky Monastery

given over to a composition of the Dormition, striking both in its size and in its monumental span.

The central apse of the cathedral contains two friezes with figures of saints full-face and a register with the Eucharist; in the conch was an image of the Virgin (now completely lost), while in the prothesis representations of different kinds of offerings and sacrifices connected with Cain and Abel, Abraham, the prophet Elijah on Mount Carmel, as also the Gospel scene of *Jesus among the Doctors* and figures of saints.

As in Nereditsa, the proto-evangelical and Gospel scenes are distributed in a comparatively haphazard way. Thus, while in the southern arm are concentrated scenes from the life of Mary and from the childhood of Christ, and five 'Feast' subjects (the *Presentation in the Temple, Baptism, Transfiguration, Raising of Lazarus, Entry into Jerusalem*), there is no set plan to their distribution on the vaults and walls. In the northern arm we find the proto-evangelical cycle (which has to be read from the top downwards, and from left to right within the limits of each register), and six 'Feast' subjects (*Crucifixion, Descent from the Cross, Descent to Hell, The Holy Women at the Sepulchre, The Descent of the Holy Ghost, The Dormition*). It is strange that the painting of *Jesus among the Doctors* was also included here. As with the southern arm, it would be useless to try to discover any chronological sequence in the order of these scenes—a fact which clearly demonstrates that in the early Russian monumental paintings of the twelfth and thirteenth centuries the Gospel narrative was treated in a considerably freer and more unorthodox way with regard to sequence than was the case in Byzantine art, which rigorously observed the order of the 'Feasts'.

The iconography of the frescoes of Snetogorsk not only deviates in a very curious way from the traditional pattern, but is also full of innovations, based on a wide use of apocryphal sources. For instance, in the scene of *The Dormition*, Mary, ascending to Heaven, is seen presenting Thomas with a cincture, while angels are bearing the other apostles on clouds—the apostles are painted full and not waist-length as was customary [110]. This episode is taken from a very ancient apocryphal narrative which tells how S. Thomas arrived too late to be present at Mary's death, but just as she was ascending heavenwards,

133

III. Detail from 'The Descent of the Holy Ghost'. Fresco, 1313. Cathedral of the Birth of the Virgin in the Snetogorsky Monastery

134

112. Detail from 'The Descent of the Holy Ghost'. Fresco, 1313. Cathedral of the Birth of the Virgin in the Snetogorsky Monastery

135

he came borne aloft on a cloud, and having sought her blessing received from her the gift of the cincture.[150] This theme was a very popular one in Western art from the thirteenth century onwards (the Italians called it *La Madonna della Cintola*), and made its first appearance in Russia on one of the metal plates for the west doors (1230–3) of the Suzdal' cathedral.[151]

Rather unusual too is the iconography of the *Descent of the Holy Ghost* [*109*], where instead of the personification of the Cosmos, widespread in Russian art, we find five figures representing different titles and nations. Again, in the scene of *Jesus among the Doctors* [*62*], we find Christ depicted not as a youth but as a mature and bearded man, a representation which accords with S. John's Gospel (viii, 14) where Christ's second sermon in the Temple was given in the third year of his mission; but this departs from the usual iconographic tradition of depicting Christ in this particular scene as an idealized youth.[152] *The Last Judgement* also contains many unusual details, such as the thrones with the 'books of destiny', figures of prophets, a crown placed in Hell with the inscription *Svyatopolk*, the name of the Prince of Kiev who murdered Boris and Gleb.[153] Finally it is most interesting to note that the proto-evangelical cycle is enriched by two specifically Russian iconographical types—*The Virgin of Mercy (Pokrov)* and *In Thee rejoiceth (O Tebe raduyetsa)*—which later enjoyed great popularity in Russian art.[154] It is no exaggeration to say that among Russian monumental painting of the twelfth and early thirteenth centuries the Snetogorsk paintings show the most unexpected decisions and the boldest deviations from accepted iconographic canons—most particularly in the Last Judgement scene where

113. Satan and the Rich Man, from 'The Last Judgement'. Fresco, 1313.
Cathedral of the Birth of the Virgin, Snetogorsky Monastery

136

original motifs from folk tales are introduced into the traditional images of 'Sea', 'Earth' and Satan [113].

Contrasting with the wealth and novelty of content in the Snetogorsk frescoes are the many archaic traits in the artistic language. Although executed in 1313, stylistically they hark back to the mature twelfth century; most of the figures are comparatively heavy in their proportion, their movements uncomplicated and angular. Like the figures in Romanesque paintings, they sprawl over the surface; their garments, elaborated with whitish tones in imitation of icon hatching, fall in sharp unrhythmic folds. Faces with robust features and large penetrating eyes still retain much of the rigidness of twelfth-century art. In many-figured compositions the artists prefer to place the figures side by side rather than one behind the other. When architecture is portrayed, the buildings have a solid unarticulated character reminiscent of the twelfth century and bear no resemblance to the light pavilion-like buildings so typical of the fourteenth century frescoes.

While stressing on the one hand the archaic flavour of the Snetogorsk frescoes, we must at the same time pay tribute to all that is novel in their style. The artists

114. Head of a Saint. Fresco, 1313. Cathedral of the Birth of the Virgin in the Snetogorsky Monastery

who worked here painted in a very courageous and energetic manner, anticipating at many points the more flexible system of painting of the fourteenth century. Sharp strong highlights are used which, like flashes, illuminate the dark faces [111, 112, 114]. This feature was already found in the Novgorod paintings of the late twelfth century but in a more static form; furthermore at that period the highlights were often utilized to create ornamental patterns [cf. 97]. In the Snetogorsk frescoes the highlights are distributed much more freely and unreservedly, and with their help the artists model the faces of the saints endowing them with an extraordinary realism and a kind of aggressive strength—one of the saints is even shown with hair standing on end [114]. The masters of Snetogorsk seem already to be affected by the spiritual doubts and new modes of thought of the fourteenth century, and the seeds from which the heresies of Pskov later sprang are already manifest in their art. This positive and forthright manner of artistic expression would doubtless have had a strong appeal for Theophanes the Greek, and it may well be that the great master did indeed have the opportunity to study these frescoes, and through them to familiarize himself with the rich tradition of painting which had flourished in Novgorod and Pskov in the centuries preceding his arrival in Rus'.

As we have already emphasized more than once, the Snetogorsk frescoes in many ways perpetuate the Novgorodian traditions of the late twelfth and thirteenth centuries; in them the influence of folk art was strong, and their realistic approach and marked pictorial qualities are already familiar to us from the paintings of Arkazhi and Nereditsa. These trends were already apparent in the thirteenth century Novgorod icons, especially in the

115 and 116. The Transfiguration. The Crucifixion. From the 'Doors of Basil', 1336. Alexandrov, Cathedral of the Trinity

more freely rendered images which decorate their borders. Thus the Snetogorsk frescoes were the logical culmination of the development of monumental painting in the twelfth and thirteenth centuries, and we cannot agree with M. V. Alpatov,[155] who associates them with the Byzantine art of the age of the Palaeologi. They do not contain any specifically Palaeologan elements, but on the contrary are a very individual expression of the technical and compositional achievements of late twelfth-century Russian monumental art. These works are painted with such tremendous picturesqueness that the spectator is easily deluded into believing himself in the presence of paintings created in the neo-Hellenistic tradition. Nevertheless, the terrain was gradually being prepared for the successful assimilation by Novgorod and Pskov of the bold artistic innovations introduced by the 'Palaeologan Renaissance'—a process connected with the later phase of development in the thirties of the fourteenth century.

After a period of temporary stagnation in the thirteenth century, when Novgorod was busily engaged in protecting her trade routes and repelling attacks from the north by the Germans and the Swedes, a new phase of intensive building began: the stone walls of the Kremlin were rebuilt, the outer fortifications were renovated, numerous churches were erected. The founding of churches was not confined to the archbishop and the rich boyars, but extended to the various guilds of craftsmen and artisans who were consolidating their

138

position all the time. Under their democratic influence, the art of Novgorod became more realistic, more human and emotional, and nowhere were these changes more radical than in the field of monumental painting which, thanks to the boom in ecclesiastical building, had very bright prospects for development. Firstly the range of themes was extended and apocryphal subjects were introduced, denoting a more liberal approach to the question of religious imagery; in the saints' faces the former rigid conventions rapidly gave way to observation from real life; figures previously heavy and static became more elegant and finely-proportioned, and were made to adopt more varied stances; the architectural background was becoming more complex and professional, often including real rather than imaginary architectural forms. All these elements contributed to the shaping of the new style in Novgorod.

It is true that the Novgorod artists drew deeply on the Byzantine art of the Palaeologue era in order to acquire a more flexible and imaginative language, but what they took they adapted to their own purposes and taste; from Palaeologan art they extracted the real essentials which they then imbued with such vitality and emotional expression that Byzantine art of the mature fourteenth century, when compared with the art of Novgorod and Pskov, seems not only fragile and ineffectual but also arid and stiff.

117. Ornamental fresco, about 1360. Church of the Archangel Michael in the Skovorodsky Monastery

That the masters of Novgorod became familiar with the fourteenth-century Byzantine models not later than the 'thirties is evidenced by the so-called 'Doors of Basil', commissioned by Archbishop Vasily (Basil) Kalika[156] for S. Sophia and made in 1336. Some of the images on these doors—for example, *The Transfiguration* and *The Crucifixion* [115, 116]—bear several traits of the new style: the figures have gained in elegance and lightness, the garments fall in restless folds, movement is boldly depicted (e.g. the apostles dropping to earth in the Transfiguration scene). These innovations are even more telling since the masters of the 'Doors of Basil' were only mediocre craftsmen.

In 1338, according to the First Novgorod Chronicle, Isaiah the Greek together with an assistant, painted the Church of the Entry into Jerusalem; the work which has not survived was also commissioned by Archbishop Vasily. We do not know where Isaiah came from—possibly from Constantinople or Salonica—but one thing is certain: he acted as champion of the 'Palaeologue Renaissance', which was already fully mature in the second decade of the fourteenth century.

139

118. Zacharias. Fresco, about 1360.
Church of the Archangel Michael
in the Skovorodsky Monastery

The earliest monumental paintings of the fourteenth century in Novgorod were the frescoes for the Church of the Archangel Michael, destroyed during the Second World War. This church, which was the cathedral of the Skovorodsky Monastery, was erected by Archbishop Moisey (Moses) in 1355;[157] the decoration was carried out about 1360, when Moisey, feeling that his end was near, retired to the monastery and was there buried on January 25, 1362[158] by Archbishop Aleksey (Alexis). The frescoes of the Church of S. Michael, when freed from their whitewash and over-painting in 1937–8, aroused great interest since they illustrated that phase of Novgorodian monumental painting which preceded the arrival of Theophanes the Greek. The paintings of the Skovorodsky Monastery

119. Archangel. Fresco, about 1360.
Church of the Archangel Michael
in the Skovorodsky Monastery

suffered many losses through architectural alterations in the beginning of the nineteenth century, when a whole row of frescoes was destroyed, but the restorers managed to uncover the following images: the Pantocrator surrounded by four archangels in the dome [119]; in the drum, five prophets, and John the Baptist and Peter of Alexandria; on the eastern pillars, walls and vaults, several Gospel scenes—*The Annunciation* [120], *The Entry into Jerusalem, The Resurrection of Lazarus, The Descent into Hell, The Assumption, The Dormition;* at the entrance to the prothesis, the martyrs Boris and Gleb; on the altar-barrier, apostles; on the vaults and transverse arches, prophets [*63, 64*]. In the overall ensemble, ornament occupied an important place, adorning the pendentives, vaults, and niches of the drum [117]; in it an acanthus motif alternated with geometrical patterns. The desire for ornamentation was so strong that in defiance of century-old traditions even the pendentives were fully covered with it, making necessary the distribution of the evangelists above the transverse arches. Such an unusual decision once again illustrates the independence of the Novgorod masters, who were not afraid to oppose tradition when it impeded their artistic plans, and it is well known that the early Russian painters were very

141

120. Angel of the Annunciation.
Fresco, about 1360.
Church of the Archangel Michael
in the Skovorodsky Monastery

attached to ornament, and by a generous use of it tried to make their work appear more solemn and festive.

In the frescoes of the Skovorodsky Monastery the characteristics of the new style are more clearly evident than in the metal plates on the 'Doors of Basil'. Instead of the massive thick-set images found in the frescoes of Nereditsa, we are here confronted by slim elegant figures, small of head and slender of limb whose draperies fall in loose free folds, their ends fluttering intricately [120], and whose movement, often expressed by three-quarter turns, is light and unconstrained. In their treatment, not a trace remains of the static frontal twelfth-century interpretation. The artists also favour complex architectural settings and rocky landscapes, and delight in free pictorial constructions with bold inter-sections and interlacings. All these elements are characteristic of the Palaeologan style in the broad sense of the word, but the Skovorodsky frescoes are also close to the work of the Palaeologan circle by virtue of the rich handling of the paint [119]. Over the flesh tints, high-lights are freely applied for modelling purposes—on the forehead, bridge of the nose, cheek-bones, neck, chin, under the eyes and above the eyebrows. But however free the treatment of the faces may be, it nevertheless retains echoes of the chiselled technique of the miniature—the highlights recalling the short little lines which came into monumental art via easel-painting where they had become an integral part of the method employed in the making of icons. Because of this, the faces in the Skovorodsky frescoes seem a little dry especially if compared with the treatment of the faces in the works of Theophanes the Greek and his disciples. In so far as the graphic element is strong in them, they provide a link with the Novgorodian icon-painting of that period.

That the frescoes in the Church of the Archangel Michael were the work of Russian or, to be more precise, Novgorod masters, is shown in the first place by their colouring which in the use of pure intense tones already contains much of the later ringing clarity of the Novgorod palette. Blue, violet, olive-green, orange-yellow, grey and brown are boldly combined, the accent being on violet and grey. All this differs fundamentally from the more subdued colour effects of Theophanes' work; here is a young strong art which, in terms of colour, strikes a major chord that is alien to the Byzantine palette. It is precisely the rich colour-scheme of the Skovorodsky frescoes, together with their lavish ornamentation, economy of outline and indigenous facial types that argues decisively for their attribution to local Novgorod masters: most probably these works were connected with the court of the Archbishop Moisey who between 1327 and 1362 backed many building projects.

The seventies of the fourteenth century saw the arrival in Novgorod from Constantinople of the outstanding artist, Theophanes the Greek—one of the great Byzantine *emigrés*, from whose ranks there emerged at a later date the celebrated Cretan Domenico Theotocopoulos, better known as El Greco. Due to her impoverished state, Byzantium could no longer provide enough work for her many artists. Furthermore, the political and intellectual climate was becoming increasingly unfavourable to Byzantine art, so that by the second half of the fourteenth century a deep crisis prevailed. The victory of the Hesychasts led to a growing intolerance and reinforced the dogmatic way of thinking, and gradually the frail shoots of humanism put out in the early phase of the Palaeologan culture were suppressed. It was these circumstances which compelled some of

121. Melchisedek. Fresco by Theophanes the Greek, 1378. Novgorod, Church of the Transfiguration

Byzantium's most illustrious sons to leave their native land and seek refuge abroad, and among them went Theophanes. In distant but free Novgorod, he found the creative freedom denied him in Byzantium; there, no longer under the vigilant eye of the Greek clergy, he was able to bring to fruition his remarkable gifts as a painter.

There still survives a most interesting letter, dated about 1415, sent by the famous ancient Russian writer Epifany the Wise to Kirill of Tver'[159] which contains very important information about the life and career of Theophanes the Greek, a friend of Epifany's. On the basis of this letter and the evidence of the chronicles, the following points seems clear: that Theophanes practised both as monumental painter and miniaturist, that he was already a mature artist on arrival in Rus' (otherwise he would not have been permitted to paint churches in Constantinople and other Byzantine towns), that he worked not only in Novgorod and Nizhniy but also in Moscow of the Grand-princes (where he arrived not later than the mid-nineties and collaborated with Andrey Rublyov), and that he was universally admired for his keen alert mind and the boldness of his experiments in painting. From Epifany's letter, it seems certain that Theophanes was born in Constantinople, since all the places where he is reported to have worked prior to coming to Rus' indicate this fact: these are, in addition to the capital, Galata (the

Genoese quarter of Constantinople), Chalcedon (on the opposite side of the Bosphorus), and the colony Caffa (now Theodosia in the Crimea) on the route leading from Constantinople into Russia. The close links between Theophanes' painting of the Church of the Transfiguration, the frescoes of the Parecclession, and the mosaics of the inner narthex of Kariye-Camii (northern and southern domes) only confirm this evidence. On coming to Rus', Theophanes did not bring with him the late Palaeologan traditions, which are notable for their arid eclecticism, but the progressive early 'Palaeologan Renaissance' style which reached its apogee in the first half of the fourteenth century. Thus it was that he planted first in Novgorod and later in Moscow those seeds which in the dried-up soil of Byzantium could no longer yield a fruitful harvest.

Once in Novgorod, Theophanes naturally began to study the local life, nor could he ignore the broad heretical movements which originated with such force in this active industrial centre. At the time of his arrival, the new heresy of the Strigol'niki, directed against the ecclesiastical hierarchy, was rapidly gaining ground. Contact with the hardworking Novgorod milieu and new intellectual currents gave a fresh stimulus to the artist's creative work, by helping him to abandon Byzantine dogmatism, widen his mental horizons and think not only more freely but also more realistically. The art of Novgorod proved equally stimulating to him, and no doubt he was first attracted by the remarkable monumental paintings dating from the twelfth century, which could not fail to overwhelm him with the power and virile force of their images

122. Noah. Fresco by Theophanes the Greek, 1378. Novgorod, Church of the Transfiguration

and the boldness of their artistic solutions. It is very likely that he also visited Pskov—which would explain the great similarity between the Snetogorsk frescoes and his own work. Through contact with all these paintings, he came to accept that concise and strong artistic language so much favoured by the people of Novgorod and Pskov.

The only monumental works by Theophanes preserved on Russian soil are the frescoes in the Church of the Saviour of the Transfiguration (Spas-Preobrazheniye) in Novgorod, which was built in 1374[160] and painted four years later 'by order' of the boyar Vasily Danilovich and the inhabitants of Il'ina Street.[161] Regrettably, only fragments of these frescoes remain, but they are in a fairly good state of preservation. In the apse are fragments of figures of bishops and of the Eucharist; on the walls and arches, the half obliterated remains of eleven figures of saints and a medallion containing the half-figure of a bishop; in the dome, the Pantocrator with four archangels and four seraphs [126] and in the drum, the patriarchs Adam, Abel [128], Noah [122, 129], Seth, Melchisedek [121], Enoch, the prophet Elijah and John the Baptist. The most important and best-preserved frescoes decorate the chapel in the north-west corner of the gallery (called the Troitskaya chapel in a sixteenth-century manuscript). The lowest register consist of an ornamental frieze of simulated drapes, above which, on the south wall over the entrance, were frontal images of saints and a half figure of the Virgin (*Znameniye*) flanked by angels; on the east and adjoining walls was shown an altar approached by four bishops, apparently part of the composition of the *Adoration of the Sacrifice*, a very popular theme in the thirteenth and fourteenth centuries; on the altar was a paten on which lay the naked image of the Infant Jesus. Above this second register was a narrow decorative frieze consisting of bricks laid obliquely, painted in accordance with the strictest rules of perspective. Finally, at the top, the principal and best preserved register with five stylites [124, 125], the Old Testament Trinity [123], medallions with John Climacus, Agathon and Acacius, and a figure of Macarius of Egypt [127].

Since we are dealing with mere fragments, it is not possible to reconstruct in our minds the decorative system of the church as a whole. Undoubtedly the frescoes were arranged in superimposed registers, and friezes of individual saints alternated with many-figured compositions, but it is difficult to know the precise content of each frieze. We are however helped by the monumental painting of the Troitskaya chapel which in view of its relatively good state gives us some idea of the original system. The amazing thing about the painting of this chapel is the unusual freedom of composition. In the second register the frontal images of saints are boldly combined with the half-figure of the Virgin (*Znameniye*) and with the bishops turned towards the altar; in the upper register medallions alternate with full-length figures and with the composition of the Trinity containing many figures. By this means, the rhythm of the painting is infused with a new and varied cadence: the static and monotonous distribution of full-face figures one beside the other, so loved by the twelfth century masters [e.g. 94], is intentionally broken by Theophanes to give place to a treatment suitable for the fullest expression of emotion. His figures seem to emerge out of hazy silver-blue backgrounds, as if they had found themselves by chance on the plane of the wall; underlying their asymmetric distribution is a deep purpose: the nervous rhythm, sometimes speeded up, sometimes slowed down, serves to convey an impression of dramatic tension. The Godhead appears as if in storm and thunder, ready

123. The Old Testament Trinity. Fresco by Theophanes the Greek, 1378. Novgorod, Church of the Transfiguration

124. Stylite. Fresco by Theophanes the Greek, 1378. Novgorod, Church of the Transfiguration

125. Stylite. Fresco by Theophanes the Greek, 1378. Novgorod, Church of the Transfiguration

126. Seraph.
Fresco by Theophanes
the Greek, 1378.
Novgorod, Church of the
Transfiguration

to vanish at a moment's notice, and later reappear, but in a different form and under different lighting.

The saints of Theophanes are notable for their keen individual characterization. Noah, Melchisedek, the stylites, Acacius, Macarius of Egypt and even the Pantocrator are all highly individualized images, and we find ourselves studying them as portraits, and very realistic ones at that. But they all share a common trait—severity. All their thoughts and feelings are bent on seeking God; to them the world is an evil place where they must struggle unceasingly against their own inner passions. But the pursuit of virtue takes its toll and this is their tragedy. They have lost their unquestioning belief in traditional dogmas, and in order to regain it they must accomplish heroic deeds as a means to moral

127. S. Macarius.
Fresco by Theophanes
the Greek, 1378.
Novgorod, Church of the
Transfiguration

and spiritual perfection; in order to leave behind the evil world and draw nearer to heaven they have to ascend high pillars, the easier to suppress the flesh and sinful thoughts. This explains their passionate intensity, their inner pathos. Powerful and strong, wise and in possession of titanic wills, they have been beset by the temptations of the world but have learnt to recognize evil for what it is and be on their guard against it. But the struggle is an unending and an arduous one. Too proud to confess their weaknesses to their neighbours, they have taken refuge within the armour of their own meditation; beneath their deceptively calm and stern exterior, all is in a state of ferment.

In an age when the winds of heresy were blowing over Europe, both east and west, the intense, acutely subjective art of Theophanes enjoyed tremendous success. Many probably

128. Abel. Fresco by Theophanes the Greek, 1378. Novgorod, Church of the Transfiguration

129. Head of Noah. Detail of no. 122

identified their own sufferings and experiences with those of his saints, and indeed it was the artist's great achievement to have been able so convincingly to portray those contradictory medieval concepts which were then on the brink of dissolution, to be radically changed and re-evaluated in the succeeding decades. In his saints, Theophanes brilliantly reflected the spiritual unrest of his age, and at the same time foreshadowed the future shaping of events.

It was the traditions of early Palaeologan culture which formed the basis of Theophanes' art, and also provided him with the source of his brilliant technique as a painter. But in his hands the technique was brought to such a degree of perfection that it became something entirely new, fertilized by his own individual talent.

Theophanes paints in a sharp, decisive, bold manner, modelling his figures with energetic strokes. The astonishing mastery with which he applies brilliant white, bluish, grey and red highlights to the dark flesh tints, is what makes his faces so extremely alive and produces that taut intense expression which most people have found so moving [127–129]. By no means always do we find these highlights on the salient protuberant parts of the face, but often on the most shadowed parts. Hence they cannot be compared with the Trecento use of light and shade which was governed by strict empirical laws.

130. Denial of Peter. Fresco, end of 1370's–80's. Novgorod, Church of Theodore Stratelates

The highlights of Theophanes are a powerful means to achieving the necessary emotional emphasis, a device to strengthen the facial expressions; one cannot help marvelling at the virtuosity he displayed in their use—they are always right on the target and always fulfil a very definite purpose. It is not fortuitous that Theophanes avoided brilliant gaudy colours, which could have detracted from the impulsiveness of his highlights. His palette is sparing and restrained, and he prefers subdued and muted tones. Figures are painted on silvery-blue backgrounds; for faces he uses a dense orange-brown tone akin to terracotta; for garments he favours pale yellow, pearl white, silvery pinks and greens. In fact all his colours are united in one silvery gamut, outside of which the one colour allowed is a terracotta possessed of extraordinary denseness and heaviness. When the highlights are applied to this terracotta, they appear especially dynamic and brilliant.

Theophanes' subsequent work was carried out in Nizhniy-Novgorod and Moscow, where between 1395 and 1405 he decorated three churches: the Church of the Nativity of the Virgin; the Cathedral of the Archangels, and the Cathedral of the Annunciation. To our great loss, not one of these has survived. In Novgorod, Theophanes exercised a powerful influence on the local painters and was the leader of a whole artistic trend which, for want of a better name, we might call the 'School of Theophanes'. With this trend are connected two schemes of monumental painting, one in the Church of S. Theodore Stratelates, the other in the Church of the Dormition on the field of Volotovo, which unfortunately was destroyed during the Second World War.

The Church of S. Theodore Stratelates was built in the years 1360–1,[162] but its frescoes [130, 131; *65, 66*] must be dated later because part of them decorate the filled-in bays between the south-east pillar and the east wall, the north-west pillar and the north wall, and the south-west pillar and the south wall. There has been considerable argument among art historians regarding the date of the decoration in this church and its attribution to Theophanes. With regard to the first point, we shall probably never know the exact date, and as to the second, while there is not sufficient evidence to ascribe these frescoes to the master himself, there can be no doubt that they are the work of his school. Here worked his closest follower who introduced a number of substantial changes into his style. Since we must allow for a lengthy interval before the style introduced by Theophanes into Novgorod could have assimilated local artistic traits, we are forced to ascribe the paintings to the end of the 'seventies or 'eighties, more probably the latter.

From the iconographical point of view the frescoes of the Church of S. Theodore Stratelates follow tradition exactly,[163] the only unusual feature being the placing of the frieze of the Passion of Christ in the apse. The individual scenes are much smaller than those in the twelfth-century fresco-cycles, and their number has correspondingly grown. Because the surface of the wall has been broken up into small segments, much of its former solid and massive qualities has been lost, and the effect is less monumental. Here are the first signs of those tendencies which when further developed were to lead in the fifteenth century to a crisis in the monumental painting of Novgorod.

Careful study of the 'Theodore' frescoes leads us to two contradictory impressions: on the one hand they are extraordinarily close to Theophanes' work, while on the other, they are so essentially different from his undisputed works that we are forced to conclude that they must be by some other hand. The free picturesque manner of painting, the generous use of brilliant highlights on reddish-brown flesh, the tenuous silvery colouring, in which violet, greyish blue, greyish yellow, grey and white tones predominate, the free composition and strongly expressed movement of the scenes—all these features remind us of the Church of the Transfiguration. But the more we observe and analyse these frescoes, the more apparent do the

131. Ezekiel. Fresco, end of 1370's–80's. Novgorod, Church of Theodore Stratelates

essential differences in style become. In the Church of S. Theodore Stratelates, the execution is less assured; the highlights do not always come in the right spot and on the whole are rather dull. Because of this, the forms lack the wonderful structural quality which is so striking in the authenticated works of Theophanes. Moreover, the figures have the deep sloping shoulders and thickset proportions typical of the Novgorod icon. The silhouettes have lost the sharpness and verve of Theophanes' touch, their rhythm is smoother and less lively.

No less laconic are the architectural settings of the frescoes in this church. Though their motifs are borrowed from fourteenth-century Byzantine painting, they are so radically changed that they too bear the stamp of the Novgorodian interpretation of form. The delicate, fairy-tale Byzantine buildings, similar to pavilions, have here become solidly-built cubic constructions [130], typical of the architecture of North Russian towns. Finally, notwithstanding the presence of Greek inscriptions alternating with the Russian, the faces are no longer Greek, but in many cases [131] exhibit typically Novgorodian traits, while the expressions, which in Theophanes' work are extremely tense and stern, become here gentle and benign. All this convinces us that the frescoes of Theodore are the work of Novgorodian masters, whose chief was undoubtedly a direct disciple, the *alter ego* of Theophanes. It is even possible that he co-operated with Theophanes in the decoration of the Church of the Transfiguration (for example in the apostles of the Eucharist). When he worked in the church of Theodore, he may have been guided and advised by his teacher.

As we already mentioned, the school headed by Theophanes the Greek is responsible for one other monumental scheme in Novgorod: the frescoes in the Church of the Dormition on the field of Volotovo [132–146; *67–73*], which were unfortunately lost when the church was destroyed by the Fascists in the Second World War. In the completeness of its ensemble and excellent state of preservation, the monumental scheme of Volotovo can be compared only with the paintings of Nereditsa. Its destruction is an irreparable loss.

The Church of the Dormition was built in 1352[164] and decorated in 1363.[165] In view of the testimony of the Chronicle, we would hardly expect to find any doubts regarding the date of these paintings, yet on this point scholars are still divided at the present day. This is due to the fact that in 1855 fragments of another system of monumental painting, of greater age and very archaic style [132] were discovered in the central part of the apse, representing the *Adoration of the Sacrifice* (John Chrysostom, Basil the Great and two angels with liturgical fan and censer stand on either side of

132. The Adoration of the Sacrifice.
Fragment of fresco, about 1363. Volotovo, Church of the Dormition

156

133. Frescoes in the Church
of the Dormition, 1380's.
Volotovo, near Novgorod

an altar on which there is a chalice). Since we have no means of knowing whether the reference in the Chronicle concerns the earlier or later paintings it is better to date the painting by its style, and then attempt to place this scheme among the Novgorod frescoes of the fourteenth century.

The question of the authorship of the Volotovo paintings is, in my opinion, much less open to dispute. Not many people would ascribe them to Theophanes, though A. I. Anisimov[166] and I. E. Grabar'[167] in their time fought persistently for this attribution, and M. K. Karger[168] insists even now on the authorship of Theophanes. A careful study of the undisputed works of Theophanes clearly shows that neither in his early nor in his mature

157

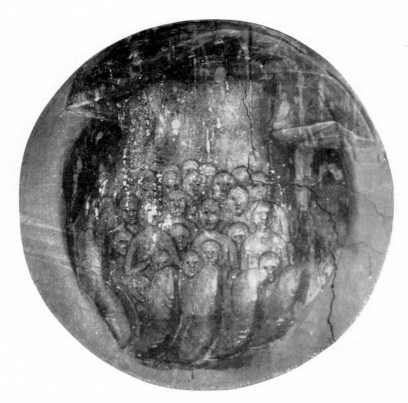

134. The Souls of the Righteous in God's Hands. Fresco, 1380's. Volotovo, Church of the Dormition

phases could he have worked in so purely Novgorodian a manner. The frescoes of Volotovo are the creation of an outstanding master of Novgorod, well acquainted with Theophanes' work but occupying an entirely independent position in relation to him.

The decoration of Volotovo combined in a very capricious way old iconographical types with new ones which became popular in the fourteenth century under the influence of the Liturgy. In the apse were representations of the Virgin enthroned with two angels; *The Eucharist* [69,70]; (the group of apostles to the right is presided over by Judas, and Paul is not included); and *The Adoration of the Sacrifice.* In 1849, G. D. Filimonov was able to see in the lower part of the apse the image of the Sacred Lamb on the paten placed on the altar, and two angels with censers and saints standing by the sides of the throne.[169] Just under the central part of this composition, which was stripped from the wall in 1855, another painting with the same theme, but more ancient (probably belonging to 1363), was discovered. Unfortunately in this fragment [132] the paten is so badly damaged that it is impossible to reconstruct its original appearance, but we have every reason to believe that here too was represented the Infant Christ. The inner meaning of this composition is easily arrived at in the light of the symbolic interpretation of the sacrament of Holy Communion.[170] Here we have a graphic illustration of the idea that the Liturgy is merely a symbol of the miraculous service of angels that takes place parallel to the Eucharist and of the real transformation of bread and wine into the body and blood of Christ. Therefore on the paten in place of the Lamb (i.e. part of the Communion bread) lies the Infant Christ, symbolizing the great mystery of the eucharistic transubstantiation. In this way the *Adoration of the Sacrifice* supplements the Eucharist, and together they form the unified concept underlying the decoration of the apse.

158

135. Scene from
'The Tale of a Prior'.
Fresco, 1380's. Volotovo,
Church of the Dormition

Also connected with the liturgy was the composition in the niche of the prothesis,
entitled in Rus' 'Mother, do not mourn for me'.[171] In it, Christ is shown stripped to the
waist, leaning on the Cross, His head resting on His shoulder and arms crossed on His
breast. Beside Him are the instruments of the Passion—the crown of thorns, spear, and
hyssop with sponge. On the arch of the niche are the half-figures of the Virgin and S.
John, lamenting over Christ. This composition too has a symbolic meaning, connected
with the prothesis where priest and deacon prepared the communion bread and wine,
with before their eyes the deeply human, pathetic image of the suffering Christ. This new

136. Christ's Descent into Limbo. Fresco, 1380's. Volotovo, Church of the Dormition

137. The Ascension. Fresco, 1380's. Volotovo, Church of the Dormition

138. The Raising of Lazarus. Fresco, 1380's. Volotovo, Church of the Dormition

139. The Transfiguration, Apostles falling. Fresco, 1380's. Volotovo, Church of the Dormition

140. Virgin and Child with Donors. Fresco, 1380's. Volotovo, Church of the Dormition

theme is very characteristic of fourteenth-century iconography, which had lost much of the austere solemnity of earlier art, and bears witness to a softening of the traditional icono-graphical types and their refashioning in a more emotional mould.

In the Volotovo paintings, we meet with two other new subjects, quite uncharacteristic of earlier monuments. On the eastern tympanum, beneath *The Descent of the Holy Ghost*, there appears an enormous hand, framed by the end of a red sleeve [134], in which a vast number of infants are held. This represents the 'Souls of the Righteous in God's Hand'.[172] From both sides two flying angels approach the hand, bringing with them new souls to be deposited in it. This is a most graphic image of the everlasting happiness of the Just secure in the Divine Hand.

The other composition, *Tale of a Prior*, decorating the south wall and divided into three parts, illustrates how a prior's charity was put to the test by Christ disguised as a wander-ing beggar.[173] To the left Christ is shown standing before the entrance to a building, dressed in rags, head uncovered and barefoot; in His left hand He holds a staff while a bag hangs at His right side. At the door we see the figure of a janitor monk, whom the beggar asks for hospitality. In the next scene [135], the janitor, unaware of Christ's true identity, approaches the prior and 'after waiting a little' hesitatingly touches his elbow and tells about the stranger. The prior ensconced in a magnificent gold armchair and with a very distinctive, almost portrait-like, face, turns to the janitor, pushing him away with his left hand while with his right he indicates his guests 'Don't you see that I am in the company of these people? Why did you let him enter? Go away'. Sitting with the prior at the table, laden down with all sorts of dishes, are three rich men; to the right a monk is serving some food from a tureen. The third episode of the composition shows the repentance of the prior who rejected the beggar, unaware of His real identity. Christ is shown in the middle of a mountainous landscape, complete with staff and bag as in the first scene; following behind is the old prior with hands outstretched to whom Christ turns and extends His right hand as a sign that he has been forgiven.

This extremely interesting composition graphically illustrates the vital role which genre painting had assumed in the monumental art of the fourteenth century; such subjects are not to be found in the twelfth and thirteenth-century murals. Even more remarkable are the ideas expressed in this composition: underlying the tale of the misguided prior who banqueting with distinguished guests did not recognize Christ in the tattered beggar figure, is conveyed the artist's own attitude to the rich, a pointed reference to the plebian opposition to the aristocracy of the boyars who had such power in the political life of Novgorod. The inclusion of such tales as this in the monumental paintings, especially at Volotovo in which the spirit of folklore was very strong, are a direct reflection of the unceasing struggle carried on against the oligarchy of the boyars

141. Archbishop Aleksey,
from 'Virgin and Child'. Fresco, 1380's.
Volotovo, Church of the Dormition

by the more democratic sections of Novgorodian society.

The remaining frescoes in the church of Volotovo more or less follow the established traditions. The walls and vaults show a series of scenes from the proto-evangelical cycle, the life of the Virgin [71–73] and the Gospel [136–139, 143–144, 146], as well as medallions with half and full-length figures of saints [133]; on the pendentives are the evangelists in the company (except for John the Theologian [68]) of personifications of Hagia Sophia, the Divine Wisdom; in the summits of the east and west transverse arches are represented the Holy Face and Christ Emmanuel; in the drum, eight prophets [67]; in the dome, the Pantocrator surrounded by four archangels, two seraphs and two cherubim; on arches, numerous medallions with patriarchs and prophets; in the west aisle, *The Resurrection* [143] and two angels.

In the middle of the south wall we find a rather unusual composition [140–142]: the Virgin together with Child sits on a semicircular throne while on either side stand the builders of the church of

142. Archbishop Moisey,
from 'Virgin and Child'. Fresco, 1380's.
Volotovo, Church of the Dormition

Volotovo—Archbishop Moisey (1324–9; 1352–9) and Archbishop Aleksey (1359–88), the former presenting the Virgin with a model of the church. Both these bishops of Novgorod, heads covered with white hoods, are shown with haloes and dressed in identical 'chasubles with crosses' which were sent from Constantinople by the Emperor John Cantacuzenus and the Patriarch Philotheus as 'special gifts' to Archbishop Moisey. His successor, Archbishop Aleksey, wore these chasubles until in 1370, by order of the Patriarch, he was obliged to remove the crosses from the chasubles because the right to wear them had been granted by Holy Synod exclusively to Archbishop Moisey.[174] In view of this fact, we might be tempted to assign the Volotovo decoration to a date prior to 1370, but such a conclusion would be premature. It is quite feasible that Archbishop Aleksey should want to see himself portrayed in these chasubles which he had worn for eleven years and of which he was probably very proud; it must be remembered too that the clergy of Novgorod did not always obey the Constantinopolitan Patriarch, and when it suited them threatened him with defection. On this account, the crosses on the chasubles of Aleksey are not a conclusive argument against a dating in the 'eighties for the Volotovo frescoes. The faces of the two archbishops are treated in an almost portrait-like way: Moisey [142] appears as a dignified old man with a long beard and earnest expression; while the portrait of Aleksey [141] is even sharper in characterization, with thin face, sunken cheeks, straggly beard, sparse eye-brows and protuberant eyes. In the painting of the fourteenth century,

143. The Resurrection. Fresco, 1380's. Volotovo, Church of the Dormition

166

144. Martha and Mary, from 'The Raising of Lazarus'. Fresco, 1380's. Volotovo, Church of the Dormition

these two portraits are an important testimonial to the artist's great skill in portraiture.

Perhaps the most characteristic trait of the Volotovo wall-paintings is the intense emotional content of the images, which are full of impetuousness and audacity and inspired by vigorous and unrestricted movement. Prophets are shown boldly turning and twisting [67]; the Magi are borne along on galloping horses, their cloaks streaming in the wind like bloated sails; Adam and Eve are irresistibly drawn towards Christ (when He descended into Hell), as if attracted by a giant magnet [136]; apostles blinded by the light radiating from Christ fall like boulders to the ground [139]; Mary Magdalen embraces the feet of the risen Christ with such passion that her whole figure seems to be caught up in one intense movement [143]. In every Gospel scene we find the same accelerated rhythm, the same heightened emotional tone, in which, however, there is nothing synthetic or forced. The atmosphere is dictated by the lively temperament of the artist, and captivates us by its naïve sincerity and warmth of human feeling.

But this intense dynamic quality is not confined to the figures alone: the draperies form sharp angles, the folds creating lightning-like zigzags [137, 139, 67]; highly-stylized

167

from the arms of Simeon so energetically that the old man can only hold on to him with the greatest difficulty [146]. In the 'Offering' scene Joachim and Anna converse so quietly and simply with the priest that the scene might have been a village church. In the next episode they go away in sadness: looking back, Anna sees only the back of the priest, who left them and refused their gifts. Such a treatment of events in the Holy Scriptures leads the spectator to imbue these scenes with everyday human content. The people in the wall-painting of Volotovo treat the Godhead quite simply. There is a radical difference between this and the frescoes of the Church of the Transfiguration. In the case of the latter the spectator would probably feel the tremendous distance separating the Almighty from the ordinary mortal; from this point of view the titanic heroes of Theophanes with their deep psychological conflicts have nothing in common with the modest, sincere, meek, slightly naïve, and not at all sophisticated, saints in the wall-paintings of Volotovo.

We have already noted the extreme picturesqueness of these frescoes which makes them so similar to the works of Theophanes the Greek. In looking at them, it almost seems as if no method could govern this lively cosmos of painting, but here the artist is helped by *line*, so highly valued by the Novgorodian artists. The summary linear outlines confine and shape figures and rocks [137, 139], architecture and draperies, by simplification giving them the effect of monumentality. The master of Volotovo is especially fond of a free parabolic design; a true citizen of Novgorod he likes clear-cut forms which the spectator can take in at a glance. He deliberately omits all superfluous detail, and eschews complex interrupted contours and jagged silhouettes. His prime concern is to express the inner significance of things, for which he relies on a terse and virile artistic language.

While from the point of view of colour the frescoes in the Church of S. Theodore Stratelates are very close to those in the Church of the Transfiguration the same cannot be said of the Volotovo frescoes, where the accent is not so much on intermediate tonal value as on much brighter and richer colours. Unfortunately, even before their destruction, these frescoes had greatly faded, making a true assessment of their colouring very difficult. The best idea of them could be gleaned from the frescoes in the west aisle, which were cleaned in the 'thirties [143], where we see the Volotovo master's great gift for colour in its full flowering. Rich cherry tones were enlivened by turquoise highlights, brownish-yellow was combined with pearl grey, yellowish-green with violet, white with pale green. Most of these colours were used to masterly advantage in the sphere of the angel which is full of the finest smoky hues.

The mural decorations of Volotovo, because of their realistic quality and keenly expressed dynamic elements, have been unjustifiably compared by some scholars to the Gothic art of the West—a theory which was most comprehensively developed by D. V. Ainalov, who made every attempt to prove the presence of Italian influences.[175] He has carefully analysed their iconography and regards their dependence on western models as an established fact. But he has oversimplified the question,[176] since the more the works of fourteenth-century Byzantine, south-Slav and Russian art become known, the more the variety of the artistic solutions devised by the Greek, Serbian, Bulgarian and Russian artists of that century becomes apparent. Quite independently of the western artists they boldly posed and solved new problems which often do coincide with those of their opposite numbers in the West. They enriched their iconography by the introduction of more human types, and a more realistic and lifelike interpretation of the religious legends seemed to them only natural. We must therefore exercise the greatest caution with regard to the conclusions of N. P. Kondakov and those who share his views, especially as he has a strong tendency to find traces of western influence in nearly all fourteenth-century Byzantine and Russian art.

Our analysis of the Volotovo frescoes has clearly proved that only a Novgorod master could have created them. His artistic formation was based on a study of Theophanes' works, but as a mature artist he went his own way. His free, strong, healthy art, reflecting in such a brilliant way and in such beautiful images the liberal spirit of Novgorod, holds great appeal in its vitality and vigour, its folkloric realism. Thanks to his sincerity and his profound understanding of human feelings, his art has dispensed with the constricting ecclesiastical fetters. While he may not have been as great an artist as Theophanes in respect of psychological depth and brilliant painterly technique, as a human being he was less inhibited and more forthright. He likes simple unpretentious Russian faces, and is not afraid to introduce the most prosaic touches into his work (for example, Christ hands to Peter a simple clay pot of the kind used in Russian villages, and the apostle is about to partake of its contents). In the episodes from the Gospel he often likes to include little slices of everyday life, and imparts to the story a geniality and warmth similar to that found in the old Russian tales. In his ornamental friezes in the Volotovo church, he makes very generous use of the flowers and plants of his native fields. Notwithstanding his dependence on the traditions of Theophanes, the deepest roots of his art were in the Russian soil, and herein resides the powerful attraction of his work.

Although the school of Theophanes dominated Novgorodian painting in the 'seventies and 'eighties, there were other movements too. The response to artistic currents from abroad, particularly to the then flourishing art of the southern Slavs, was immediate and strong in fourteenth-century Novgorod. A good example of this south-Slav influence is the mural decoration of the Church of the Saviour (Spas) in Kovalyovo, built in 1345[177] and painted in 1380,[178] which shows once again the very close cultural connexions between the two countries in the fourteenth and fifteenth centuries, not only in literature and painting, but eventually in architecture.

Originally the whole of the Kovalyovo church was decorated, but only a part of the frescoes survived—the best being on the north wall, apse, dome, drum and in the west chapel.[179] These, too, perished when the church was destroyed by the Germans, and all that now remains for the study of this very important monument of Novgorodian painting are a few photographs [147–148; *74–78*].

In this church, the many-figured compositions and the single images do not form a sophisticated architectonic system, but are placed at random, and the frames not only fail to coincide with one another but are often quite out of alignment. The masters who worked here based their technique on easel painting and their work has the appearance of icons painted in the medium of fresco. They were so taken up with the subject matter of each composition that they disregarded the broader problem of uniting the compositions into one coherent decorative whole, subordinated to the principles of strict tectonics. These principles, so precious to the artists of the eleventh and twelfth centuries, did not

147. The Transfiguration. Fresco, 1380. Kovalyovo, Church of the Saviour

receive much attention in the fourteenth century when the trend was towards freer and more picturesque creations. Nowhere, however, were they so decisively neglected as in the church of Kovalyovo—a fact which singles it out even in Novgorod where the decorative schemes on the whole were already much freer than in the Byzantine churches.

The murals in this church have Russian inscriptions with strong southern Slav characteristics. Predominant in the bright almost gaudy palette were tones of reddish-brown, white, green, blue, violet, yellow and orange. The faces, painted on a green undercoat, had dense areas of light and a touch of red on the cheeks. Compared with the frescoes of Theophanes' circle, they betray a certain lack of fluidity in execution and a drier treatment; there is a certain woodenness about the often inaccurate drawing [77, 78]. In these works there is not the same attractive rhythmic ease of the Volotovo frescoes; the simple faces lack the acute psychological depth of the 'portraits' of Theophanes. These paintings combine, in a somewhat eclectic way, influences from the methods used by Theophanes [76]; new techniques of icon-painting (note especially the practice typical in icon-painting of portraying the highlights as short fine lines, 148); and many traits of south Slav art in both iconography and style.

If we compare these frescoes with other Novgorod wall-paintings of the second half of the fourteenth century, we are struck by how un-Russian they are. We do not find here the purely Russian type of face, much less the terse, laconic forms so characteristic of the artists of Novgorod. The more they are studied, the more it becomes evident that their authors (who worked as a team, and not a very harmonious one at that) either followed some foreign models, or were themselves foreign masters working in Novgorod.

In his time, Gabriel Millet rightly stressed several parallels between the cycles of the Passion in the Kovalyovo church and works of the Macedonian and Serbian schools (decoration of the Church of S. Nicolas in Kastoria, many Serbian wall paintings in the Church of S. Nikita near Churcher, the Church of S. Akhily at Arilye, the Church of the Virgin at Grachanitsa).[180] The iconography, extremely rare for so early a period, also points to the Balkans—as for example the composition of *The Queen of Heaven standing at Thy Right Hand* [74], which decorated the north wall.[181] Christ is seen on a throne wearing the Saccos decorated with crosses, with the Omophorion over it, while to His right stands the Virgin, in imperial garb and wearing a crown. On the head of Christ is a mitre which in the eleventh century had a two-fold significance: being a reference both to the imperial diadem and the crown of thorns, interpreted as a symbol of the King of Kings, i.e., Christ. This composition, with the addition of John the Baptist, became very popular in Russian icon-painting in the sixteenth and seventeenth centuries, under such titles as The Saviour as the Supreme Bishop, the King of Kings, or the Queen of Heaven standing at Thy Right Hand. It originated in Serbia, where the earliest examples of it are preserved (a miniature in the Serbian Psalter in the Staatsbibliothek, Munich, fol. 58; a fresco in the Church of the Archangel Michael at Lesnovo painted in 1341–8; a fresco at Zaum near Ochrida dated 1361, and one in the Church of S. Demetrius in the Markov Monastery of c. 1370); and from the Balkans it came to Novgorod. Another connexion with the Balkans is the Tetramorph in the dome of the Kovalyovo, uniting the four symbols of the evangelists, of which the closest parallel is the symbol of the evangelists divided into two pairs in the Church of the Saviour at Ravanitsa, built in 1381. Finally, the style of the Kovalyovo

148. Holy Monk. Fresco, 1380. Kovalyovo, Church of the Savie

frescoes is based on southern Slav sources. For the elegant impeccably-dressed figures of the holy warriors it is easy to find convincing stylistic analogies in the decoration of the Church of the Virgin at Grachanitsa (*c.* 1321) and the Church of the Virgin in the Monastery of the Patriarchate of Pech (1324–37); for the figures of anchorites and holy monks [148], there are parallels in the Church of the Saviour at Ravanitsa (*c.* 1381, see John the Almsgiver). A very large number of south Slav traits are also to be observed in the decoration of the dome [75] and drum, and in the prothesis composition 'Do not

149. Heads of Apostles, from 'The Dormition'. Fresco, last decade of 14th century.
Novgorod, Church of the Nativity at the Cemetery

mourn for me, Mother', where the faces have a somewhat subdued expression as in the frescoes of Ravanitsa.

It is probable that the artists who worked here came from Athos, which acted as a communicating link between Russian and south Slav monasteries. They may have been brought or recommended by Kiprian who first came to Russia in 1373–4 as an 'Apocrisiarios of the Patriarch' and later through a series of complex intrigues and manoeuvres was made Metropolitan of All Russia. A native of the Balkan peninsula, he had in his youth been a monk at Athos, and it is possible that from there he engaged the masters.

These close contacts between Novgorodian and south Slav art during the late 1370's were not fortuitous. This was the decade which saw the rapid spread of the so-called *Strigol'niki* heresy in Novgorod—a heresy which originated in the artisan milieu and openly threatened the existence of the established (i.e., Greek Orthodox) Church in Novgorod. The supporters of the heresy were cruelly persecuted and, if we are to believe the Third Chronicle of Novgorod, in 1376 the 'Strigol'niki Heretics, perverters of the Holy Faith, have been put to death by being thrown from the bridge'. Besides constituting a threat to the official church, this movement was also directed against the power of the wealthy boyars. In such circumstances it is not difficult to understand why the sponsor of the Kovalyovo decoration, Afanasy Stepanovich, might well have preferred to employ artists connected with Athos, a monastic and orthodox milieu. In the years when the heresy was raging, the defence of the established religion was prompted by very real social and political interests, and only in this light can we understand many peculiarities in the decorative ensemble of this church. For instance, the generally ascetic approach, revealed in the emphasis on scenes from the Passion and in the admonishing inscriptions on the monks' scrolls (e.g., 'Monk, forsake the world in order to save your soul'); the fact that included among the images of the saints are a very large number of anchorites and monks [148; 76] who were fanatical opponents of the iconoclasts (one of them, Moses Murin, is shown holding an icon of the Saviour); the presence of such solemn and ceremonial scenes as *The Queen of Heaven standing at Thy Right Hand;* the fact that the compositions are more canonical, stiff and sterile than the frescoes of Volotovo and the Church of S. Theodore; the drier style of painting more akin to icon-painting. These features in the Kovalyovo murals indicate that ascetic and dogmatic traits were on the increase, and the free interpretation so typical of the Volotovo master had completely disappeared. These paintings can therefore be considered as a reaction to the *Strigol'niki* heresy, a fact which explains why so much use was made of the traditions of Athos, introduced into Russia either by Serbian artists, or Russian artists trained in one of the Serbian monasteries.[182]

A further deviation from the free traditions of Theophanes can be observed even more clearly in a later work—the frescoes in the Church of the Nativity at the Cemetery, probably executed in the last decade of the fourteenth century. Unfortunately they are in a very bad state of preservation[183] and the colours have lost much of their former intensity. The dominant tones are brownish-red, brownish-yellow, green and violet; devoid of any luminosity they form a heavy dense gamut. The green foundation of the faces is enlivened by an almost pure ochre, over which touches of white and vermilion are applied. Our first impression is that the treatment is much drier [149] and totally different from the method used at Volotovo—here the artists based their technique on icon-painting, whence they borrowed the fine short white lines which have taken the place of the energetic and juicy strokes of Theophanes.

The frescoes in the Church of the Saviour in Kovalyovo, of the Annunciation on Gorodishche and of the Nativity at the Cemetery prove clearly that in the eighties and nineties of the fourteenth century the tradition of painting created by Theophanes gradually disappeared, to be replaced both in icon-painting and monumental painting by the linear and graphic approach which finally predominated.

In Novgorod in the fifteenth century, monumental painting was completely over-shadowed by icon-painting and frescoes became merely an enlarged type of icon, and fresco ensembles another branch of icon-painting. Since the churches were now being built on a smaller scale, there was less wall-surface for decoration. This gave rise to a crisis in monumental art. The interior of a fifteenth-century Novgorod church had something of the intimacy of a small chapel, testifying to the existence of new artistic ideals—more personal and less civic-minded than those of the fourteenth century. These churches could only accommodate a small number of persons—they were more in the nature of private places of worship for wealthy donors and members of their families. The character of the decoration correspondingly changed: it consisted of small-scale images which looked as if they had been transferred from the icon-panel to the wall. In contrast to the murals of the earlier period, the forms have now become diminutive, and the former broad bold manner of painting has been replaced by a linear treatment borrowed from the icons.

In the Museum of History and Art in Novgorod some fresco remains from the Church of S. Sergius at the Archbishop's Court are preserved, dating from 1459.[184] Scenes from the life of S. Sergius of Radonezh are set out in a frieze composition, where small figures are shown in complex architectural settings. In their general character these frescoes differ very little from icons, and the same impression is gained from the interesting wall-paintings in the Church of S. Simeon (1468) at the Zverin Monastery[185] which still await cleaning. The parts so far uncovered reveal some registers with half-figures of saints, a portrait of the archbishop Iona carrying a model of the church which was restored in the seventeenth century, and an image of the archdeacon Stephen. Their bright clear colours (white, pink, pale and dark blue, cherry) are strongly reminiscent of the icon-painter's palette. As the frescoes were completely repainted in 1845, and the new compositions differ from the old, we cannot yet form an accurate idea of the original decorative ensemble. However, it is already clear that it was entirely different from fourteenth-century schemes. Here all is on a miniature, almost toy-like, scale. The scenes arranged in friezes resemble icons placed in rows; especially popular are friezes, containing small half-length figures in frontal poses, placed on the tops of pillars, over pillars, on walls, over windows, over pendentives, breaking up the surface of the walls and depriving them of their monumental aspect. Since the figures are so small, the effect is totally different from that provided by the monumental figures of Nereditsa.

The same conception and interpretation of wall-painting is to be found in the Church of S. Nicolas in the Monastery of Gostinopol'ye. Before this church was destroyed by the Fascists, several trial cleanings were carried out which showed the underlying frescoes to be in a good state of preservation.[186] The cleaned fragments of S. Nicolas in the apse [79], and SS. Laurus [80] and Florus on the south-west and north pillars clearly show how much the style of fresco-painting had changed by the 1370's. Fine clear lines replace the former lush highlights, the heavy shadows have a disagreeable harshness; even the icon-painter did not treat his subject in such an arid way. This shows that Novgorod monumental painting of the fifteenth century had decisively broken with the great traditions of the preceding century, and was in a state of deep crisis.

Taken as a whole, the wall-paintings in the Novgorod churches represent one of the highest peaks in the development of Russian monumental art. The best works, in which the deeply-felt ideals of the people received their most complete expression, belong to the second half of the twelfth and last third of the fourteenth century. But despite the tremendous gulf between the art of these two periods, they do share some common traits, viz. the unusual vivacity of the figures, which express loftily and clearly a physical and spiritual strength; the free interpretation of the traditional religious themes; the bold artistic solutions and the variety of techniques employed; and, finally, the folklore freshness and spontaneity of the imagery.

150. King David. Fresco, 1408. Vladimir, Cathedral of the Dormition

Chapter IV

THE STATE OF MOSCOW UNDER THE GRAND-PRINCES

THE FLOURISHING of Novgorod and Pskov as centres of culture took place during that stage in the evolution of Old Rus' when the country was in the throes of decentralization. The disunity brought about by the feudal system in its early stages gave rise to the formation of local schools of art, the discovery of local artistic talent and the strengthening of native traditions. Whereas in the spheres of architecture and icon-painting this process of development is easily traced, in the case of monumental painting the task is far more difficult since few of the once vastly numerous church paintings of Old Russia have survived to our day, particularly after the losses suffered during the Second World War. The surviving monuments are inadequate to fill the many lacunae which abound in the history of early Russian art, and nowhere unfortunately is this so apparent as in the history of the monumental painting of Moscow, of which only a few examples have come down to us.

The fourteenth century saw the rise of Muscovy. The struggle which had been joined against the Golden Horde in the early seventies of this century was led by the Prince of Moscow, Dmitry Donskoy (1359–89). Following on the famous battle of Kulikovo in 1380, in which the Russian armies inflicted a crushing defeat on the Tartars, the political importance of the Principality of Moscow began to grow rapidly. This vital battle, which had enabled the Russian people to savour for the first time the meaning of national unity, led to an awakening of national consciousness, which in turn provided a new climate for the development of the art of the fifteenth century.

Had it not been for the co-operation of the Church, the rapid successes of the Muscovite princes would hardly have been possible. By this time the Metropolitan Peter had already transferred his residence from Vladimir to Moscow, and during the reign of Ivan Kalita ('The Money-Bags'), the new Metropolitan Theognostes permanently established himself in the city. This factor played a very important part in consolidating the status of the prince of Moscow, for henceforth the 'Metropolitan of All-Russia' had his seat in the prince's capital and supported him with his authority. The successor to Theognostes, Aleksey, was the first Russian metropolitan to be a Muscovite by birth, and his enlightened policies while head of the government during the minority of Prince Dmitry Ivanovich paved the way for the future political ascendancy of Moscow. In 1448 the Russian Church finally became independent of the Church of Byzantium, and the Metropolitan Iona was elected by an assembly of bishops, all of whom were Russian.

The progress in the consolidating of national forces was extremely slow throughout the first half of the fifteenth century, a fact which can be explained by the then vigorous decentralizing forces: the weakening of the power of the Moscow prince at the time of Vasily Dmitriyevich (1389–1425), the Lithuanian invasion, the attack of Edigei Khan on Moscow in 1408, and the three-fold capture of Moscow by the princes of Galicia. Eventually, however, the princes of Moscow succeeded in establishing their supremacy and although Vasily Vasil'yevich the Dark was blinded during the struggle by order of his captor Dmitry Shemyaka, he nevertheless succeeded not only in defeating the Galician princes but in taking up arms against Novgorod, Pskov and Ryazan', and in liquidating the majority of the provincial principalities. In this way the ground was gradually prepared for the reign of the all-powerful Ivan III.

Nothing is known of the early monumental painting of Muscovy, apart from the fact that in 1344 the Metropolitan Theognostes, a Greek of Constantinopolitan birth, commissioned Greek masters to paint his court Church of the Virgin, and that according to the chronicles, the work was finished within a year.[187] It is possible that these masters came from Constantinople, where Theognostes had been educated and where he had many friends.[188] It was during the thirties and forties that Muscovy was in close contact with Constantinople and therefore had the opportunity to acquire some first-rate artists from that city. There can be no doubt that these artists would have been adherents of the new 'Palaeologan' style which was in full flower during the forties, but since the paintings of the Church of the Virgin have perished, we cannot draw any precise conclusions about their style.

Also contained in the chronicles of the same year (1344) is a reference to the painting of the court Cathedral of the Archangel[189] by a team of Russian artists headed by Zakhariya, Dionisy, Iosif, and Nicolay. Despite their number, the commission was not completed in one summer owing to the extent and complexity of the work. These frescoes have also been lost, but the evidence of some examples of the Muscovite easel-painting of the first half of the fourteenth century strongly suggests that the team which worked in the Cathedral of the Archangel probably followed an artistic trend which was already obsolete and traditions which were archaic.

By 1345, the names of Zakhariya and his colleagues had disappeared from the chronicles to be replaced by a new group of artists led by Goitan, Semen, and Ivan. These are described by the chronicler as 'Russians by birth, but pupils of the Greeks',[190] and must therefore have acted as disseminators of the Palaeologan traditions. By order of Anastasiya, wife of the Grand-prince Simeon Ivanovich, Goitan, Semen, Ivan and their pupils painted the monastery church of the Saviour-on-the-Bor, and the work, as in the case of the Cathedral of the Archangel and the Church of John Climacus, was not completed before 1346.[191] The chronicler of that year says nothing about the identity of the masters who worked during that time, but only records the fact that the paintings of three Moscow churches were by then finished.

These snippets of information supplied by the chronicles provide an interesting picture of the artistic life of Moscow during the mid-forties of the fourteenth century. Evidently by this time some concentrated work on the decoration of stone churches was being carried out by Russian artists and visiting Greek artists with their Russian protégés. Apparently there was a certain amount of rivalry between the two groups who followed different artistic trends. The forties marked the turning point in the development of Muscovite art; during these years the new style began to make headway and to acquire for the first time adherents among the Muscovite artists, some of whom had been trained by the Greeks.

The rapid boom in the progress of Muscovite art began in the last decade of the fourteenth century—a time when Moscow was showing a keen interest not only in Byzantine art but also in southern Slavonic art. Following on the Turkish conquest of Bulgaria and Serbia many Bulgarian and Serbian craftsmen fled to Rus'. With the Balkan peninsula in the grip of the Turks, Moscow was acquiring greater significance both as the nerve-centre of the Slavonic world and as a rallying point for organizing the forthcoming campaign against the Golden Horde. Hence the arrival on the Moscow scene of Theophanes the Greek during the nineties is not surprising. In the Muscovite people he was to find an enlightened and appreciative audience for his remarkable artistic talents.

Five works executed by Theophanes in Moscow are referred to by the chroniclers and Epifany the Wise, but all of them have unfortunately perished.[192] In 1395, helped by Semyon the Black and his pupils, he decorated the Church of the Nativity of the Virgin; in 1399, once again with the assistance of pupils, he worked in the Cathedral of the Archangel; in 1405, together with the monk Prokhor of Gorodets and Andrey Rublyov, he painted the Cathedral of the Annunciation. As well as these ecclesiastical commissions, Theophanes also carried out two secular ones: a mural decoration showing a view of Moscow for the palace of the Grand-prince Vladimir Andreyevich of Serpukhov and Borovsk; and a series of magnificent murals for the palace of the Grand-prince Vasily Dmitriyevich. Epifany the Wise provides two interesting details regarding the subject-matter of Theophanes' work in Moscow, viz. that on the wall of the Cathedral of the Archangel Theophanes depicted the city of Moscow, and in the Cathedral of the Annunciation he painted the *Tree of Jesse* and the *Apocalypse*. Having listed the paintings executed by Theophanes in Moscow, Epifany gives an unusually vivid account of the working methods of the renowned master. 'When he portrayed or painted all this he was never seen by anyone to look at models, as certain of our icon-painters do, who, in perplexity, constantly stare [at them], looking hither and thither, and do not so much paint with colours as just look at models. In his case, however, his hands seem to do the painting while he himself is perpetually walking about, chatting to visitors and pondering wise and lofty thoughts in his mind, seeing goodness with his thoughtful sensitive eyes'. One has only to recall the frescoes in the Church of the Transfiguration to appreciate how true this 'literary portrait' of the turbulent Theophanes is.

The evidence of the chronicles and the letter of Epifany unequivocally testify that Theophanes had many pupils in Moscow and that he willingly worked alongside the Muscovite artists, among whom was the greatest artist of Old Russia, Andrey Rublyov (c. 1370–c. 1430). There can be no doubt that Rublyov felt the influence of the distinguished Greek painter, through whom he became acquainted with the highest traditions of Byzantine monumental painting. Contact with Theophanes' work not only heightened Rublyov's remarkable gift for colour, taught him the finer points of composition and helped him to acquire a more polished technique, but also enriched his concept of man whose complex spiritual world, after acquaintance with the creations of the Greek artist, must have taken on a new dimension for him. However, Rublyov was never a direct pupil of Theophanes. He was a product of the traditions of the Moscow school, and in all probability his teacher was that Prokhor of Gorodets with whom he had worked in 1405 in the Cathedral of the Annunciation. Moreover, Rublyov's artistic ideals were far removed from those of the Greek artist. A monk of the Monastery of the Holy Trinity, he nurtured all his life the precepts of the founder of that monastery, S. Sergius of Radonezh, who had

151. S. Laurus. Fresco, end of 14th to beginning of 15th century.
Zvenigorod, Cathedral of the Dormition

worked for peace and understanding among men. The images of Theophanes, tragic and full of inner conflict, probably had little appeal for him; his own strivings were towards an art which would be straightforward and lucid. Coming into contact during his lengthy career with those sections of Russian society which were most active in the struggle for total freedom from Tartar domination, Rublyov no doubt felt a keen awareness of the absolute need to break with alien traditions. He must have come to realize that this new era of national fervour also required a new art, which could express the thoughts and feelings of its time in forms not only entirely original but also aesthetically perfect. Setting out along this road, Andrey Rublyov was to become the greatest Russian master of the fifteenth century.

As far as we know, Rublyov's earliest monumental works are two frescoes in the Cathedral of the Dormition on Gorodok in Zvenigorod, erected about 1400 by Prince Yury of Zvenigorod. Although an attempt has recently been made to attribute the building of the Zvenigorod church to the second decade of the fifteenth century,[193] this hypothesis appears unconvincing to us and we prefer the earlier dating.

Rublyov's frescoes in the Cathedral of the Dormition decorate the altar pillars [151]. A half-length figure of S. Laurus, contained within a circle, has survived on the upper part of the south pillar. Under this, a triumphal cross, and the figures of Varlaam and Ioasaph are painted. A fragment of the half-length figure of S. Florus within a medallion was found on the upper part of the north pillar (the head is lost); on the lower part an analogous triumphal cross, and the figures of S. Pacomius and an angel were discovered [83]. Only the depictions of Florus and Laurus can be attributed to Rublyov himself—the paintings on the lower part of the columns reveal a different hand, possibly that of an artist belonging to an older generation. The two saints are here represented as patrons of warriors (strictly speaking, they were revered as patrons of horse-breeding, but since cavalry in those days played a decisive role in warfare, they were not infrequently regarded as patrons of fighting men).

The image of Laurus with his open, clear character is appealing. Shown against the background of a three-toned circle, he wears a light-green robe over which a cherry-coloured cloak is thrown, while a yellow halo surrounds his head. In the free and picturesque treatment of the face with its lush strokes, one senses vivid echoes of Theophanes' art. One cannot for instance help recalling the image of Acacius in the Church of the Transfiguration,

152. S. Acacius. Fresco, 1378. Novgorod, Church of the Transfiguration

also shown against the background of a three-toned medallion [152]; yet, in other respects, how dissimilar the two figures are! Theophanes' Acacius betrays a strained and sad elation, it seems that all is seething and surging within him; he looks out with an unseeing eye, as if gripped by the sight of God appearing to him 'in thunder and tempest'. Rublyov's Laurus appears quite differently. The expression on his clear and unruffled countenance is one of extreme serenity; he is not wracked by doubts, his whole being is at peace. His person radiates an unshakable steadfastness, achieved not at the price of renouncing the world but by the nourishing strength of his own moral power.

Besides this difference in the treatment of the subject, there are also marked stylistic differences between the two artists. The nervous picturesqueness of Theophanes' manner with its pronounced asymmetry, gives place in Rublyov to flowing parabolas which form a nearly-symmetrical silhouette. The restless strokes of the former are replaced by calm, finely drawn markings; the folds of Acacius' cloak, with their agitated unrestrained movement now grow straighter and simpler; the complex chromatic palette of Theophanes becomes not only brighter but also more pure. In this early work Rublyov already shows himself to be a master of pure classical form.[194]

In order of chronology, Rublyov's next monumental work was the decoration of the Cathedral of the Dormition in Vladimir which, according to the chronicles, he completed in 1408, with the assistance of the 'icon-painter Daniil'.[195] Since Rublyov's name is mentioned second, we can assume that Daniil was the older of the two artists. Almost twenty years later, they were again to work together in the Cathedral of the Monastery of the Holy Trinity, and evidently were linked by close ties of friendship, for even the old

153. The Last Judgement. Fresco, 1408. Vladimir, Cathedral of the Dormition

sources refer to them as 'friends'.[196] Probably they were members of the same team, which obviously must have been famous and never at a loss for commissions.

The fact that on the orders of the Grand-prince of Moscow the two celebrated artists were sent to Vladimir for the purpose of restoring its ancient church, was symptomatic of the lively interest displayed by the people of the time in the treasures of their national heritage. As we know, it was under Dmitry Donskoy that the systematic restoration of buildings dating from the era of Rus' independence began, and the dispatch of Rublyov and Daniil to Vladimir was just another episode in this praiseworthy scheme.

Unfortunately the greater part of the frescoes for the Cathedral of the Dormition have now perished. The few that survive are in the western sector of the church, and show fragments of a large composition of the Last Judgement. The authors have skilfully succeeded in blending the paintings with the architecture: governed by the rhythm of the wall surface, the frescoes are architectonic in the best sense of the word [153]. The light, almost weightless figures seem to force the vaults to curve, the pillars to stand apart, the arches and walls to soar; in fact these elegant figures contribute in no small way to making the architecture itself assume an air of ethereal elegance.

In the central nave of the cathedral, on the vault under the gallery, a figure of Christ is shown within an aureole of seraphim [153]: with His right hand He points the way for

184

154. Apostles, from 'The Last Judgement'. Fresco, 1408. Vladimir, Cathedral of the Dormition

the Just, and with His left the way for sinners. Also depicted are the sun, moon, stars, angels furling the mantle of heaven, and the symbols of the four kingdoms—the Babylonian kingdom, symbolized by a bear; the Macedonian, by a griffon; the Roman, by a winged dragon; and the kingdom of Antichrist, by a horned beast. With great artistry, the animals have been composed in a circle and are strongly reminiscent of the drawings on Greek wine-cups.

The frontal part of the vault in the central nave is decorated with one of the most beautiful of all the paintings: *The Empty Throne (Etimasia)*, on either side of which are placed the apostles Peter and Paul with accompanying angels [153]. The remaining ten apostles with angels standing behind them are shown on the curves of the vault [Frontispiece, 154].

On the arch itself we see two trumpeting angels busily engaged in summoning mankind to the Last Judgement [159]. Above one of them is a gigantic hand holding the 'souls of the Just' in the guise of infants. On the same arch we also find the prophets Isaiah and David [150] in medallions. Placed low down on the north pillar of the central nave, Daniel is shown prostrate on the ground while an angel standing over him points to the Judgement scene as if to say 'Behold, your prophecy has come to pass'. On the south pillar opposite there is a corresponding group showing *The Chorus of Holy Women* [161]. On an arch, below the apostles, Earth and Sea are personified in the act of giving up their dead. *The Chorus of Hierarchs* is depicted on the south arch, under the gallery of the central nave.

Stretched across the northern incline of the vault in the south nave is a large composition of the *Entry of the Elect into Paradise* [160]. Peter and Paul stand next to one another, the latter showing the way which leads to the 'land of eternal happiness'. On one of the walls, under the vault, the gates of heaven are depicted, guarded by a cherub with a fiery sword; and here the Good Thief is to be seen—the first man to gain entry into heaven. On the opposite wall, we see the Virgin flanked by angels, while on the southern slope of the vault is a representation of *Abraham's Bosom*. Abraham, Isaac and Jacob [156] sit under the trees of Paradise; on the bosom of Abraham, held within his enfolding arms are the 'souls of the Just' in the guise of boys, while similar souls stand alongside [155].

Finally, on the arches of the south nave are six saints—Peter, Onuphrius [*84*], Sabas, Anthony the Great [157], Artemius, and Avraamy—of which the two latter belong to the paintings dating from the twelfth century. An extensive cycle showing the Torments of Hell which once existed in the left, north-west part of the cathedral, has been completely lost.

In the surviving frescoes of the Cathedral of the Dormition, two stylistic groups can be clearly distinguished. This accords with the information supplied by the chronicles which speak of the two masters, the 'icon-painter Daniil' and the 'monk Andrey' as having worked here. Although of the same team, each must have painted in his own manner.

One of the masters—without any doubt the elder of the two—executed such compositions as *Abraham's Bosom* [155], *The Entry of the Elect into Paradise* [160], the *Virgin with Angels*, and the *Young John the Baptist with the Angel*. This artist is still very closely bound to the traditions of the fourteenth century: he paints boldly and freely; his draughtsmanship while not always accurate is very expressive, his figures are somewhat

155. The Souls of the Just in Abraham's Bosom. Fresco, 1408. Vladimir, Cathedral of the Dormition

heavy. His heads are asymmetrical in form with faces which are purely Russian in type and imbued with an air of touching candidness. His art is distinctive in its great feeling for the patriarchy and its deep sincerity. This master can most probably be identified with the icon-painter Daniil, though unfortunately the absence of any works bearing his signature prevents us from corroborating this hypothesis.

The second master, to whom can be attributed *Christ among the Seraphim* [153], *The Apostles with Angels* [Frontispiece, 154, 158], *Trumpeting Angels* [159], *The Symbols of the Four Kingdoms, Etimasia with the apostles Peter and Paul* [153], *The Angel with the prophet Daniel*, the groups of the Just, both men and women [161], the

187

156. Head of Jacob. Fresco, 1408. Vladimir, Cathedral of the Dormition

prophets Isaiah and David, S. Onuphrius [84], Anthony the Great [157], and others, belongs to a younger generation which has already cast off the traditions of the fourteenth century. His draughtsmanship, compared to that of the first master, is more precise and accurate. Instead of employing daring, asymmetrical effects, he makes use of flowing parabolic lines, his favourite compositional device being the circle because of its straight-forward clarity. In fact, his heads are markedly circular in outline. He is a superlative craftsman, capable of giving his elegant figures a delicate silhouette and conferring on them by means of an extraordinary softness and nobility of expression an enchanting grace (the trumpeting angels are particularly noteworthy in this respect). This second master, whom we have every reason to believe is Andrey Rublyov, stands out, by comparison with the first as an artist of a more perceptive nature and greater spiritual sensitivity. In his crystal-clear art, there is something of the truly classical.

It is impossible to say what overall impression the composition of the Last Judgement would have made on us had its right side, with the scenes of Hell's Torments, survived. One has the feeling, however, that it, too, would have differed substantially from Byzantine portrayals of the same theme. In Byzantium the stress was generally laid on the idea of punishment and divine vengeance, whereas in the paintings of the Cathedral of the Dormition

157. Anthony the Great. Fresco, 1408.
Vladimir, Cathedral of the Dormition

a more humanitarian spirit prevails, and it is precisely this element which unites the two masters, Daniil and Rublyov, however different in temperament they may have been. Not a shade of severity is to be found in the angels, apostles, saints, nor the righteous men and women; on the contrary, they all appear thoroughly warmhearted and of kindly disposition. Even in the scene of the Last Judgement, a certain benign quality prevails. The artists who worked in this cathedral made a decisive break with the Byzantine tradition which was such a potent factor in the frescoes of the Nereditsa: they humanized their images and gave greater prominence to the language of emotions. In this latter connexion, the apostle Peter [160] is one of the most expressive of all the figures: turning to the Just, who follow him in great multitude, he seems to be addressing words of approval; his whole bearing speaks of his trust in the inherent goodness of mankind—hence the radiant welcoming expression on his face. And although he has a certain individuality his face approximates to more the idealized portrayal of the time: he stands for spiritual strength and moral integrity which in the eyes of the artist were the most valuable qualities of the Russian character.

189

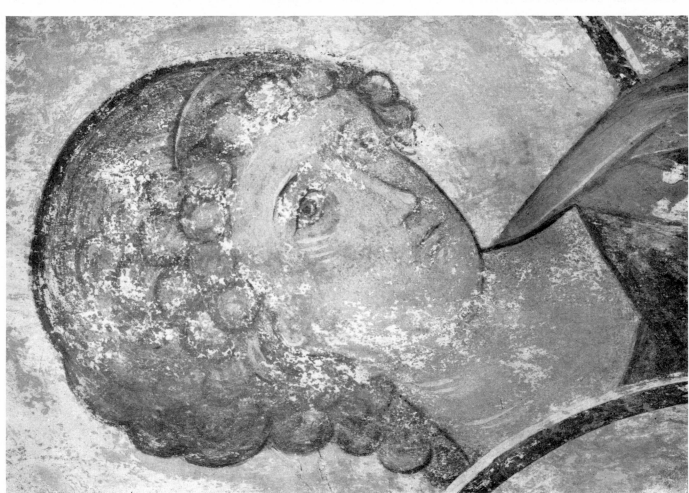

158 and 159. Angels. Frescoes, 1408. Vladimir, Cathedral of the Dormition

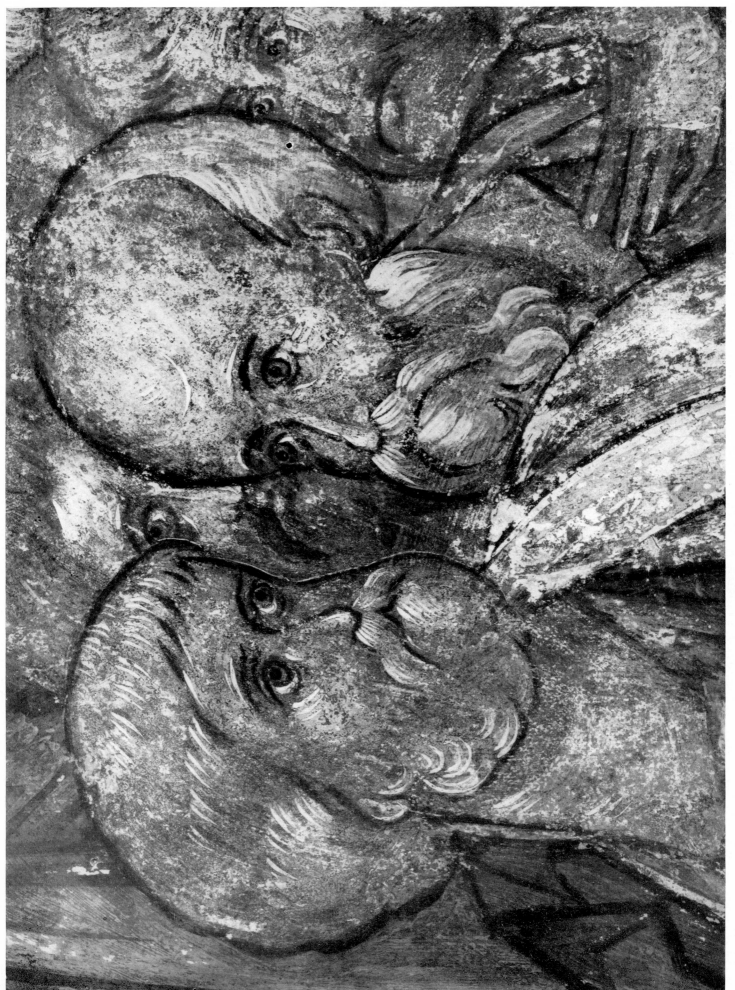

160. Apostles, from 'The Entry of the Righteous into Paradise'. Fresco, 1408. Vladimir, Cathedral of the Dormition

161. Chorus of Holy Women. Fresco, 1408. Vladimir, Cathedral of the Dormition

The works of Rublyov and his circle usher in one of the periods of highest artistic achievement in the entire history of Old Russian culture. This is particularly clearly seen in the realm of icon-painting the finest examples of which were created in the first half of the fifteenth century.

From the second half of the century onwards, notable changes begin to take place in the social and political structure of Old Rus'. Under Ivan III (1462–1505) and Vasily III (1505–33), Muscovy brings the remaining independent principalities of Yaroslavl', Rostov, Novgorod, Pskov, Tver' and Ryazan' under its control. The continuous and boundless expansion of the territories of the principality of Moscow makes it so powerful that it can free itself from dependence on the Golden Horde; a favourable peace with Lithuania is also concluded and a series of crushing defeats inflicted on the Livonian order. Thus, step by step, Moscow takes its place in the international arena. Diplomatic relations are established with Germany, the Venetian Republic, Turkey, Hungary, Denmark, and Persia. The erstwhile humble princes of Moscow had become the heads of the centralized Russian State which, following the fall of Byzantium in 1453, was now the new stronghold of Orthodoxy and the centre of the Slavonic world.

Needless to say these developments did not go unnoticed by the Russian writers of the time, and their political theories were utilized in the building up and consolidation of the Muscovite state. Moscow came to be regarded as the 'Third Rome', assuming the former role of Byzantium as direct heir to the Universal Empire. Already by 1492, we find the Metropolitan Zosima calling Ivan III 'ruler and autocrat of all-Russia', the 'new Emperor Constantine', and referring to Moscow as 'the new city of Constantine'.[197] A little later, the Elder Filofey, a monk of the Eleazarov Monastery in Pskov, was to formulate these ideas in even more precise terms in his epistle to Ivan III. Until then, writes Filofey, there had been two Romes: the first had fallen through moral degeneration, the second, Byzantium, succumbed to the 'Agarian oppression'; the third, Moscow, stands unshakable, and as for a fourth—'there will be none'.[198] The Muscovite state is regarded as the direct successor to the Kievan one, and the genealogy of the Moscow princes is traced back, via Ryurik, to the Roman Emperor Augustus ('The Story of the Princes of Vladimir').

With the growth of centralization local artistic traditions gradually lose their hold, and from the sixteenth century onwards become absorbed into the all-Russian style, that is to say, the style which had come into being in Muscovy. Cognisant of his new-born power, Ivan III naturally begins to look around for forms of expression commensurable with his lofty position. With increasing frequency he couples the title of Tsar with his earlier title of Grand-prince. Pomp begins to play a more substantial part in court ceremonial, and the language of diplomatic procedure takes on a new refinement and sophistication. The monuments of architecture, painting and sculpture created during the age of feudal disunity no longer seem sufficiently adequate for expressing the new type of centralized state governed by the grand-prince of Moscow, ruler of All-Russia. Hence, the appearance on the artistic scene of a new phenomenon—the summoning of architects from Italy to erect magnificent stone palaces and churches in the Moscow Kremlin; hence the appearance of an element unknown to the artists of Rublyov's time, that of festive grandeur.

The most renowned Muscovite artist of the late fifteenth century was Dionisy (*c.* 1440–*c.* 1508). Most of his work was done with the help of a team of artists which comprised, between the sixties and eighties, Mitrofan, the priest Timofey, Yarets, and Kon', and later (after 1484) his two sons Feodosy and Vladimir. In 1481 Dionisy painted the icons for the iconostasis of the Cathedral of the Dormition in the Moscow Kremlin, a fact which seems to imply that he was considered the leading artist of the time. The work was commissioned by Vassian, who was archbishop of Rostov and a close friend of Ivan III:

193

not only was he his confessor, but he also kept peace between Ivan and his brothers and, in 1479, christened his son Vasily. Between the eighties and nineties of the fifteenth century, Dionisy appears to have worked mainly on the Moscow Kremlin which was being speedily built at that time and where the artist was engaged in completing the commissions of the Grand-prince. Between the years 1500 and 1502, Dionisy executed his last work with the help of his sons: the frescoes for the Church of the Nativity of the Virgin in the Ferapontov Monastery.

Dionisy lived at a time when ecclesiastical dogma was assuming a greater importance and when a policy of systematic ruling in this respect was laid down by the government. The effects of this can be seen in Dionisy's art which in its general spirit is less free and individual than the art of Rublyov and his circle. There is much significance in the fact that it is more difficult to recognize different hands in the works of Dionisy's school than in those of the Rublyov circle. Moreover, although he made use of a wider variety of themes and was very fond of icons depicting scenes from the life of a particular saint—a relatively rare practice in the Muscovite painting of the early fifteenth century—there is nevertheless a greater element of standardization in his painting. For instance, in the faces of his saints, the little noses, small eyes and rounded outlines of the heads recur with a tiring repetitiveness. Equally standardized are his elongated figures and the lack of variety in their gestures and movements. The influence of dogmatic thinking is apparent in all this, and it is furthermore significant that Dionisy's son, Feodosy, corresponded with Iosif Volotsky and proved himself a ruthless opponent of the heresy of the Judaisers and a strong and zealous champion of Orthodoxy.[199]

From the activity of Dionisy and his school, only two monumental works remain, namely, some frescoes in the Moscow Cathedral of the Dormition, and the paintings in the Church of the Nativity of the Virgin in the Ferapontov Monastery. Surviving from the Cathedral of the Dormition are the remains of frescoes in the Peter and Paul Chapel (*Forty Martyrs of Sebaste*, a scene from the life of S. Peter); *The Three Hebrew Children in the Furnace*, in the prothesis; numerous figures of monks, hermits, Josaph and Barlaam, Christ-Emmanuel with seraphim, on the stone altar-barrier;[200] the *Adoration of the Magi* [164], the *Praise of Our Lady* (*Pokhvala Bogoroditsy*), and the *Nativity of the Virgin*, in the Pokhval'skiy pridel. All these paintings, contemporary in execution and similar in style to the creations of Dionisy and his workshop, were apparently completed in time for the consecration of the cathedral in 1479 (or at any rate not later than 1481 when Dionisy and his assistants received the commission for a wooden iconastasis to be placed above the stone altar-barrier).[201] There are strong indications that at the time of its consecration only the chancel of the cathedral had been decorated, and that the greater part of the paintings for the church itself were executed much later, in 1513–14, a fact which is supported by the evidence of all the Moscow chronicles.[202]

The best-preserved of these frescoes are in the Pokhval'skiy pridel. Occupying the vault is a monumental composition of the *Praise of Our Lady*, in which Mary enthroned is surrounded by half-length figures of prophets bearing the traditional scrolls. On the north wall is depicted the *Adoration of the Magi* [164], and on the south the *Nativity of the Virgin*, though only the upper portion of each composition remains since the lower part has been cut off through the insertion of a new floor. Even at a rapid first glance, one is immediately struck by the great stylistic affinity between the frescoes of the Pokhval'skiy pridel and the paintings of the Ferapontov Monastery. There are the same exaggeratedly elongated figures, the same refinement, the same architectural settings, the same circular throne with similar ornamental attachments [cf. 163]. There is also much affinity in the bright festive colouring with its tender tones—light-blues, golden-ochres, pinks, lilacs, pale-greens, pearl-greys, alongside which the thick raspberry colour, cleverly exploited by the artist, acquires a particularly strong timbre. Nevertheless, despite these similarities, the frescoes in the Pokhval'skiy pridel possess other features which distinguish them from the paintings in the Ferapontov Monastery. Instead of a delicate, almost miniature-like treatment of form, the approach is broader and more monumental—a feature well-illustrated by the figures of the prophets, whose prominent noses, largish eyes and irregularly-shaped heads have little in common with the delicately treated faces of Dionisy's figures. Neither do the ledges of the rocks, with their sharp bold outlines look like the product of his brush. At least two masters were involved in the painting of the Pokhval'skiy pridel. To one, whose style is very akin to that of Dionisy, can be attributed the paintings on the walls and the half-length figure of one of the prophets (the figure nearest to the wall), to the other, whose style is more archaic, can be attributed the paintings on the vault. As a general summing-up, it is safe to say that the early group of frescoes in the Cathedral of the Dormition is undoubtedly connected with the activities of Dionisy's team, but in the light of our present knowledge it is impossible to say how far the master himself was involved in the work.

The chief creation of Dionisy, about which there is no dispute, is the decorative scheme he carried out in the Church of the Nativity of the Virgin in the Ferapontov Monastery.

Proof of his authorship is provided by an ancient inscription surviving in the soffit of the north door, which states that between 1500 and 1502 the paintings were executed by Dionisy together with his sons Feodosy and Vladimir [162–175; *85–88*].[203] Since by this time the master was already advanced in age, it is extremely probable that a large part of the work was done by his assistants. Moreover, remembering that Dionisy's sons had been working with him since 1484, by 1500 they would have been at the height of their creative powers. This further emphasizes the fact that even when dealing with Dionisy's undisputed work, the problem of his specific contribution still remains a difficult one.

The Ferapontov Monastery was founded at the end of the fourteenth century by Ferapont, a close friend of Kirill Belozersky. Both men maintained energetic contacts with the Trinity-Sergiev Monastery, jealously safeguarding the precepts laid down by S. Sergius of Radonezh. From the fifteenth to seventeenth centuries, through the acquiring of vast

162. Detail from 'The Return of the Prodigal Son'. Fresco, 1500–2. Church of the Birth of the Virgin in the Ferapontov Monastery

163. 'In Thee Rejoiceth'. Fresco, 1500–2. Church of the Birth of the Virgin in the Ferapontov Monastery

164. The Adoration of the Magi. Fresco, about 1479. Moscow, Cathedral of the Dormition, Pokhvalskiy Chapel

165. Frescoes, 1500–2. Church of the Birth of the Virgin in the Ferapontov Monastery

landed interests, the Monastery grew very powerful and became one of the strongholds of Muscovite culture in the north of Rus'. Not infrequently, Muscovite statesmen would retire there in their old age. It was quite possibly on the advice of one of these that the famous artist from the capital was invited north for the purpose of painting the cathedral church, founded at the end of the fifteenth century and dedicated to the Nativity of the Virgin.

The exceptional richness and highly festive quality of the decorations in the Ferapontov Monastery make an immediate impact—there is something truly exultant in the gay, joyous colours of the frescoes covering the walls and vaults. Making extensive use of local minerals in the preparation of their colours, the artists produced a palette of such dazzling beauty that, by comparison, the colour schemes of fourteenth-century Russian painting seem dull, even a trifle gloomy. The tender light-blue tones blend with the pale greens, the golden-yellows with the pinks, the pale violets with the turquoises, the whites with the cherry tones, the silver-greys with the pale lilacs. The whole gamut is heightened to its fullest extent, producing a special transparent quality and at the same time a sort of cool, matt effect.

With great largesse the artists have covered the interior of the church and the entrance portal with scores of images, all united by a single concept, namely, the glorification of the Virgin: the entire scheme of decoration is in fact an ecstatic hymn to the glory of the Mother of God. Thus we find greatest prominence given to those compositions most intimately connected with her: the *Acathistus of the Virgin* [174], the *Praise of Our Lady*, *In Thee Rejoiceth* [163], the *Virgin of Mercy* (*Pokrov*), and the frequently recurring *Annunciation*. But a curious feature of this 'temple' to Mary is the absence of scenes from her life-cycle which would, naturally, have had to terminate with her dormition or death—an omission which can probably be attributed to the artists' reluctance to introduce a note of gloom into their jubilant chorale.

The figures in the Ferapontov frescoes are elegantly slender in build with high waists and long legs; their small heads poised on delicate sloping shoulders give them an air of aristocratic self-assurance [166–168]. Their movements are restrained and unhurried as if controlled by the strict requirements of court etiquette, and we will not find a single passionate gesture or brusque energetic motion in the entire paintings; here, as in the icons created by Dionisy, an element of calm adoration predominates. The figures bow respectfully either to Mary, to Christ, to a saint, or to a tsar [170, 174, 175], with that slow dignified bearing which is proper to all ceremonial occasions. Entirely in keeping with this general atmosphere is the treatment of the draperies, which are luxurious and magnificently regal [170, 172, 173]: heavy brocade alternates with silk and taffeta, wide borders and collars are studded with precious stones. Particularly sumptuous is the apparel of the warriors and martyrs whose robes, in the diversity of their cut, colour and adornment show the inordinate interest which the artists took in the outward appearance of their characters. This feature clearly underlines the different approach of Rublyov and Dionisy to the human image. Whereas, for Rublyov, the inner world of man and his rich spiritual life were all-important, for Dionisy, the physical aspect and outward trappings held a greater appeal and, indeed, at times absorbed too much of his attention. Hence the propensity for striking chromatic effects in the ceremonial and festive attire and for flowing, pleasing lines which

166. The Archangel Michael. Fresco, 1500-2.
Church of the Birth of the Virgin in the Ferapontov Monastery

are purely decorative in intent; hence the diminished interest in salient psychological characteristics; hence the stereotyped faces in which the canons of icon-painting begin to predominate.

A curious inconsistency in the paintings of the Ferapontov Monastery is that whereas on the one hand they contain architectural and landscape backgrounds [170, 172, 174] of a more diverse character than those found in fourteenth and early fifteenth century art, these elements are nevertheless completely lacking in any three-dimensional quality. The work of Dionisy and his sons shows a predilection for complex architectural structures often inspired by real buildings, for hillocks with projecting crags, columns, semi-circular thrones, footstools and tables. Each of these motifs in itself offers a three-dimensional challenge to the artists' skill [168], but we find they have all been subordinated to the plane of the wall through the use of inverted perspective. Thus the wall surface retains its flatness; in orientating the composition towards the plane, the illusion of the structure of objects has been sacrificed. In the Ferapontov paintings both the buildings and the figures give the impression of floating in a disembodied way; there seems to be no central focal

point, and the functional inter-
dependence of the compositional
elements is extremely weak. The
subjects seem to run into one
another, their feet scarcely touching the ground; moreover, they
often overstep the limits of the
framework [163], recalling a
practice which was widespread
in gothic miniature-painting; in
some instances the figures even
tread on one another's feet [171].
From the spectator's point of
view, the position of these figures
in space has not been made clear.
With such methods, Dionisy and
his assistants aimed at conveying
an impression of other-worldli-
ness and spirituality; their figures
and buildings, deprived of volume, have a weightless, ethereal
quality. Whereas the Florentine
artists inspired by the example
of Antonio Pollaiuolo made the
fullest use of contour to render
the plastic volume of a figure
or object, Dionisy, on the other
hand, flattens to the utmost the
silhouette in order to minimize
the volume contained within it.
For instance, his seated figures
[174] have all but the most
tenuous contact with their seats,
as if some invisible magnet were
drawing them upwards; when a
figure is standing, it appears to
be in a state of mild levitation.
Such conventions were not practised by the masters of Rublyov's
school. One can detect in the art
of Dionisy's time a strengthening
of the principles of planar stylization which gives to the image a
much more abstract appearance.

167. The Archangel Gabriel. Fresco, 1500–2.
Church of the Birth of the Virgin in the Ferapontov Monastery

168. The Birth of the Virgin. Fresco, 1500–2. Church of the Birth of the Virgin in the Ferapontov Monastery

169. Serving Maid,
from 'The Birth of the Virgin'.
Fresco, 1500–1502.
Church of the Birth of the
Virgin, Ferapontov Monastery

Yet another peculiarity in the Ferapontov paintings, which diminishes the natural appearance of the image, is the replacement of lush vigorous highlights by fine linear markings [172, 175]. Apart from the fact that this entails a more standardized type of modelling, it also produces a more intense flattening out of form. In the faces of Dionisy's saints, particularly when compared with the highly individualized faces of Theophanes' stylites, there is already a certain element of monotony, underlining the influence of icon-painting which depersonalizes the image and discourages individual nuances. One type for instance is repeated some hundred times with scarcely a variation, and then only of a purely external kind, such as beard, moustache, etc. In this way, the foundations for the icon-painting of the sixteenth century, with its tedious repetition of types, were laid.

On entering the Ferapontov church, one is immediately struck by the unusual complexity of the iconographic scheme, especially when compared with those found in fourteenth-century works. The depiction of the *Œcumenical Councils* and the *Acathistus of the Virgin* are completely new themes in the repertoire of Russian iconography. They were however widely used in the Serbian art of the thirteenth–fourteenth centuries (Sopochani, *c.* 1265; the Church of S. Demetrius in Pech, *c.* 1324; the Church of the Virgin in Pech, shortly after 1337; the Church of the Saviour in Dechani, 1335–50; the Church of the Virgin in Mateych, *c.* 1356; the Church of S. Demetrius in the Markov Monastery, *c.* 1375).[204] There can be no doubt that the large numbers of Serbian immigrants who fled to Rus' before the oncoming Turks contributed to the enrichment of the iconography of church painting in Russia in the sixteenth century.

As already mentioned, the Ferapontov cathedral is dedicated to the Nativity of the Virgin, and this to a very large extent conditioned the distinctive character of the iconographic system employed. On the main west portal [165], a magnificent *Deesis* is depicted in which the Virgin is shown interceding for the human race before the figure of Christ enthroned; below this come the *Birth of the Virgin* [168, 169] and two episodes from the infancy of Mary. On the sides of the portal [166, 167], the figures of the archangels Michael and Gabriel are stationed, and above the portal the half-length group of the Virgin and Child [165]. This latter representation—the so-called *Znameniye*—symbolized the Incarnation of the Son of God sung by the hymnographers, John of Damascus and Cosmas of Mayuma, both of whom are shown in a poetical posture on either side of Mary.

In the interior of the church, pride of place is given to the image of the Virgin, but instead of being featured as an historical character in the proto-evangelical story, she is represented as an object of glorification, or as symbolic of a number of sometimes quite abstruse theological concepts. In the conch of the apse, we see her enthroned with her Son, accompanied by two kneeling angels. Lower down is a frieze containing the figures of bishops (it is significant that the traditional composition of the Eucharist theme is absent in the altar). Placed above the triumphal arch is a monumental portrayal of the *Virgin of Mercy*, which has a national significance in that it shows Mary as patron and protectress of the Russian state.[205] With a shroud in her hand and surrounded by throngs of people in Russian national costume, she is set against the background of the ancient city of Vladimir, which at the end of the fifteenth century was regarded as a symbol not only of the ecclesiastical but also of the political unity of Rus'. Finally, on the forefront of the triumphal arch is a depiction of *Znameniye*. Thus the decoration of the vital section of this church has been

170. The Œcumenical Council. Fresco, 1500–2. Church of the Birth of the Virgin in the Ferapontov Monastery

given over to the three-fold image of the Virgin, reminding the faithful not only of her unique and glorious role but of her power to intercede with her Son on behalf of all who seek her help.

There are four registers of frescoes in the Ferapontov church. Stretching along the lower levels of the walls is an attractive frieze of white simulated drapes with ornamental medallions, while above this are situated the *Œcumenical Councils* [170], together

205

with figures of saints, and higher still, paintings illustrating the hymns of the 'Acathistus' [174]. A series of evangelical scenes occupies the lunettes and vaults [171, 173].

As is known, the *Acathistus of the Virgin* was composed of thirteen hymns. Of these, the first six still contain some fleeting references to the life of Mary, though their main concern is with her praise and glorification; in the following seven, however, all mention of her life has gone and the hymns are one continuous eulogy to the various symbolic meanings of the Virgin. The 'Acathistus' cycle commences in the chancel of the Ferapontov church,[206] where we see two versions of the Annunciation, based on the texts 'The angel standing before her was sent from heaven to say: Rejoice', and 'In order to make the wondering mind understand'. This hymn of praise in honour of Mary, composed by George Pisides, is further illustrated in a whole series of frescoes stretching uninterruptedly along the south and west walls and adorning the pillars of the cathedral. Here we find seventeen episodes from the life of Mary and Christ, the majority of which take the form of an intricate symbolical exposition. Since the main accent is placed on honouring and glorifying the Mother of God, the motif of 'standing before' recurs repeatedly, thus introducing a certain ceremonial tone [174]. The same intent, namely, the glorification of Mary, is reiterated in the representations *In Thee Rejoiceth* (south wall [163]), and *Praise of Our Lady* (north wall).

Since the dogmas concerning the incarnation of the Word of God and the teachings resulting therefrom regarding the exalted role of Mary in the drama of Redemption were first expounded in the Ecumenical Councils, parts of the north and south walls (those nearest to the west wall) are given over to representations of these various Councils—especially the Seventh which sanctioned the honouring of icons portraying the image of the Virgin. It is also worthy of note that even in *The Last Judgement*, the traditional west-wall composition, the Virgin plays an unusually prominent role. Amid celestial bliss, enthroned as heavenly empress, surrounded by angels and members of the human race whom she has helped to save, Mary is seen interceding before the awesome Judge for the salvation of the whole of mankind.

Thus, a single underlying theme runs right through the decorative scheme of the Ferapontov Monastery church, viz. the exaltation of the Virgin as Queen of Heaven, the glorification of her as our intercessor, and at the same time the honouring of the feast of her Birth 'which heralds the joy to the entire universe'.

The frescoes in the church which are not connected with the cult of the Virgin include: in the cupola, the traditional half-length figure of the Pantocrator surrounded by angels; on the pendentives, the evangelists; in the apexes of the vaults, four images of Christ; on the transverse arches, medallions with saints and martyrs; in the summits of the arches, the *Conversations of three bishops* (Basil the Great, Gregory of Nazianzus, and John Chrysostom)—quite a rare subject in which participation in the teachings of Christianity is symbolized by people drinking from cups;[207] on the cants of the windows in the altar, the Ancient of Days, the Christ Child on a paten and a paten with a star. In the conch of the prothesis, is shown a half-length figure of John the Baptist with wings; on the cants of the windows, the Christ Child on a paten, and cherubim; in the apse, angels and deacons. On the north and south walls are two symmetrically-placed compositions: the *Vision of*

171. The Healing of the Blind Men. Fresco, 1500–2. Church of the Birth of the Virgin in the Ferapontov Monastery

Brother Leonty and the *Vision of Peter of Alexandria*, while also on these walls and on the vaults are scenes from the life of Christ [171] together with illustrations of several of the Gospel parables—*The Widow's Mite, The Publican and the Pharisee, The Return of the Prodigal Son* [87], *The Unprofitable Servant* [172], and *The Unworthy Wedding Guest.* The subjects selected from the Gospels are mainly those in which Christ manifests His divine power to the unbelieving. Finally, in the diaconicon can be seen a beautifully painted half-length figure of S. Nicholas [88], accompanied by less-competently executed scenes from his life.

Of all these iconographical themes, some were traditional and, consequently, canonical; others, such as the *Councils* [170] may have been included at the express wish of the donor, as a timely reminder of certain fundamental ecclesiastical dogmas then under attack from

172. The Unprofitable Servant. Fresco, 1500–2. Church of the Birth of the Virgin, in the Ferapontov Monastery

the heretical sect of the Judaizers. Gennady, archbishop of Novgorod, during his energetic campaign to suppress this heresy, kept in close touch with the Ferapontov Monastery,[208] where he found men who shared his views and whose library possessed all the works necessary for exposing the heresy's errors. Hence the inclusion of the *Councils* in the Ferapontov paintings seems perfectly natural and logical. They symbolized the immutability and the strength of ecclesiastical dogmas.

A mere enumeration of the subjects portrayed in the decoration of the Church of the Nativity of the Virgin makes it clear how complicated the iconography of early Russian church painting had grown by the sixteenth century. Many new images with profound symbolical connotations had appeared—images whose significance, without due elucidation, was becoming increasingly obscure to the ordinary man. Throughout the sixteenth

173. The Wedding at Cana. Fresco, 1500–2. Church of the Birth of the Virgin in the Ferapontov Monastery

century, which lies outside the chronological limits of this present work, the tendency grew even stronger. With a determination which could have been put to a better use, the centralized government and the Church began to exploit religious painting in a didactic way to further their own ends. As a result, monumental painting gradually lost that clear, architectonic character which proved so appealing in the fresco ensembles created in the period from the eleventh to fourteenth centuries. At the same time, a strong element of standardized formalism, connected with the government's suppression of individual

174. The Acathistus of the Virgin. Fresco, 1500–2. Church of the Birth of the Virgin in the Ferapontov Monastery

thought and the enforcement by the Church of strictly binding canons, crept into art, deeply affecting the types of models hitherto used. In these conditions, fertile creative thought in art saw a gradual decline. Henceforth, the artists of Old Russia were no longer to follow the path which led to profundity in artistic conception and realization, but that which led to shallow refinement of the image and virtuosity in technique. Church painting now took on the appearance of a mottled tapestry in which sophisticated craftsmanship had taken the place of inspired creation.

The fact that the early Russian frescoes of the eleventh to the fourteenth centuries, representing the pinnacle of achievement in Russian monumental art, did not exert any influence over the art of other nations, does not in any way detract from their intrinsic

175. Detail from 'The Last Judgement'. Fresco, 1500–2. Church of the Birth of the Virgin in the Ferapontov Monastery

aesthetic importance. Early Russian monumental art was built up on the foundations of Byzantine art, whose traditions were most closely adhered to in the art of Kievan Rus'. And although during the twelfth, thirteenth and fourteenth centuries, Russian art was constantly absorbing new elements from visiting Byzantine and southern Slavonic masters—e.g. the frescoes of the Cathedral of S. Demetrius in Vladimir, the works of Theophanes the Greek, the paintings of Kovalyovo, etc.—it had rapidly acquired an artistic idiom of its own, forthright and manly, simple and expressive. This was the idiom employed in the twelfth century by the authors of the Novgorod frescoes (Arkazhi, Nereditsa), and again by the Novgorodian artists of the fourteenth century, while not a little of the same artistic language is still manifest in the work of Andrey Rublyov. But at each new phase in the history of the emerging nation, this language underwent subtle changes and developed new forms of expression. In the case of the Novgorodian artists of the twelfth century, we have monumental grandeur, inspired by popular feeling with images on an epic scale. When we turn to the Snetogorsk paintings, we find a patriarchal feeling of enchanting sincerity, and a spirit of rebelliousness bordering on heresy. In the work of the master of Volotovo the salient feature was strong emotionalism and a freedom of thought divorced from any kind of ecclesiastical restraint. With Theophanes the Greek new heights were reached: in his acute awareness of psychological nuances, and in his ability to convey the inner conflicts of man's soul with clarity and insight he had no equal. Distinguishing the work of Andrey Rublyov was a deep poetic feeling coupled with spiritual lucidity, and the moral purity radiating from his images was never to be repeated. Finally, in the creations of Dionisy, supreme elegance and grace prevail in an atmosphere of triumphant, pervasive festivity.

As we cast a last backward glance along the road travelled by the artists of Old Russia between the eleventh and fourteenth centuries, we cannot but marvel at how, within the comparative limitations of the medieval outlook on life, these artists could achieve such a richness in shades of emotional meaning. Indeed, this is all the more remarkable when we consider that we have been dealing with church paintings, whose primary purpose was to reinforce the teachings of the Church. Hence, in Old Russian monumental painting, we value and respect an art which is vigorous and free, devoid equally of the dogmatism of Byzantium and the conformist spirit of western scholasticism. Through contact with indigenous folk-art traditions, the imported Byzantine art-forms underwent a process of rejuvenation on Russian soil, and thus produced in the frescoes of Old Russia one of the healthiest and most full-blooded currents in the whole history of medieval painting.

NOTES TO THE TEXT

1. B. Rybakov, *Remeslo drevney Rusi* (Crafts in Ancient Rus'), Moscow, 1948, p. 501.

2. I. Sreznevsky, *Materialy dlya slovarya drevne-russkogo yazyka* (Materials for a dictionary of the ancient Russian language), St. Petersburg, 1893–1912, vol. I, cols. 866, 1088; vol. II, cols. 539, 940.

3. See M. Prisyolkov, *Troitskaya letopis', rekonstruktsiya teksta* (Troitskaya Chronicle, Reconstruction of the text), Moscow-Leningrad, 1950, pp. 366–7. The Russian artists who decorated the Church of S. Michael in Moscow were characterized by the chronicler in the following way: 'Among them were the eldest the icon-painters Zachariya, Iosif and Nikolay.' The master Goitan, mentioned in the chronicle for 1345, is called the elder of the icon-painters.

4. The Ipat'yevskaya Chronicle for the year 1259. This relates how Prince Daniil of Galich, intending to build the town of Kholm, called craftsmen from all the neighbouring countries, and several young men and masters fleeing from the Tartars obeyed his call.

5. D. Abramovich, *Kievo-Pechersky Paterik* (Kievo-Pechersky Patericon), Kiev, 1930, p. 173.

6. L'vovskaya Chronicle for the year 1481.

7. Cf. M. Tikhomirov *Drevnerusskije goroda* (Ancient Russian Towns), Moscow, 1946, pp. 127–8; B. Rybakov, op. cit., pp. 496–501. The Greek artists, mentioned in the Troitskaya Chronicle for the year 1344, are described as 'painters of the metropolitan', and Russian artists working in the same year as 'Russian painters of the Grand Prince Simeon Ivanovich.' See M. Prisyolkov, *Troitskaya Chronicle*, p. 366. The books of the second half of the 14th century frequently contain supplements mentioning the execution of artistic tasks by the 'Bishop's craftsmen' and 'Bishop's youths'. See B. Rybakov, op. cit., p. 688.

8. M. Karger, *Drevniy Kiev* (Ancient Kiev), I, Moscow-Leningrad, 1958, pp. 310–16, 469, 473, 478, 479, plate XXXV, figs., 64, 96–1, 98–1, 134, 137.

9. Troitskaya Chronicle for the year 1344 'and the rest of the members of their team', i.e., painters. Nikol'skaya Chronicle for the year 1345 ('and the other apprentices and the members of the team.'). 2nd Chronicle of Pskov for the year 1420: 'The people of Pskov engaged the master Fedor and his team to make a roof with wood and lead for the Church of the Holy Trinity' (this reference concerns a team of builders).

10. B. A. Rybakov (op. cit., p. 510) rejects on insufficient grounds the existence of wandering artisans in ancient Rus'.

11. Troitskaya Chronicle for 1405; L'vovskaya Chronicle for 1481.

12. Povest' vremennykh let for 989.

13. D. Abramovich, *Kievo-Pechersky Paterik*, pp. 9–11.

14. Ibid., p. 172.

15. N. Voronin, 'Politicheskaya legenda v Kievo-Pecherskom Paterike' (Political legend in the Kievo-Pechersky Patericon), in *Trudy Otdela drevnerusskoy literatury*, 1955 (XI), pp. 96–102.

16. 1st chron. of Novgorod for 1196.

17. 1st chron. of Novgorod for 1338.

18. 3rd chron. of Novgorod for 1378.

19. Troitskaya and Nikonovskaya chronicles for 1344.

20. Troitskaya and Nikonovskaya Chronicles for 1345. In the text of the Troitskaya Chronicle reconstructed by M. D. Prisyolkov only Goitan is mentioned.

21. Troitskaya Chron. for 1395.

22. Troitskaya Chron. for 1399.

23. Troitskaya Chron. for 1405.

24. O. Demus, *Die Mosaiken von San Marco in Venedig*, Baden bei Wien, 1935, p. 66.

25. Cf. V. Lazarev, *Mozaiki Sofii Kievskoy* (Mosaics of the Sophia of Kiev), Moscow, 1960, p. 153.

26. V. Lazarev, *Freski Staroy Ladogi* (Frescoes of Staraya Ladoga), Moscow, 1960, pp. 68–9.

27. V. Lazarev, 'Snetogorskiye rospisi' (Wall paintings of Snetogorsk), in *Soobshchenija Instituta Istorii Iskusstv Akademii Nauk S.S.S.R.*, fascicle 8, 1957, p. 106.

28. V. Myasoyedov, *Freski Spasa-Nereditsy* (Frescoes of Spas-Nereditsa), Leningrad, 1925, p. 16; M. Artamonov, 'Mastera Nereditsy' (Masters of Nereditsa), in *Novgorodskiy istoricheskiy sbornik*, fascicle 5, Novgorod, 1939, p. 46.

29. Yu. Dmitriyev, 'Zametki po tekhnike russkikh stennykh rospisey X–XII vv: Zhivopis' i mozaika' (Notes on the technique of Russian wall-paintings of the 10th to 12th centuries: Paintings and Mosaics), in *Ezhegodnik Instituta Istorii Iskusstv Akademii Nauk S.S.S.R.*, 1954, p. 243.

30. I. Grabar', 'Feofan Grek' (Theophanes the Greek), in *Kazanskiy Muzeynyy Vestnik*, 1922, No. 1, p. 8.

31. Troitskaya Chron. for 1344.

32. Troitskaya Chron. for 1345. Nikonovskaya Chron. for 1345. In the text of the Troitskaya Chronicle, reconstructed by M. D. Prisyolkov, the names of Semen and Ivan are not mentioned.

33. Savva Chyornyy, 'Zhitiye prepodobnogo Iosifa, igumena Volokolamskogo' (Life of the Reverend Joseph, Prior of Volokolamsk), in *Chteniya v Moskovskom Obshchestve lyubiteley dukhovnogo prosveshcheniya*, 1865, p. 23. Dosifey later became Bishop of Krutitsk, and Vassian Bishop of Kolomna.

34. Yu. Dmitriyev, op. cit., p. 245.

35. e.g. Andrey Rublyov worked twice with Daniil Chernyy, once in the Cathedral of the Dormition at Vladimir and once in the Cathedral of the Trinity in the Troitse-Sergiev Monastery; and on another occasion he worked with Theophanes the Greek and with Prokhor from Gorodets in the Moscow Cathedral of the Annunciation.

36. Cf. Yu. Dmitriyev, op. cit., p. 244.

37. 'Povest' o Evfimii, arkhiyepiskope novgorodskom' (Tale of Yevfim, Archbishop of Novgorod), *Pamyatniki Starinnoy russkoy literatury*, edited by Count G. Kushelyov-Bezborodko, fascicle 4, St. Petersburg, 1862, p. 21.

38. Troitskaya chron. for 1344; Nikonovskaya chron. for 1344.

39. Chronicle of Avraamka for 1463. Cf. Yu. Dmitriyev, op. cit. pp. 244–5.

40. V. Bogusevich, 'Masterskije XI veka po izgotovleniyu stekla i smal'ty v Kieve' (11th century workshops manufacturing glass and smalt in Kiev), in *Kratkiye Soobshcheniya Instituta Arkheologii Akademii Nauk Ukrainskoy S.S.R.*, fascicle 3, Kiev, 1954, pp. 14–20; M. Karger, Drevniy Kiev, p. 410.

41. Cf. V. Lazarev, *Mozaiki Sofii Kievskoy*, p. 155.

42. V. Lazarev, *Mozaiki Sofii Kievskoy*, pp. 139–40; Yu. Dmitriyev, op. cit., p. 277.

43. Yu. Dmitriyev, op. cit., pp. 277–8.

44. V. Levitskaya, 'Po povodu glavy VIII knigi A. V. Vinnera "Materialy i tekhnika mozaichnoy zhivopisi"' (on Chapter VIII of the book by A. B. Vinner, 'Materials and technique of Mosaic-painting'), in *Vizantiyskiy Vremennik*, 1956 (IX), p. 263.

45. V. Levitskaya, op. cit., p. 263.

46. V. Lazarev, *Mozaiki Sofii Kievskoy*, pp. 143–51.

47. M. Makarenko, 'Naidavnisha stinopis' knyazhoy Ukraini' (The oldest wall-painting of the princely Ukraine), in '*Ukraina*', *Naukoviy tr'yokhmisyachnik*, Books 1–2, Kiev, 1924, p. 12.

48. L. Durnovo, *Tekhnika drevnerusskoy freski* (Technique of ancient Russian frescoes), Moscow, 1927.

49. T. Gaponenko, *Monumental'naya Zhivopis'* (Monumental Painting), Moscow–Leningrad, 1931.

50. T. Gaponenko, op. cit., p. 37.

51. Yu. Dmitriyev, op. cit., pp. 249–61. Cf. N. Chernyshyov, *Isskustvo freski v drevney Rusi* (The art of fresco in ancient Rus'), Moscow, 1954, pp. 51–5, 71–5.

52. Cf. V. Lazarev, *Mozaiki Sofii Kievskoy*, p. 58.

53. Cf. V. Lazarev. *Freski Staroy Ladogi*, pp. 54–8.

54. Ipat'yevskaya Chron. for 1288.

55. Cf. Yu. Dmitriyev, op. cit., p. 262.

56. V. Lazarev, *Freski Staroy Ladogi*, p. 32.

57. V. Shchavinsky, *Ocherki po istorii tekhniki zhivopisi i tekhnologii krasok v drevney Rusi* (Essays on the history of the technique of painting and the technology of colours in Ancient Rus'), Moscow–Leningrad, 1935, pp. 66–86; Yu. Dmitriyev, op. cit., pp. 245–9; R. Chernyshyov, op. cit., pp. 15–21, 52–3, 71–3.

58. V. Shchavinsky, op. cit., p. 69.

59. Cf. R. Oertel, 'Wandmalerei und Zeichnung in Italien, Die Anfänge der Entwurfszeichnung und ihre monumentalen Vorstufen', in *Mitteilungen des kunsthistorischen Institutes in Florenz*, 1940 (V), pp. 277–302; Mostra di affreschi staccati, Firenze, 1957, pl. X, XIV; U. Procacci, *La tecnica degli antichi affreschi e il loro distacco e restauro*, Firenze, 1958, pl. II, IV, VI, XVI.

60. Cf. R. Oertel, op. cit., p. 281.

61. U. Procacci, op. cit., pp. 26, 27, pl. IX.

62. B. Biagetti, 'Indagini sul procedimento disegnativo di Michelangiolo', in '*Michelangiolo Buonarroti nel IV centenario del Giudizio Universale*' (*1541–1941*), Firenze, 1942, p. 201, pl. IX.

63. R. Oertel, op. cit., pp. 221, 273–6. Oertel is mistaken when he claims that in mosaics the preparatory design was made on the first coat of the plaster bed. It was in fact made on the second layer.

64. This can be explained primarily by the fact that the painters of the ancient Russian frescoes did not go in for careful chiaroscuro modelling which was a more time-consuming technique.

65. N. Chernyshyov, op. cit., p. 52.

66. Yu. Dmitriyev, op. cit., pp. 252–6.

67. Yu. Dmitriyev, op. cit., p. 253.

68. Yu. Dmitriyev, op. cit., p. 264. In the wall-paintings of the Ferapontov monastery incised lines were more widely used. See N. Chernyshyov, op. cit., p. 73.

69. For further details cf. Yu. Dmitriyev, op. cit., pp. 266–70.

70. N. Chernyshyov, op. cit., pp. 53–4, 74–5.

71. See P. Luk'yanov, *Istoriya khimicheski'kh promyslov i khimicheskoy promyshlennosti Rossii* (History of the chemical trade and industry in Russia), IV, Moscow, 1955, pp. 64–74. See also his 'Kraski Drevney Rusi' (Colours in ancient Rus'), in *Priroda*, 1956, No. 11, pp. 77–81.

72. N. Chernyshyov, op. cit., pp. 75–82.

73. N. Chernyshyov, op. cit., pp. 55–7, 75, 82. The ancient blue azurite does not adhere to moist plaster without a supplementary fixing agent. The fixative used for this purpose was wheat-glue.

74. R. Oertel, op. cit., pp. 223, 231, 239.

75. D. Abramovich, *Kievo-Pechersky Paterik*, p. 12.

76. I. Grabar', *Feofan Grek*, p. 5. I quote this extract in my own words.

77. H. Hahnloser, 'Das Musterbuch von Wolfenbüttel', in *Mitteilungen der Gesellschaft für Vervielfält. Kunst*, Wien, 1929.

78. H. Hahnloser, *Villard de Honnecourt, Kritische Ausgabe des Bauhüttenbandes, ms. fr. 19093 der Pariser National-bibliothek*, Wien, 1935.

79. C. Cippola, 'La pergamena rappresentante le antiche pitture della Basilica di S. Eusebio in Vercelli', *Miscellanea di storia Italiana*, ser. III, vol. VI, Torino, 1901, pp. 1ff.; A. Brizio, *Catalogo delle cose d'arte e di antichità d'Italia, Vercelli*, Roma, 1935, pp. 107–8. Cf. R. Scheller, *A Survey of Medieval Model Books*, Haarlem, 1963.

80. D. Abramovich, *Kievo-Pechersky Paterik*, p. 11.

81. I. Sreznevsky, *Materialy dlja slovarya drevne-russkogo yazyka*, III, col. 275.

82. See K. Swoboda, 'Geometrische Vorzeichnungen roma-nischer Wandgemälde', in *Alte und neue Kunst, Wiener Kunstwissenschaftliche Blätter*, 1953 (II), drittes Heft, pp. 81–100.

83. We can deduce this on the basis of Vladimir's prayer, which he uttered at the consecration of the Desyatinnaya Church (Russian Primary Chronicle and the 1st Chronicle of Novgorod for 996). See N. Nikol'sky, *Materialy dlya povremennogo spiska russkikh pisateley i ikh sochineniy, X–XI vv.* (Materials for a chronological list of Russian writers and their works, 10th–11th centuries), St. Petersburg, 1906, pp. 41–3.

84. N. Sychyov, 'Drevneyshiy fragment russko-vizantiyskoy zhivopisi' (The oldest fragment of Russian-Byzantine painting), in *Seminarium Kondakovianum*, 1928 (II), pp. 92–104; Id. Iskusstvo srednevekovoy Rusi (The art of medieval Rus'), p. 184, in *Istoriya iskusstva vsekh vremen i narodov* (History of the art of all times and of all peoples), fascicle 4, Leningrad, 1929.

85. *Povest' Vremennykh let* for 1036 and 1037.

86. The full argument in favour of this date is given in my article 'Novyye dannyye o mosaikakh i freskarch Sofii Kievskoy' ('New facts on the mosaics and frescoes of S. Sophia at Kiev'), in *Vizantiyskiy Vremennik*, 1956 (X), pp. 161–5.

87. On the lost mosaics of the bema see V. Lazarev, *Mosaiki Sofii Kievskoy*, pp. 93–7.

88. *Povest' vremennykh let* (Russian Primary Chronicle), essays and commentaries by D. S. Likhachyov, Moscow-Leningrad, 1950, I, p. 12; II, pp. 218–19. Cf. M. Prisyolkov, *Ocherki po tserkovno-politicheskoy istorii Kievskoy Rusi* (Essays concerning the ecclesiastical and political history of Kievan Russia), St. Petersburg, 1913, pp. 160–2. For further details on the composition of the evangelical cycle see V. Lazarev, *Novyye dannyye o mozaikakh i freskakh Sofii Kievskoy*, pp. 165–72.

89. Concerning the symbolism of the wall paintings on the galleries see V. Lazarev, op. cit., pp. 172–7.

90. M. Karger, 'Portrety Yaroslava Mudrogo i yego sem'i v Kievskoy Sofii' (Portraits of Yaroslav the Wise and of his family in S. Sophia of Kiev), in *Uchyonyye Zapiski Lenin-gradskogo Gos. Universiteta*, 1954, No. 160, seriya istori-cheskikh nauk, fascicle 20, pp. 143–80; V. Lazarev, 'Novyye dannyye o mozaikakh i freskakh Sofii Kievskoy. Gruppovoy portret semeystva Yaroslava' (New facts on the mosaics and frescoes of S. Sophia of Kiev. A group-portrait of the family of Yaroslav), in *Vyzantiyskiy Vremennik* 1959 (XV), pp. 148–69.

91. B. Rybakov, 'Zapis' o smerti Yaroslava Mudrogo' (Record of the death of Yaroslav the Wise), in *Sovetskaya Arkheo-logiya*, 1959, No. 4, pp. 245, 249. This graffito was dis-covered not long ago in S. Sophia of Kiev by S. A. Vysotsky.

92. When in the 1840's the frescoes in S. Sophia of Kiev were overpainted in oils, the identification of these saints was determined by the guess-work of ignorant restorers and their equally unenlightened advisers. It is well known that at the time of this restoration only twenty old Greek inscriptions were preserved. For this reason we must be extremely cautious in the identification of the saints.

93. N. Kresal'ny, *Sofiyskiy Zapovednik v Kieve* (The Sophia preserve at Kiev), Kiev, 1960, p. 233; M. Karger, *Drevniy Kiev* (Ancient Kiev), vol. II, Moscow–Leningrad, 1961, pp. 157–75.

94. A. Grabar, 'Les fresques des escaliers à Sainte-Sophia de Kiev et l'iconographie impériale byzantine', in *Seminarium Kondakovianum*, 1935 (VIII), pp. 102–17; Id., *L'Empereur dans l'art byzantin*, Paris, 1936, pp. 62–74, 144–7.

95. Ch. Diehl, *Manuel d'art byzantin*, II, Paris, 1925, p. 404; A. Grabar, *L'Empereur dans l'art byzantin*, p. 106.

96. Nic. Choniates, *De Andronico Comneno*, I, II, pp. 432–4 (ed. Bonn).

97. Lavrent'yevskaya Chron. for 1096.

98. Cf. N. Sementovsky, *Skazaniye o lovakh velikikh knyazey kievskikh* (Tale of the hunts organized by the Grand princes of Kiev), St. Petersburg, 1857.

99. On the right wall of the tower a man is represented bearing a head and leg of a wild boar.

100. The manuscript by N. V. Charlemagne is preserved in the archives of the Sofiyskiy Museum at Kiev. The lost hunting scenes must have been similar in theme to the miniatures in the Cynegetica of Oppian (Marc. gr. 479). See M. Bonfioli, 'Le rappresentazioni di Caccia del Codice Marciano Greco 479—Oppiano', in *Felix Ravenna*, 1956, fasc. 20, pp. 31–49. On the animals in the hippodrome of Constantinople see J. Théodoridès, 'Les animaux des jeux de l'hippodrome et des ménageries impériales à Constantinople', in *Byzantinoslavica*, 1958 (XIX), pp. 73–84. It is very curious that although the lion was the favourite animal of the spectators of the hippodrome at Constantinople, not one of these animals appears on the walls of the towers of S. Sophia of Kiev.

101. N. P. Kondakov, 'O freskakh lestnits Kievo-Sofiyskogo sobora' (On the frescoes of the staircases in the Cathedral of Sophia at Kiev), in *Zapiski Imp. Russkogo Arkheologicheskogo Obshchestva*, 1888 (III), pp. 288–306; I. Tolstoy and N. Kondakov, *Russkiye drevnosti v pamyatnikakh iskusstva* (Russian antiquities in the monuments of art), fascicle IV, St. Petersburg, 1891, pp. 147–60. Kondakov oversimplifies these problems when he connects the subject-matter of the decoration of both towers exclusively with the Hippodrome of Constantinople. Not only were the towers not decorated simultaneously, but their paintings differ in content from one another. Furthermore the hunt scenes have no connexion with the themes of the Hippodrome, but form a totally different group. Finally it is necessary to keep in mind that, unlike the cathedral itself, whose decoration forms a strictly logical entity, the frescoes of the towers are not a logical unity but are purely ornamental in intent.

102. O. Demus, *Byzantine Mosaic Decoration*, London, 1947.

103. See Yu. Aseyev, *Ornamenty Sofii Kievskoy* (Ornaments of the Sophia of Kiev), Kiev, 1949.

104. A. Grabar, *Martyrium*, II, Paris, 1946, pp. 315–16.

105. On this fragment S. Thekla was represented.

106. *Puteshestviye antiokhiyskogo patriarkha Makariya v Rossiyu v polovine XVII veka, opisannoye yego synom ar-* khidiakonom Pavlom Aleppskim (Travels of Makarios, Patriarch of Antioch, to Russia in the middle of the 17th century, described by his son, Archdeacon Paul of Aleppo), fascicle 2, Moscow, 1897, pp. 51–2.

107. M. Karger, 'K voprosu ob ubranstve inter'yera v russkom zodchestve domongol'skogo perioda' (On the question of pre-Mongol interior decoration in Russian architecture), in *Trudy Vserossiyskoy Akademii Khudozhestv*, 1947 (I), p. 28; *Istoriya kul'tury Drevney Rusi* (History of the Culture of Ancient Rus'), II, Moscow–Leningrad, 1951, pp. 266–8; M. Karger, *Drevniy Kiev*, II, pp. 261–86.

108. Yu. Aseyev, 'Novyye dannyye o sobore Dmitriyevskogo monastyrya v Kieve' (New facts on the cathedral of the Dmitriyevsky Monastery at Kiev), in *Sovetskaya Arkheologiya*, 1961, N.3, pp. 291–6.

109. *Puteshestviye Makariya*, fascicle 2, p. 73.

110. D. Abramovich, *Kievo-Pechersky Paterik*, pp. 9–11.

111. D. Ainalov, 'Die Mosaiken des Michaelklosters in Kiev', in *Belvedere*, 1926 (9/10), pp. 201–16.

112. G. Galassi, 'Musaici di Kiev a San Michele arte Russa', in *Felix Ravenna*, 1956, fasc. 19, pp. 18–29.

113. Cf. F. Shmit, *Iskusstvo drevney Rusi Ukrainy* (The art of Ancient Rus' and the Ukraine), Kharkov, 1919, p. 84.

114. N. Polonskaya, 'Arkheologicheskiye raskopki V. V. Khvoyko v mest. Belgorodke' (The archaeological excavations carried out by V. V. Khvoyko in the years 1909–10 in the borough of Belgorodka), in *Trudy Moskovskogo predvaritel'nogo komiteta po ustroystvu XV arkheologicheskogo s'yezda*, I, Moscow, 1911, p. 59.

115. See N. Makarenko, 'Drevneyshiy pamyatnik iskusstva Pereyaslavskogo knyazhestva' (The oldest monument of art in the principality of Pereyaslav), in *Sbornik statey v chest' grafini Uvarovoy*, Moscow, 1916, pp. 373–404; Id., *Stargorod'ska Bozhnitsya ta ii malyuvannya* (Starogod'ska church and its paintings), Kiev, 1928; M. Karger, *Drevney Kiev*, II, Moscow–Leningrad, 1961, pp. 420–2, 424.

116. See A. Prakhov, 'Kievskiye pamyatniki vizantiysko-russkogo iskusstva' (The Kievan monuments of Byzantine-Russian art), in *Drevnosti, trudy Moskovskogo Arkheologicheskogo Obshchestva*, 1887 (XI), fascicle 3, pp. 9–25; P. Shmit, *Iskusstvo drevney Rusi Ukrainy*, pp. 86–93; N. Sychyov, *Iskusstvo srednevekovoy Rusi*, pp. 207–9; V. Lazarev, 'Zhivopis' i skul'ptura Kievskoy Rusi' (Painting and Sculpture in Kievan Rus'), pp. 214–20 in *History of Russian art*, I, Moscow, 1953.

117. Cf. N. Sychyov, op. cit., pp. 208–9.

118. See N. Artleben, 'Drevniye freski, otkrytyye v Spaso-Preobrazhenskom sobore v Pereyaslavle Zalesskom' (The ancient frescoes discovered in the Spas-Preobrazhensky Cathedral at Pereyaslavl' Zalessky), in *Trudy Vladimirskogo gubernskogo statisticheskogo komiteta*, 1864, fascicle 1, pp. 77–85.

119. Cf. V. Lazarev, *Mozaiki Sofii Kievskoy*, pp. 73–4.

120. Ipatyevskaya Chron. for 1162.

121. V. Ikonnikov, *Opyty issledovaniya o kul'turnom znachenii Vizantii v russkoy istorii* (Results of the research on the cultural significance of Byzantium in Russian history), Kiev, 1869, p. 53.

122. A. Vinogradov, *Istoriya Uspenskogo Sobora* (History of the Cathedral of the Dormition), Vladimir, 1905, p. 95.

123. See N. Sychyov, 'Predpologayemoye izobrazheniye zheny Yuriya Dolgorukova' (Suggested image of the wife of Yury Dolgoruky), in *Soobshcheniya Instituta Istorii Iskusstv Akademii Nauk S.S.S.R.*, fascicle 1, Moscow–Leningrad, 1951, pp. 51–62.

124. Lavrent'yevskaya Chron. for 1233.

125. See Yu. Dmitriyev, 'Stennyye rospisi Novgoroda, ikh restavratsiya i issledovaniye—raboty 1945–8 godov' (Wall-paintings of Novgorod, their restoration and research—work undertaken in the years 1945–8), in *Praktika restavratsionnykh rabot*, Moscow, 1950, pp. 135–9, 142–6.

126. As revealed by the restoration carried out in 1944–5, the half-length figure of the Pantocrator and upper parts of the figures of the archangels (except one figure) had been painted on a new coat of plaster not earlier than the 16th century. See Yu. Dmitriyev, op. cit., pp. 137–9.

127. 3rd chron. of Novgorod for 1108. Another argument against ascribing the early group of wall-paintings in the Cathedral of S. Sophia at Novgorod to Greek artists is the presence of old Slav inscriptions near the figures of the saints in the arches of the light-apertures.

128. P. Kazansky, *Istoriya pravoslavnogo russkogo monashestva* (History of Orthodox Russian monachism), Moscow, 1855, p. 152—is of the opinion that Antony of Rome came to Rus' from South Italy.

129. *Pamyatniki starinnoy russkoy literatury* (The monuments of ancient Russian literature), I, St. Petersburg, 1860, pp. 267–8.

130. F. Buslayev, *Pamyatniki drevnerusskoy dukhovnoy pis' mennosti* (Monuments of ancient Russian ecclesiastical literature), in the works of F. I. Buslayev, III, pp. 110–13.

131. The old historians of the Russian church (incl. E. E. Golubinsky) denied the Greek origins of Niphont. Now this origin is confirmed by his lead seals. See N. Porfiridov, *Drevniy Novgorod* (Ancient Novgorod), Moscow, 1947, p. 169; Id., 'Imennyye vladychnyye pechati Novgoroda' (The seals with the names of the archbishops of Novgorod), in *Sovetskaya Arkheologiya*, 1958, No. 3, pp. 222–3, fig. I–1.

132. 1st chron. of Novgorod for 1164.

133. Ch. Diehl, *Manuel d'art byzantin*, II, Paris, 1926, pp. 586, 588; Ph. Schweinfurth, *Geschichte der russischen Malerei im Mittelalter*, Haag, 1930, p. 111; D. Talbot Rice, 'Later Byzantine Painting, I, The Twelfth and Thirteenth Centuries', in *Eidos*, 1950, No. 3, p. 16.

134. 1st Chron. of Novgorod for 1189.

135. Yu. Dmitriyev, *Stennyye rospisi Novgoroda*, pp. 146–153.

136. 1st Chron. of Novgorod for 1144.

137. P. Underwood, 'Third Preliminary Report on the restoration of the frescoes in the Kariye Camii at Istanbul by the Byzantine Institute, 1956', in *Dumbarton Oaks Papers*, 1958 (XII), pp. 271–82; Fourth Preliminary Report, 1957–8, *Dumbarton Oaks Papers*, 1959 (XIII), pp. 216–28.

138. Cf. V. Lasareff, 'La scuola di Vladimir-Susdal': due nuovi esemplari delle pitture di cavaletto russa dal XII al XIII secolo (per la storia dell'iconostasi)', in *Arte Veneta*, 1956 (X), pp. 9–18.

139. 1st Chron. of Novgorod for 1199. Because of the great hurry to finish the decoration, it was completed in an exceptionally short time (about one month).

140. Such processions of saints in the apse are totally unknown in the Orient, but are to be found in many Western buildings (San Silvestro in Tivoli, *c.* 1100; Santa Maria in Trastevere, *c.* 1145; Santa Francesca Romana, *c.* 1161, etc.).

141. N. P. Sychyov—N. Syčev, 'Sur l'histoire de l'église du Sauveur à Neredicy près Novgorod', in *Deuxième recueil, dédié à la mémoire de Theodore Uspenskij*, 1 ère partie, Paris, 1932, pp. 84–92, explained the presence in the Deesis of John the Baptist and of Martha in the following way: the founder of the Church, the grand prince Yaroslav Vladimirovich bore the Christian name of John, and his wife the name of Martha. But A. Frolov—'Sainte Marthe ou la Mère de Dieu', in *Bulletin of the Byzantine Institute*, 1946, I, pp. 79–82—correctly refuting such an arbitrary interpretation of the Deesis, considers the inscription with the name of Martha as a distortion of the monogram of the Holy Mother of God ($\overline{\text{MP}}$ $\overline{\Theta\text{Y}}$). In Nereditsa we meet with another distortion of a similar type (near the image of the Orans in the dome we find the monogram $\overline{\text{MP}}$ $\overline{\Theta\text{P}}$). These errors in the inscriptions clearly indicate that the work was done by local Novgorod masters and not by visiting Greek masters.

142. I. Tolstoy and N. Kondakov, *Russkiye drevnosti v pamyatnikakh iskusstva*, fascicle VI, St. Petersburg, 1899, p. 137.

143. Ch. Amiranachvili, 'Quelques remarques sur l'origine des procédés dans les fresques de Néredicy', in *Deuxième recueil dédié à la mémoire de Théodore Uspenskij*, 1 ère partie, Paris, 1932, p. 114.

144. Yu. Dmitriyev, 'Isobrazheniye ottsa Aleksandra Nevskogo na nereditskoy freske XIII veka' (Image of the father of Alexander Nevsky in a Nereditsa fresco of the 13th century), in *Novgorodskiy istoricheskiy sbornik*, fascicles 3–4, Novgorod, 1938, pp. 39–57.

145. Ch. Diehl, *Manuel d'art byzantin*, II, pp. 568, 588; Ph. Schweinfurth, *Geschichte der russischen Malerei im Mittelalter*, Haag, 1930, pp. 100, 108, 109; G. Hamilton, *The Art and Architecture of Russia* (The Pelican History of Art), Harmondsworth, Middx., 1954, p. 54.

146. G. Filimonov, *Tserkov' sv. Nikolaya Chudotvortsa na Lipne* (Church of S. Nicolas the Wonderworker on Lipna), Moscow, 1859; V. Myasoyedov, Nikola Lipnyy (S. Nicolas on Lipna), in *Sbornik Novgorodskogo Obshchestva lyubiteley drevnosti*, III, Novgorod, 1910, pp. 1–14; Yu. Dmitriyev, 'Tserkov' Nikoly na Lipne v Novgorode' (Church of S. Nicolas on Lipna at Novgorod), in *Pamyatniki iskusstva razrushennyye nemetskimi zakhvatchikami v S.S.S.R.*, Moscow–Leningrad, 1948, pp. 67–75; Id. *Stennyye rospisi Novgoroda*, pp. 161–5. In the dome the Pantocrator with archangels was represented; in the drum, prophets; in the pendentives, evangelists; between the pendentives, crosses with flowers; in the apse, a semifigure of the Virgin of the type *Znameniye* between two archangels and saints; lower down, a frieze with the figures of bishops; above the triumphal arch, *The Transfiguration* and *The Descent of the Holy Ghost;* in the summits of the transverse arches, Deesis in medallions; on the pillars of the apse, *The Annunciation*, cherubim and S. Theodore and S. Mercury; on the vaults and walls, gospel scenes (*Presentation of the Virgin in the Temple, Presentation in the Temple, Baptism, The Agony in the Garden,* etc.) and figures and semifigures of saints. In the prothesis, dedicated to Mary, are bishops in omophorions (one of them Chariton); above the entry to the prothesis, *The Resurrection of Lazarus* and the Old Testament Trinity; in the diaconicon dedicated to John the Baptist there are young warriors; above the entry to the diaconicon, *The Descent into Hell* and *The Three Hebrew Children in the Furnace*. On the walls the frescoes were arranged in four registers above the frieze, imitating a marble panel. The gospel story commenced in the lowest register and terminated in the upper zone and on the vaults. The middle register was occupied by figures of saints, large in comparison with the figures in the gospel scenes.

147. 1st and 2nd chron. of Pskov for 1310.

148. Evidence found in the note on the margins of the Parimeynik of Pskov dating from the 14th century. See A. Nekrasov, 'Iz oblasti literaturnykh istochnikov drevnerusskogo iskusstva' (From the field of literary sources of ancient Russian art), in *Sredi Kollektsionerov*, 1922, Nos. 11–12, pp. 35–6.

149. This proto-evangelical cycle includes the following scenes: *The Rejection of the Gift, Annunciation to Joachim, Annunciation to Anna, The Meeting at the Golden Gate, First Seven Steps of the Virgin, The Presentation of Mary, The Competition of the Suitors, The Betrothal of the Virgin, Joseph taking leave of Mary, Trial of the Virgin by the cursed water, Pokrov, 'In Thee Rejoiceth'* (western wall of the northern arm); *Birth of the Virgin, Presentation of the Virgin* (eastern wall of the south arm). In the south arm, where cleaning of the frescoes is still in progress, we will probably discover several new scenes from the proto-evangelical cycle. Concerning the iconography of this cycle see V. Lazarev, 'Snetogorskiye rospisi' (Wall paintings of Snetogorsk), in *Soobshcheniya Instituta Istorii Iskusstv Akademii Nauk*

S.S.S.R., fascicle 8, 1957, pp. 81–90, 109–10. J. Lafontaine-Dosogne, *Iconographie de l'enfance de la Vierge dans l'Empire byzantin et en Occident*, Brussels, 1964, pp. 49, 64, 66, 73, 81, 87 n. 3, 115 n. 2, 123 n. 12, 131 n. 5, 132, 140, 181, 194, 204, 206.

150. C. Tischendorf, *Apocalypses apocryphae*, Lipsiae, 1866, pp. 113–36.

151. I. Tolstoy and N. Kondakov, *Russkiye drevnosti*, fascicle 6, St. Petersburg, 1899, p. 67, fig. 103. Concerning the iconography of this subject see V. Lazarev, *Snetogorskiye rospisi*, pp. 90–3, 110–11.

152. N. Pokrovsky, *Evangeliye v pamyatnikakh ikonografii, preimushchestvenno vizantiyskikh i russkikh* (The Gospel in the monuments of iconography, predominantly Byzantine and Russian), St. Petersburg, 1892, pp. 154–5.

153. The composition *The Last Judgement* is full of apocalyptic motifs, some of which we do not meet in earlier works.

154. In the fresco showing the *Pokrov*, the figure of the Virgin-Orans is placed in the centre. The shroud extends over her. On either side are represented figures of flying angels, and below are two groups, one comprised of bishops, the other of laity. This subject, so extremely rare for such an early period, and not met with in any Byzantine works, was probably created on Russian soil. We find it for the first time on the western doors of the Cathedral of Suzdal', executed between 1230 and 1233 (I. Tolstoy and N. Kondakov, *Russkiye drevnosti*, fascicle 6, fig. 103).
Even more unusual for the early 14th century is the composition *In Thee Rejoiceth*. It is found in the fresco of Snetogorsk in a rudimentary form. The stress on the central axis, so characteristic of later icons and frescoes, is absent in the Snetogorsk fresco. For more details about these iconographic types see V. Lazarev, *Iskusstvo Novgoroda*, pp. 110–11; Id., *Snetogorskiye rospisi*, pp. 88–90, 110.

155. M. Alpatov und N. Brunov, *Geschichte der altrussichen Kunst*, Augsburg, 1932, p. 341.

156. See V. Lazarev, 'Vasil'yevskiye vrata 1336 goda' (Vasil'yevskiye doors dating from the year 1336), in *Sovetskaya Arkheologiya*, 1953 (XVIII), pp. 386–442. The Vasil'yevskiye doors were transported by Ivan the Terrible to Alexandrovskaya Sloboda, where they are now kept. The plates adorning them are executed in gold foil, in a technique slightly reminiscent of etching: the design is scratched into the black varnish which totally covers a plate of copper; after that the parts cleared of varnish are etched by acid, worked over with mercury, and gilded. This technique, already known to Pliny (Pliny, lib. 33 sect. 32, 42), was introduced into Rus' from Byzantium.

157. 1st Chron. of Novgorod for 1355; the Chronicler of Novgorod to the Churches of God for 1355.

158. Archmandrite Makary, *Arkheologicheskoye opisaniye tserkovnykh drevnostey Novgoroda i yego okrestnostey* (Archeological description of the ecclesiastical antiquities of Novgorod and its surroundings), part I, Moscow, 1860, p. 616.

159. See V. Lazarev, *Feofan Grek i yego shkola* (Theophanes the Greek and his school), Moscow, 1961, pp. 111–12.

160. 1st Chron. of Novgorod for 1374.

161. 3rd Chronic. of Novgorod for 1378. M. K. Karger—'K voprosu ob istochnikakh letopisnykh zapisey o deyatel'nosti zodchego Petra i Feofana Greka' (On the sources of the references in the chronicles of the activities of the architect Peter and of Theophanes the Greek), in *Trudy otdela drevney russkoy literatury Instituta russkoy literatury Akademii Nauk S.S.S.R.*, 1958 (XIV), pp. 567–8—suggests that the testimony of the late 3rd Chronicle of Novgorod may be based on the ancient lost inscription in the Church of the Transfiguration.

162. 1st Chron. of Novgorod for 1360–1.

163. The conch of the apse was decorated with a figure of the Virgin with Child enthroned between two angels (only unimportant fragments are preserved). Lower down is a register containing scenes from the *Passion*, an unusual theme for this location. This register continues on the north and south walls. Below is a frieze with the traditional Eucharist, from which only some fragments have been preserved. The lower part of the apse was filled by figures of bishops holding scrolls, now nearly all perished (probably the same composition was represented here as in the Church of Volotovo—i.e., *Adoration of the Sacrifice*). On the triumphal arch are represented Aaron and Melchisedek; on the pillar of the apse *The Annunciation*. In the prothesis we see various images of saints and *The Three Hebrew Children in the Furnace;* in the diaconicon, martyrs. The walls and vaults of the church are decorated by a large number of scenes from the life of Christ, below which run friezes with standing figures of saints. On the western wall of the central nave are located badly preserved scenes from the life of Theodore Stratelates and Theodore Tiron. On the north wall of the western nave the *Forty Martyrs of Sebaste* are shown. The composition which decorates the dome is made up of traditional elements (Pantocrator between archangels and cherubim, seven prophets and John the Baptist).

164. 1st Chron. of Novgorod for 1352.

165. 1st Chron. of Novgorod for 1363.

166. A. Anisimov, 'La peinture russe du XIV siècle (Theophane le Grec)', in *Gazette des Beaux Arts*, 1930, pp. 169–77.

167. I. Grabar', 'Feofan Grek', in *Kazanskiy Muzeynyy Vestnik*, 1922, No. 1, p. 15.

168. M. Karger, *Novogorod Velikiy* (Novgorod the Great), Moscow, 1946, p. 61.

169. G. Filimonov, *Arkheologicheskiye issledovaniya po pamyatnikam* (Archeological Research of Monuments), I, Moscow, 1859, p. 59.

170. On this iconographic type see V. Lazarev, *Freski Staroy Ladogi*, pp. 23–6.

171. Cf. V. Lazarev, 'Kovalyovskaya rospis' i problema yuzhnoslavyanskikh svyazey v russkoy zhivopisi XIV veka' (Wall paintings of Kovalyovo and the problem of South Slavonic connexions with Russian painting of the 14th century), *Ezhegodnik Instituta Istorii Iskusstv Akademii Nauk S.S.S.R.*, 1957, pp. 250–4.

172. This relatively rare subject is represented in the Church of the Holy Apostles at Thessalonica (*c.* 1315), on one of the miniatures of the Serbian Psalter at Munich (14th century) and in the Church of the Holy Trinity at Manasiya (1418).

173. Cf. L. Matsulevich, *Tserkov' Uspeniya Presvyatoy Bogoroditsy v Volotove* (Church of the Dormition at Volotovo), St. Petersburg, 1912, pp. 21–2.

174. The Metropolitan Makary, *Istoriya russkoy tserkvi* (History of the Russian Church), IV, St. Petersburg, 1886, pp. 327–8; P. Tikhomirov, *Kafedra novgorodskikh svyatiteley* (The Cathedral of the Archbishops of Novgorod), I, Novgorod, 1891, pp. 195–6.

175. D. Ainalov, *Vizantiyskaya zhivopis' XIV stoletiya* (Byzantine painting of the 14th century), Petrograd, 1917, pp. 124–47.

176. In a supplement to my monograph on Theophanes the Greek I gave a detailed critique of the theory of D. V. Ainalov.

177. 2nd Chron. of Novgorod for 1345. The Boyar Ontsifer Zhabin of Novgorod built this church.

178. The text of an inscription now lost on the interior western wall above the entrance: 'In the year 6888 (i.e., 1380) this temple of the Lord God and of our Saviour Jesus Christ was decorated under the rule of Grand Prince Dmitry Ivanovich and in the time of His Grace the Archbishop of Novgorod, Aleksey, at the order of the serf of God Ofanasy Stepanovich and of his wife, Mariya, and the decoration was finished in the month of August'. Cf. Archimandrite Makary, *Arkheologicheskoye opisaniye tserkovnykh drevnostey v Novgorode*, part I, p. 579.

179. In the apse were images of the *Eucharist* and bishops, on pillars figures of deacons, on the lower parts of the walls and pillars rows of saints (some in small arches, supported by delicate columns). Among the latter it was possible to recognize the Baptist, Moses Murin, Euphrosyn, Seth with disc, Constantine and Helen, and the princes Boris and Gleb. Adorning the upper parts of the walls and vaults were gospel scenes, of which the following survived up to the time of the war: *The Transfiguration, Mourning of Christ, Entombment, Crucifixion* (north wall), *Jesus among the doctors* (above the entrance). In the prothesis and on the north wall were two compositions rare in Russian decorations: '*Do not mourn for me, Mother*', which we know already from the wall-paintings of Volotovo, and quite separately the '*Queen of Heaven Standing at Thy Right Hand*'. At a vault near the entrance were the remains of a half-length Deesis. The dome was filled with a traditional semifigure of the Pantocrator, surrounded by four archangels and four cherubim, one of which was used as the symbol of the evangelist Mark in the tetramorph. Finally in the drum there were figures of eight prophets.

180. G. Millet, *Recherches sur l'iconographie de l'évangile au XIV, XV et XVI siècles*, Paris, 1916, pp. 506, 532, figs. 196, 544, 545.

181. For more details on this type see V. Lazarev, *Koval-yovskaya rospis'*, pp. 254–60.

182. The perished remains from the decoration in the Church of the Annunciation on Gorodishche reveal great stylistic similarities with the wall-paintings of Kovalyovo (the composition '*Do not mourn for me, Mother*' with half-figures of John the Theologian and S. Rhodion in the prothesis and figures of John Chrysostom, Basil the Great (?) and two angels standing on either side of the altar in an eastern niche—all of which were discovered as recently as the 1930's). In these fragments the faces are not of Russian but South Slav type. The manner of painting was akin to that of the second master who worked on the dome of the church of Kovalyovo. Very striking analogies to the frescoes of the church on Gorodishche are to be found in the Serbian decoration of the Church of the Saviour in Ravanitsa. L. A. Matsulevich was in favour of assigning the fragments of the church on Gorodishche to the mid-fourteenth century, but without doubt such a dating is too early. The similarity of style to the frescoes of Kovalyovo suggests a much later date—*c.* 1380. See L. Matsulevich, 'Fragmenty stenopisi v sobore Snetogorskogo monastyrya' (Fragments of wall-paintings in the cathedral of the Monastery of Snetogorsk), in *Zapiski otdeleniya russkoy i slavyanskoy arkheologii Russkogo Arkheologicheskogo Obshchestva*, 1915, (X), pp. 52–5.

183. The lower registers are completely lost. In the conch of the apse the Virgin of the type *Znameniye* is represented with angels standing at her sides; in the dome the Pantocrator, surrounded by four archangels and four cherubim; in the drum, prophets; in the summits of transverse arches, the Holy Face and Emmanuel; in the pendentives, evangelists; on the north-eastern pillar, the angel of the Annunciation; on walls and vaults, scenes from the life of Christ (*The Nativity of Christ, The Annunciation to the Shepherds, Presentation in the Temple, Jesus among the doctors, Baptism, Christ and the Samaritan Woman, Resurrection of Lazarus, Crucifixion, The Descent from the Cross, Transfiguration*); on the western wall, the vision of S. Pachomius; on the northern wall, *The Dormition* (only fragmentarily preserved); on pillars, semi-figures of Ephraim Syrus and of an unknown saint, and figures of Solomon and David.

184. Cf. V. Peredol'sky, 'Zapiska o sostoyanii veliko-novgorodoskoy stariny' (Note on the state of the antiquities of Novgorod the Great), in *Sbornik Novgorodskogo Obshchestva lyubiteley drevnosti*, III, Novgorod, 1910, p. 8.

185. Cf. Yu. Dmitriyev, *Stennyye rospisi Novgoroda*, pp. 170–2. Trial cleanings took place in the years 1923, 1924 and 1948.

186. The perished decoration of the Church of S. Nicolas contained the following images: Virgin with Child, enthroned between two angels; *The Eucharist* and the order of bishops (apse); Pantocrator, four angels and four seraphim (dome); prophets (drum); evangelists (pendentives); *Bearing of the Cross, Agony in the Garden, The Kiss of Judas* (western wall);

Beheading of John the Baptist (southern wall); *Finding of the Head of John the Baptist* (northern wall); figures and semi-figures of saints (vaults, pillars, walls).

In the Church of the Dormition in the village of Melyotovo in the region of Pskov fragments of badly damaged decoration are preserved, dating from 1465. In the years 1933 and 1949 some of the fragments were recovered from beneath the later additions of plaster and whitewash (*Last Supper, Washing of the Feet, Incredulity of Thomas, Vision of Peter of Alexandria*, legendary episodes from the life of Mary, figures of saints). Yu. N. Dmitriyev claims to see in the cleaned fragments the hands of two painters, one of whom he connects with the Central Russian school and the other with the school of Pskov. See Yu. Dmitriyev, 'Melyotovskii freski i ikh znacheniye dlya istorii drevnerusskoy literatury' (The frescoes of Melyotovo and their importance for the history of ancient Russian literature), *Trudy Otdela drevne-russkoy literatury*, 1951 (VIII), pp. 403–12.

187. Nikonovskaya Chron. for 1344.

188. Cf. G. Zhidkov, *Moskovskaya zhivopis' serediny XIV veka* (Moscow painting in the middle of the 14th century), Moscow, 1928, pp. 68–9.

189. Nikonovskaya Chron. for 1344.

190. Nikonovskaya Chron. for 1345.

191. Nikonovskaya Chron. for 1346.

192. See M. Prisyolkov, *Troitsskaya letopis', rekonstruktsiya teksta* (Troitskaya Chronicle, Reconstruction of the text), Moscow–Leningrad, 1950, pp. 445, 450, 459; V. Lazarev, *Feofan Grek i yego shkola*, pp. 7–13.

193. M. Tikhomirov, 'Andrey Rublyov i yego epokha' (Andrey Rublyov and his period), in *Voprosy Istorii*, 1961, No. 1, p. 10; M. Il'yin, 'Iz istorii moskovskoy arkhitektury vremen Andreya Rublyova' (On the history of Moscow architecture in the time of Andrey Rublyov), ibid., 1960, No. 18, pp. 89–98.

194. In the Cathedral of the Birth of the Virgin in the Savvin-Storozhevsky monastery in Zvenigorod four figures of anchorites and ascetics are preserved on the altar barrier built of white stone. The style is close to that of Andrey Rublyov. It is possible that either Andrey Rublyov himself or one of his closest collaborators worked here. See *Istoriya russkogo iskusstva*, III, Moscow, 1955, pp. 122–4; G. Vzdornov, 'Freskovaya rospis' altarnoy pregrady Rozhdestvenskogo sobora Savvino-Storozhevskogo monastyrya v Zvenigorode' (Wall-paintings of the altar-barrier in the Cathedral of the Birth of the Virgin at the Savvin-Storozhevsky Monastery), in *Drevnerusskoye iskusstvo*, Moscow, 1963, pp. 75–82.

195. 2nd Sofiyskaya, Voskresenskaya and Nikonovskaya Chronicles for 1408. The 2nd Sofiyskaya Chronicle is based on a version of the year 1456.

196. I. Sakharov, *Issledovaniya o russkom ikonopisanii* (Research on Russian icon painting), booklet 2, St. Petersburg, 1849, supplements, p. 14.

197. *Russkaya Istoricheskaya Biblioteka* (Russian Historical Library), vol. VI, No. 118.

198. Cf. V. Malinin, *Starets Eleazarova monastyrya Filofey i yego poslaniya* (Elder of the Monastery of Elizarov Philotheus and his epistles), Kiev, 1901, p. 383. Cf. N. Andreyev, 'Filofey and his Epistle to Ivan Vasil'yevich', in *Slavonic and East European Review*, 1959 (XXXVIII), pp. 1–31.

199. Cf. V. Georgiyevsky, *Freski Ferapontova monastyrya* (Frescoes of the Ferapontov monastery), St. Petersburg, 1911, p. 34.

200. Frescoes on the stone altar-barrier hidden behind the wooden iconostasis were discovered in 1812, after Napoleon's soldiers had removed the icons from the iconostasis. Unfortunately these frescoes have not been studied. The small number of fragments which can be seen indicate a great stylistic similarity with the works of Dionisy and his circle. Among the figures decorating the altar-barrier can be recognized: Aleksey, man of God; Parthenius; John Climacus; Ioan Kushchnik; Paul, the first hermit (Pavel Fiveyskiy); Theodosius the Great; Isaac Sirus; Ephraim Sirus; Euthymius the Great; Anthony the Great; Sabas of Jerusalem; Simeon the Stylite; Arsenius the Great; Pimen the Great; Nil Postnik; Sisoy the Great.
Cf. the editorial essay 'Drevniye freski za ikonostasom Moskovskogo Uspenskogo sobora' (Ancient frescoes behind the iconostasis of the Cathedral of the Dormition in Moscow), in the magazine *Svetil'nik*, 1915, No. 1, pp. 3–7. S. A. Usov—*Drevnosti, Trudy Imp. Moskovskogo Arkheologicheskogo Obshchestva*, 1883 (IX), fascicles 2–3, pp. 44–7—claims, probably rightly, that the choice of saints was dictated by the important events in the political and ecclesiastical life of Moscow which took place on their respective feast days. These days reflect events only up to 1481. Should the supposition be correct, it confirms once more the assignment of the decoration of the stone altar-barrier to a time near to the consecration of the Cathedral.

201. L'vovskaya Chron. for 1481; 2nd Sofiyskaya Chron. for 1482.

202. 2nd Sofiyskaya, L'vovskaya and Nikonovskaya Chronicles for 1514. See also the fragment of the Russian Chron. for 1515. Cf. M. Tikhomirov, 'Iz Vladimirskogo letopistsa' (From the 'Chronicler of Vladimir'), in *Istoricheskiye Zapiski*, 1945, No. 15, p. 294.

203. The inscription: 'In the year 7008 (1500) in the month of August, on the 6th, the day of the feast of the Transfiguration of our Lord Jesus Christ the decoration of the Church was commenced and was finished 2 years later on the 8th of September, the day of the feast of the Birth of our most holy Queen Mary, God's Mother. The decoration took place under the rule of Ivan Vasil'yevich, orthodox Grand Prince of all the Russias and of Vasily Ivanovich, Grand Prince of all the Russias, and in the time of the Archbishop Tikhon, and the painters were the icon painter Dionisy and his children. O Lord Christ, King of all, O God, do not permit them to suffer eternal torments.' See V. Georgiyevsky, *Freski Ferapontova monastyrya* (Frescoes of the Ferapontov monastery), St. Petersburg, 1911, pp. 17–18.

204. *The Œcumenical Councils* are also represented in the Church of Peter and Paul in Tyrnovo (end of 14th beginning of 15th centuries) and in the Metropolis at Mistra (*c.* 1312), and Acathistus in the Pantanassa at Mistra (*c.* 1428).

205. An interesting analysis of this subject is contained in the unpublished dissertation which the late E. S. Medvedeva presented in 1947, under the title 'Iconography of the Russian Feast of the Pokrov'. Cf. I. Danilova, 'Ikonograficheskiy sostav fresok Rozhdestvenskoy tserkvi Ferapontova monastyrya' (Iconographical content of the frescoes in the Rozhdestvenskaya Church of the Ferapontov monastery), in *Iz istorii russkogo i zapadnoyevropeyskogo iskusstva*, Moscow, 1960, p. 121.

206. Cf. I. Danilova, op. cit., pp. 121–4.

207. Cf. V. Georgiyevsky, op. cit., p. 88; I. Danilova, op. cit., p. 120.

208. See the epistle dated 2 February, 1489, from the archimandrite Gennady to Ioasaf, former archbishop of Rostov and Yaroslavl', in *Chteniya v Obshchestve istorii i drevnostey rossiyskikh*, 1847, book VIII, pp. 4–5.

NOTES ON
OLD RUSSIAN MURALS & MOSAICS

Fig. 1. Archangel. Mosaic, 1043–6. Kiev, S. Sophia.

DESCRIPTIVE NOTES

Cathedral of S. Sophia, Kiev

PANTOCRATOR. Mosaic in the dome. 1043–6.   14, 19

This is one of the most monumental images of the art of the eleventh century. The diameter of the medallion is four metres, the distance from the top of the dome to the floor about twenty-eight and a half metres. Good state of preservation, except that the gold background on the right and the beard have been restored with tempera. On the figure's right hand a small rectangular area has been left uncleaned; the darker colour of this rectangle clearly shows how the mosaic looked before restoration.

Of all the representations of the Pantocrator done in the eleventh and twelfth centuries the Kievan mosaic is closest to that of Hosios Lucas (E. Diez and O. Demus, *Byzantine Mosaics in Greece*, Cambridge, Mass., 1931, Pl. II, fig. 12; O. Demus, *Byzantine Mosaic Decoration*, figs. 13a, 19, 23, 26, 27b). In the enormous half-length figure of the Pantocrator there is a unique combination of pure peasant force and archaic restraint. The heavy figure, massive head, short neck, square shoulders, large, clumsy hands, the harsh, not very rhythmical folds of the cloak—all give an entirely individual note to this image, which is so unlike the Byzantine Pantocrators at Nicea, S. Sophia of Constantinople, Daphni, Cefalù and elsewhere. In these there is incomparably more refinement and gloss, but none of the freshness of expression or monumentality of conception. The mosaicist who laid the medallion of the Pantocrator also executed the figures of the *Virgin Orans* [20] and the Archangel [1]. He was evidently a specialist in large portraits.

F. I. Shmit attributes this mosaic to the twelfth century, but there is no basis for such an attribution (F. Shmit, *Kievskiy Sofiyskiy Sobor*—The Cathedral of S. Sophia, Kiev, Moscow, 1914, pp. 12–13).

ARCHANGEL. Mosaic in the dome. 1043–6.   1

Of the four figures surrounding the medallion of the Pantocrator, only one has survived, and even this is not complete as both wings have suffered damage in parts. Moreover, the lower part of the garment and the feet were restored by the famous Russian artist Vrubel'. The figure is 3·85 metres high. It is unusually clumsy with its large head and bulky shoulders. In his right hand the archangel holds a sphere decorated with a cross which symbolizes the martyrdom of Christ, and in his left hand, a labarum with the opening words of a hymn of glory to Christ (Apocalypse IV, 8). A similar composition, a Pantocrator surrounded by archangels, used to decorate the dome of the Church of Theotocos' Pharos (about 864) in Constantinople.

APOSTLE PAUL. Detail of mosaic in the drum. 1043–6.   2

At one time the drum contained figures of the twelve apostles. Of these only the upper part of the figure of the Apostle Paul has survived, although all were still in existence in the seventeenth century, when they were seen by Paul of Aleppo (*Puteshestviye antiokhiyskogo patriarkha Makariya v Rossiyu v polovine XVII veka, opisannoye yego synom arkhidiakonom Pavlom Aleppskim*—The Travels of Makarios, the Patriarch of Antioch, to Russia in the Middle of the Seventeenth Century, Described by his Son, Archdeacon Paul of Aleppo—2nd edition, Moscow, 1897, p. 69). The face is similar to that of S. Paul in the arch of the narthex in Hosios Lucas. It is clear that this artist was also responsible for parts of the *Eucharist* and the *Deesis*. In the former he laid the left figure of Christ [22], and the left angel [23], and the first four apostles with Peter at their head [21] and in the latter, the half-length figure of John the Baptist [18]. His work is characterized by a comparatively wide setting of tessarae, in which the interstices between the cubes stand out very noticeably.

CHRIST-THE-PRIEST. Mosaic above east transverse arch. 1043–6.   4

For a long time this image was hidden under a disfiguring coat of oil-paint. The preservation is good. Diameter of the medallion, 1·16 metres. The first to discover the real meaning of this image, which had long been wrongly considered a portrait of Emmanuel, was D. V. Ainalov (D. Ainalov, 'Novyy ikonograficheskiy obraz Khrista'—A New Iconographic Image of Christ—*Seminarium Kondakovianum*, 1928, II, pp. 19–23). In the mosaic Christ is represented with a thin moustache and beard, short thick hair and a tonsure; in His left hand he holds a scroll. The type of face is very unusual. The portrait is taken from an ancient apocrypha which tells of the election of Christ, by a general vote, to the twenty-two priests of the temple of Jerusalem. A. A. Vasil'yev, who published two Greek texts from this apocrypha (12th and 15th–16th centuries), believes it to be pre-Justinian (A. A. Vasiliev, *Anecdota Graeco-Byzantina*, pars prior, Mosquae, MDCCXCIII). In his opinion the apocrypha originated from the Jewish Christians, since it was according to Jewish thought that the qualities of both king and priest were combined in the Messiah. The portrayal of Christ as a priest, thus stressing the significance of priesthood, may have been occasioned by the Church's struggle against the heretical tendency to deny the ecclesiastical hierarchy. The Nikon Chronicle mentions, for instance, under the year 1004, a heretic called Andreyan Skopets, who came out against the laws of the Church, and against bishops, presbyters and monks.

Apart from S. Sophia, the representation of Christ as a priest occurs in three other instances—in the Church of Nerezi, 1164 (cupola of the south-west chapel), in the Church of Nereditsa, 1199 (apse), and in the Church of Bertubani, 1213–22 (refectory). The hand of the master who laid this mosaic can easily be recognized in the portraits of Gaius, Crispus and Lysimacus in a series of medallions of the Martyrs of Sebaste. He is characterized by a vigorous treatment of form, by bold, sometimes rather imprecise drawing, and by a liking for bright and mottled colours.

EVANGELIST MARK. Mosaic on the north-west pendentive. 1043–6.   3

Good state of preservation. Height of figure, 1·64 metres. The figure of the evangelist, the chair, footstool, small table, lectern—all these are carefully positioned on the surface so as to avoid the foreshortening due to perspective. This accounts for the angularity and the frozen quality of the movements.

Fig. 2. The Apostle Paul. Mosaic, 1043–6. Kiev, S. Sophia.

The mosaicist who laid the figure of Mark worked in the archaic tradition. He also did the two figures on the extreme left of the *Eucharist* and the figure of the archangel Gabriel in the *Annunciation*. He was clearly unsuccessful in his attempt to portray the figure of Mark in the three-quarter view which the Byzantine masters usually used for the evangelists. Nor did he satisfactorily represent the direction of Mark's look, which is turned towards the Gospels; the pupil of Mark's left eye, which is badly misplaced, makes the eye appear to bulge and as a result he seems to have a squint. In spite of these defects, however, this monumental figure is undeniably expressive. The face, full of deep concentration and inner power, is particularly remarkable. The Greek text on the open pages of the codex is taken from the Gospel of S. Mark (i, 1–2).

THE VIRGIN FROM THE DEESIS. Mosaic above the main apse. 1043–6.   17

Excellent state of preservation. Diameter of the medallion, 0·84 metres. The Virgin, like the half-length figures of Christ and John the Baptist, is shown without a halo; this was for purely practical reasons as there was not enough space for one. This artist, one of the more experienced masters who worked in the S. Sophia, was also responsible for the figure of Mary in the *Annunciation* [16, in colour], the figure of Aaron and the entire right side of the *Eucharist* composition.

JOHN THE BAPTIST FROM THE DEESIS. Mosaic above the central apse. 1043–6.   18

Excellent state of preservation. Diameter of medallion, 0·85 metres. This face is very similar to that of John the Baptist from the *Baptism* in Hosios Lucas. The wide setting of the

tesserae reveals the hand of the master who did the figure of the apostle Paul [2], and most of the figures in the left-hand part of the *Eucharist* [22, 23].

THE VIRGIN ORANS. Mosaic in the apse. 1043–6.   20

Good state of preservation. Height of the figure, 5·45 metres. The head (0·90 metres) is one-sixth of the height of the figure. The lower part of the body (2·80 metres) is disproportionately short in relation to the size of the head, proportions being only three to one. Had the master taken perspective foreshortening into account, he should have lengthened the lower part of the body. This he did not do, with the result that the figure seems short and large-headed, and assumes a somewhat archaic character. The Greek inscription, which follows the curve of the arch framing the conch, is from Psalm xlv, 6.

Generally the apses in Kievan churches were decorated with the figure of Mary in the *Orans* attitude. In the churches of Byzantium, however, a variety of attitudes can be seen. There the Virgin was often depicted with the Child in her hands, either standing or enthroned. The Kievan addiction to one particular inconographic type is reminiscent of a favourite pagan mythological image of the 'great goddess', represented by a woman standing with raised hands, facing the spectator. For the Slavs this was a traditional legendary image, taken from antiquity, and when Christianity arrived to displace heathendom, the Mary *Orans* took the place of the 'great goddess', who had embodied the life-giving forces of the earth. The *Orans* of S. Sophia came to be known by the people as 'the unshakable wall' (*nerushimaya stena*). Possibly the aesthetic appreciation of this figure took on a special significance owing to its sense of solidarity and its expression of spiritual strength. However there is no doubt that this name was inspired by church anthems in which the Virgin is constantly compared to an 'unshakable' and 'immovable' wall. In the Middle Ages the Virgin was regarded, above all, as an intercessor and patroness, and, more particularly, as the patroness of the individual town and as someone who guaranteed the safety of its ramparts. This was the role of the famous

Fig. 3. S. Mark. Mosaic, 1043–6. Kiev, S. Sophia.

Orans in the Church of Blachernae in Constantinople; here Mary appeared as the protectress of the walls of Byzantium (see N. Kondakov, *Iconografiya Bogomateri*—The Iconography of the Virgin—II, Petrograd, 1915, p. 72). Evidently this interpretation of the *Orans* image, or one similar to it, was imported from Byzantium into Kievan Rus', where the portrayal of Mary with raised hands came to be treated not only as a symbol of the Church Militant, but also as a personification of the patroness of the town of Kiev and its people. It is precisely in this light that Hilarion sees the image of the Virgin in his famous 'Slovo o zakone i blagodati'—A Word on Law and Grace (see *Pamyatniki drevnerusskoy tserkovnoy literatury*—The Works of Old Russian Religious and Didactic Literature—edited by A. I. Ponomaryov, fascicle 1, St. Petersburg, 1894, pp. 74–5).

THE EUCHARIST. Mosaic in the apse. 1043–6.   21–24

This is the largest of the mosaic compositions that have survived. The preservation is good although the two apostles on the extreme right are completely lost, except for their feet. The figures are between 1·90 and 2·05 metres in height. Two Greek inscriptions run across the gold background, bearing the words of the two parts of the Holy Communion: 'Take this and eat; this my body, broken for you for the forgiveness of sins' and 'Drink from it all of you. For this is my blood, blood of the covenant, shed for many for the forgiveness of sins'. (Matthew xxvi, 26–9; Mark xiv, 22–5; Luke xxii, 17–21). Although the features of the apostles are not yet sufficiently individual to be recognized at first glance, they can nevertheless be identified on a more careful analysis. The first to approach Christ are Peter on the left, and Paul on the right. Behind Peter comes John, followed by Luke, Simon and Bartholomew, and Philip (or possibly Thomas) ends the procession: only the last figure in the left-hand group cannot be identified with certainty. On the right, Paul is followed by Matthew, Mark and Andrew.

The *Eucharist* is one of the most ancient subjects depicted in Christian art. Its dogmatic content, allowing no misinterpretation, was a direct reflection of those impassioned arguments that surrounded its mystery and were particularly acute in Asia Minor and Syria. From the ninth century onwards, illustrations of the *Eucharist* can often be found in Greek psalters, and it was probably by way of these psalters that the subject of the Eucharist was taken up and elaborated upon in monumental painting. The Crucifix of Pope Pascal (814–24) gives grounds for such reasoning, inasmuch as angels ministering to Christ already feature on it. The mosaic of S. Sophia is the earliest known monumental work showing an elaborated version of the Eucharist. But there is not the slightest doubt that for the source of this variant one must refer to the art of Constantinople in the ninth and tenth centuries.

The Kievan mosaic is remarkable for its monumentality. Stressing the two-dimensional quality of the whole composition, the mosaicists systematically avoid anything that might disturb this principle. Thus they deprive the altar of any volume, reducing it to a flat, ornamentally elaborated rectangle. The ciborium they also project in plane, omitting the fourth column, and by so doing they avoid any hint of foreshortening. In the majestically striding figures they never make use of superimposition but carefully observe the rule whereby one figure is placed next to another at more or less regular intervals. All this taken together helps to create a unique artistic effect: to the onlooker it appears that the action takes place in a spaceless and timeless setting, which is ruled by its own, entirely peculiar laws. The portrayal of the Eucharist was primarily an illustration of dogma; and since that is precisely what the Church was trying to achieve, there was need for an abstract structure and form, which could express the particular symbolic content.

The part of the mosaic which has survived was executed by three mosaicists and the two figures on the extreme right, which are lost, were probably done by a fourth. The entire right half of the remaining composition, including Christ and the angel, is the work of one man. He also laid the figures of Aaron and the Virgin in the Annunciation [16, in colour] and the half-length figure of the Virgin in the Deesis [17]. Another did the left side of the composition, except for the two figures on the far left. To him can also be attributed several other mosaics, including the apostle Paul [2]; John the Baptist from the Deesis [18]; Gregory of Nazianzus, S. Nicholas and Archdeacon Stephen from the order of saints; and Vivianus, one of the Martyrs of Sebaste. A characteristic of his work is his wide setting of the cubes. Finally, the third mosaicist executed the two figures on the far left. It was he also who laid the evangelist Mark on the pendentive [3] and the archangel Gabriel in the *Annunciation*. This third master had a particularly strong leaning towards any archaic type of representation.

ORDER OF SAINTS. Mosaic in the apse. 1043–6.   25, 26, *6–8*

Of the mosaic portraying eight bishops and two archdeacons, only the upper portions have survived. The mosaic on the north side of the apse extends to the waists of the figures and that on the south side to their knees. The missing parts of the figures have been restored with oil painting. Average height of the figures—about 2·30 metres.

The mosaic on the north shows, from left to right, Epiphanius of Cyprus, Pope Clement, Gregory of Nazianzus, Nicholas Thaumaturgus and Archdeacon Stephen; that on the south Archdeacon Lawrence, Basil the Great, John Chrysostom, Gregory of Nyssa and Gregory Thaumaturgus. On the walls between the windows there used to be mosaics of the apostles Peter and Paul, but no trace of these remains. In selecting the Fathers of the Church, those who compiled the programme for the decoration of the cathedral chose the customary group, with two exceptions, for it is not very often that one finds Epiphanius of Cyprus and Pope Clement included with the Fathers of the Church. The works of Epiphanius were well known to Kievan Rus' through Slav translations produced not later than the eleventh century. As far as Clement was concerned, he was particularly revered by the Slavs. His relics, brought from Korsun' by Grand-prince Vladimir, were preserved in the Desyatinnaya church. For Kievan Rus' these relics were something national and sacred (see I. Franco, 'S'vyatiy Kliment u Korsuni'—S. Clement in Korsun'—*Zapiski naukovogo tovaristva imeni Shevchenka*, Book 2, 1902, pp. 1–44; Book 4, 1902, pp. 45–144; Book 6, 1903, pp. 145–80; Book 3, 1904, pp. 181–208; Book 4, 1904, pp. 209–56; P. Duthilleul, 'Les reliques de Clement de Rome', *Revue des études byz.*, 1958, 16, pp. 85–98).

The mosaic on the north side of the apse, executed in a paler range of colours, has not nearly the quality of that on the south side. The figures of Epiphanius and Clement were executed by the master who laid the half-length figure of Christ in the Deesis: he is characterized by a somewhat

Fig. 4. Christ-the-Priest. Mosaic, 1043–6. Kiev, S. Sophia.

Fig. 5. Pryscus, Martyr of Sebaste. Mosaic, 1043–6. Kiev, S. Sophia.

Fig. 6. Gregory Thaumaturgus. Detail from the 'Order of Saints'.
Mosaic, 1043–6. Kiev, S. Sophia.

Fig. 7. John Chrysostom. Detail from the 'Order of Saints'.
Mosaic, 1043–6. Kiev, S. Sophia.

uncertain style, an uncomplicated use of lines, and pale tones which tend to flatten the image. The other three figures of the north mosaic (Gregory of Nazianzus, Nicholas Thaumaturgus and Stephen) are the work of another master. In the faces with their bulky, pronounced features, and in the wide setting of the tesserae, one can easily recognize the hand of the 'master of the apostle Paul' [2]. All five figures on the south side of the apse were laid by one and the same mosaicist; he must be considered the main, as well as the most gifted, artist and must have been in charge of all the mosaics in S. Sophia. He reserved for himself the most prominent part of the lower register in the apse, in the justified belief that there the onlooker would be most able to appreciate his remarkable art. And indeed, he greatly surpassed his colleagues in his skill in portraying individual features, in the correctness and expressiveness of his drawing, and in the refinement of his colour compositions. For example, in the treatment of the ascetic face of John Chrysostom [7] he makes use of short, broken lines, with a downward emphasis. This can be seen in the triangle on the bridge of the nose, the triangular form of the shadow between the eyebrows, the wedge-shaped shadows on the cheeks, the moustache drooping sadly downwards, and the pointed chin. The shapes of the crosses on the omophorion fully correspond with this linear rhythm; the crosses are elongated, angular, and geometrically dry. The face of Gregory Thaumaturgus is executed in an entirely different manner [6]. The mosaicist achieves a general expression of grace with the aid of soft, seemingly flowing lines, and rounded forms, which find a parallel in the rounded arms of the crosses on the omophorion. It is in such details, at first inconspicuous, that the development of the drawing, perfected by generations of medieval artists, is most apparent.

THE VIRGIN OF THE ANNUNCIATION. Mosaic on the south-east pillar. 1043–6.

16, Colour Plate

Good state of preservation. Height of figure, 2·23 metres. On the left there is an inscription in Greek: 'I am the Lord's servant; as you have spoken, so be it' (Luke i, 38). In her hand Mary holds a skein of purple yarn which was given to her by the Judaic priests for the preparation of the Veil of the Temple. This episode, which had already been recorded on a mosaic in the Church of S. Sergius in Gaza, goes back to apocryphal sources, the Protevangelium Jacobi xi, 1). The mosaicist who laid the figure of Mary also did the whole right side of the *Eucharist* [e.g. 24].

THE MARTYRS OF SEBASTE. MEDALLIONS OF HALF-LENGTH FIGURES. Mosaics on the south and north transverse arches. 1043–6.   27, 5

Preservation good on the whole, except for damage to the gold backgrounds of the portraits of Vivianus and Pryscus, and on the left side of Pryscus's face. The diameters of the medallions range from 0·87 to 0·98 metres. Above each medallion there is an inscription in Greek giving the name of the martyr portrayed. Each martyr holds a cross in his right hand, and a diadem adorned with precious stones in his left. The portraits of Nicholas [27] and Aetius do not approach in quality those of Vivianus, Pryscus [5] and Chydius. In the first two there are many errors of draughtsmanship; the lines are heavy and unrhythmical, the modelling of the faces lacks subtle gradations of tone and in several places yellow-orange cubes have been used in place of gold ones. These medallions were not done by the most skilled masters but by their local assistants, who clearly worked in an archaic style. A comparison of the Kievan mosaics with the frescoes of Cappadocia and the mosaics of the Cathedral in Monreale shows that the iconography of the Martyrs of Sebaste was quite freely interpreted. As a result, where the same martyrs are portrayed, the features are completely different in each representation.

Frescoes in the Cathedral of S. Sophia, Kiev

The frescoes of S. Sophia have suffered greatly from the ravages of time and from the truly barbaric restorations of 1844–52, when they were completely overpainted in oils. Their very bad state of preservation soon became evident when the oil-painting was first removed in 1928. They have suffered a great deal of physical damage in that the paint has often been badly scratched or rubbed away, and their colours have weakened and become tarnished as a result of age, white-washing, and the covering of hot, drying oil which the ignorant restorers of the nineteenth century used as their own special primer when they painted the frescoes in oils. Most of the frescoes still bear traces of a very thin coat of oil-paint in those areas where nothing had remained of the original and where

Fig. 8. The Order of Saints. Mosaic, 1043–6. Kiev, S. Sophia.

Fig. 9. The Denial of Peter. Fresco, 1043–6. Kiev, S. Sophia.

Fig. 10. The Wedding at Cana. Fresco, 1043–6. Kiev, S. Sophia.

Fig. 11. The Descent of the Holy Ghost. Fresco, 1043–6. Kiev, S. Sophia.

Fig. 12. The Visitation. Fresco, 1046–61/7. Kiev, S. Sophia.

231

the overpainting was therefore not removed during the most recent restoration. Although only the finest possible coat of oil-paint has been retained the presence of oil is nevertheless evident. Naturally the frescoes of S. Sophia reproduced in this book are those which appeared to be in the best state of preservation.

THE WEDDING AT CANA. Fresco on the south side of the gallery. 1043–6. *10*

The fresco of the *Wedding at Cana* has lost its upper layers of paint and thus the tonal gradations have disappeared also, so that the viewer can gain little idea of anything other than its compositional structure. Nothing has survived of either the upper left or the upper right parts of the original painting and in these areas the oil-painting of the mid-nineteenth century has been left. The *Wedding at Cana* is divided into two registers. In the upper register Christ is shown reclining by the table with three companions; to the right stands the servant, to the left there used to be the figure of a woman approaching Christ. In the lower register the moment of the actual miracle is recorded: Christ, approaching the vessels, changes the water into wine, and to the left a servant draws water from a well. Similar representations of the *Wedding at Cana*, across two registers, often occur in the miniatures of tenth to twelfth century Greek gospels (Cod. Leningr. gr. 21, fol. 2; Cod. Parm. Palat. 5, fol. 89v). See V. Lazarev, 'Novyye dannyye o mozaikakh i freskakh Sofii Kievskoy'—New data on the mosaics and frescoes of the S. Sophia in Kiev—in *Vizantiyskiy Vremennik*, 1956 (X), pp. 173–4.

THE DENIAL OF PETER. Fresco on the north wall of the transept. 1043–6. *28, 9*

Bad state of preservation. At both left and right no trace of the original painting remains. In some places, for instance in the garments and in the faces, a thin layer of oil-paint restoration has been preserved. The scene is taken from S. Mark's Gospel (xiv, 66–8): Christ was with Caiaphas and Peter was warming himself by the fire outside, when the maid of the high priest approached him and said: 'You were there too, with this man from Nazareth'. But Peter denied his Master, saying: 'I know nothing, I do not understand what you mean'. The lonely figure of Peter is full of expression. In the middle distance the court-house is depicted.

GROUP OF APOSTLES FROM 'APPARITION OF CHRIST TO THE ELEVEN'. Detail of the fresco on the south wall of the transept. 1043–6. *29*

The entire right half of the composition and a considerable part of the left side are completely lost. The head and the right side of the figure of Christ, the figure of Paul, and the heads of the four apostles following him, have been preserved. Six apostles could once be seen approaching the figure of Christ from the right; five more approached from the left. Christ is shown in a stern frontal pose. His hands rest on the heads of Paul and Peter. The episode depicted here is derived from S. Matthew's Gospel (xxviii, 16–20), where the appearance of the risen Christ to eleven of his disciples on a mountain in Galilee is described. Drawing near to the apostles Christ 'spake unto them, saying, All power is given to me in heaven and earth. Go ye therefore, and teach all nations, baptizing them in the name of the Father, and of the Son, and of the Holy Ghost'. This scene had a very special meaning for the people of Kievan Rus', who had only recently been baptized. As Burke proved, the iconography of this subject began to be formulated at the end of the third and beginning of the fourth century. (W. Burke, 'A Bronze Situla in the Museo Cristiano', *Art Bulletin*, 1930, XII, pp. 163–78). The composition of this fresco has close parallels among the Greek miniatures (Cod. Paris. gr. 510, fol. 426; Lenigr. gr. 21, fol. 11; Athen. MS. 820, fol. 20).

THE DESCENT OF THE HOLY GHOST. Fresco on the west wall of the transept. 1043–6. *11*

Bad state of preservation. In some places, where the original drawing is completely lost, thin outlines in oils have been left by the restorers. The apostles are shown sitting on a semicircular seat, with Peter and Paul in the centre. Above, there is a segment symbolizing heaven. The groups of people usually depicted below are absent here. In the treatment of the composition, this fresco closely resembles the Greek miniature of Cod. Vatic. gr. 1162 (fol. 2v) and the mosaic of Monreale.

THE PROTO-EVANGELICAL CYCLE. Frescoes in the apse, and on the south wall of the bema in the diaconicon. 1046–61/7. *31–35, 12*

State of preservation relatively good. There is some superficial damage and partial loss to the top layer of paint. Only very few paintings are unspoilt by oil-paint. At one time the half-length figure of Anna could be seen in the conch of the prothesis, dedicated by Yaroslav to the memory of his mother and his wife. Of this figure only the remnants of the bent left arm, shoulder, and the upper part of the head and halo have survived. The scenes of the proto-evangelical cycle are arranged on the walls of the apse in four registers. The narration begins with the top register. The fresco to the left is lost; most probably it depicted the *Annunciation to Joachim*. To the right the *Annunciation to Anna* is shown; the cooing doves in the basin of the fountain remind her of her childlessness. The second register continues along the south wall of the bema and portrays three scenes: the *Meeting at the Golden Gate of Jerusalem*, the *Birth of the Virgin*, and the *Presentation of the Blessed Virgin Mary*, with an additional episode, *Mary fed by the hand of an Angel*. The third register also shows three scenes: the *Betrothal of the Virgin*, the *Annunciation at the Spring*, and the *Presentation by Mary of the Temple Veil to the Priest* (the last scene was interpreted wrongly by N. P. Kondakov, D. V. Ainalov, and E. K. Redin as *Mary Receiving the Purple for the Temple Veil* and by J. Lafontaine-Dosogne as *Farewell of Mary*). A comparison with the miniatures of Cod. Vatic. gr. 1162 (fol. 109 and 142) will confirm that my interpretation is correct. Finally, in the lower register, the proto-evangelical cycle concludes with representations of the *Annunciation* and the *Visitation*. Cf. J. Lafontaine-Dosogne, *Iconographie de l'enfance de la Vierge dans l'Empire Byzantin et en Occident*, Brussels, 1964, pp. 38, 182.

The proto-evangelical cycle, derived from apochryphal sources, was already well known to early Christian art (cf. the columns of the ciborium of the fifth century in San Marco), Byzantine art (Castelseprio, Daphni, Cod. Vatic. gr. 1162, etc.) and Georgian art (Ateni). But it became much more widespread in Rus', where we find it in many monuments of the eleventh and early twelfth centuries (e.g., S. Sophia in Kiev, the Cathedral of the Spaso-Mirozhsky Monastery in Pskov, the Church of the Annunciation near Arkazhi, the Church of Nereditsa, the Cathedral of the Nativity of the

Fig. 13. Half-length figure of a Youth and Profile of an Old Man.
Fresco, 1046–61/7. Kiev, S. Sophia.

Virgin in the Snetogorsk Monastery, etc.). Evidently scenes from this cycle with their emotional appeal were particularly attractive to the people of ancient Rus'.

The frescoes in the diaconicon, which differ somewhat in their manner of execution from the paintings in the central cross of the cathedral, could have been completed after its first consecration in 1046; but they were certainly done no later than 1061/7, when the second consecration took place. The frescoes were painted by Kievan artists who came from a mixed Byzantine-Russian workshop. The un-Byzantine type of faces, the massive architectural settings, the grossly elongated proportions of the figures—all indicate the work of Kievan masters.

HALF-LENGTH FIGURE OF A YOUTH, AND PROFILE OF AN OLD MAN. Sketches in the conch of the apse in the northern exterior nave. 1046–61/7.   *13*

Preservation satisfactory. In many places the top layer of paint is missing.

The heads of the youth and the old man have been visible for a long time through the blue paint of the background of the conch, but they have usually been regarded as the work of restorers of the nineteenth century. After their final cleaning, not long ago, it became clear that both these portraits were painted in dark blue on the still moist surface of the original plaster, and were later covered by the light blue paint of the background. Consequently, we have here the sketches of an eleventh century artist which can be attributed to the class of 'Autonome Zeichnungen' (see B. Degenhart, 'Autonome Zeichnungen bei mittelalterlichen Künstlern', *Münchener Jahrbuch der bildenden Kunst*, 1950 [I], pp. 93–158). Evidently the half-length figure of the youth with classical features depicts S. George and was drawn either by an artist trying his hand, or by an experienced master instructing a pupil. The head of the ageing bearded man, presented in profile, is so individual that one would like to treat it as a portrait of one of the artists working on the scaffolding. Such sketches made on moist plaster, then lying hidden under a covering coat of paint, must have been common in medieval monumental painting, particularly if we take into account the high cost of parchment, and, later, of paper. When the fresco painter stood on the scaffolding in front of the wall prepared for painting,

he had excellent opportunity to experiment first with his brush, and use the large surface for quick sketches. Similar sketches were discovered on the wall of the Baptistry in Padua (see *Pitture murali nel Veneto e tecnica dell' affresco*, Venezia, 1960, pp. 61–2, pl. 24) and on one of Signorelli's frescoes in the Cathedral of Orvieto (see A. Bertini Calosso, 'Disegni tracciati ad affresco da Luca Signorelli nel Duomo di Orvieto,' *Rivista d'Arte*, 1941 [XX], pp. 194–202).

UNKNOWN VIRGIN MARTYRS. Frescoes in the central nave and in the diaconicon. 1046–61/7.   *14, 15*

State of preservation satisfactory. The surface is badly damaged and much of the top layer of paint is missing. In various places there is some very delicate oil-paint restoration; a small area of nineteenth-century overpainting still remains near the shoulder of the right-hand figure.

THE APOSTLE PAUL. Fresco in the prothesis. 1046–61/7. *16*

State of preservation relatively good. The greatest losses in colour are in the nimbus and in the background. The head, hands and clothing give a true idea of the style of mid eleventh-century painting.

S. NICHOLAS. Fresco in the central nave. 1043–6.   38

State of preservation relatively good. The greatest damage to the surface of the paint is in the nimbus and in the background.

UNKNOWN SAINT. Fresco in the central nave. 1043–6. *17*

State of preservation relatively good. The greatest damage to the surface of the paint is in the nimbus, in the background, and in the hands. The flush on the cheeks has blackened. There is no evidence to support the traditional name of *The Healer Kir*.

Figs. 14 and 15. Virgin Martyrs. Frescoes, 1046–61/7.
Kiev, S. Sophia

233

Fig. 16. The Apostle Paul. Fresco, 1046–61/7. Kiev, S. Sophia.

Fig. 17. Unknown Saint. Fresco, 1043–6. Kiev, S. Sophia.

HEBREW YOUTH. Fresco in the central nave. 1043–6.   46

State of preservation satisfactory. The surface is badly damaged and much of the top layer of paint is missing, particularly in the background, nimbus, clothing and hands. Next to it are depicted two more Hebrew children.

UNKNOWN BISHOP. Fresco on the north-east pillar support-ing the dome. 1043–6.   21

State of preservation bad, except for the face. The pupils of the eyes are lost and the red in the cheeks has blackened. On forehead and above the head there is some mid nineteenth-century overpainting in oil, left intact by recent restorers. The figure of the bishop is below the mosaic of Aaron, from which it is separated by a slate cornice. This cornice is the dividing line between the mosaics and frescoes.

UNKNOWN SAINT. Fresco on the west pillar in the south transept. 1046–61/7.   37

State of preservation relatively good. On its lower part there is a later addition, where the fresco is completely lost. The saint is depicted in priestly robes, with a candle (?) in his left hand.

UNKNOWN SAINT. Fresco in the drum of the north dome of the gallery. 1043–6.   18

One of the best preserved frescoes, giving a good idea of the modelling of the face. In the vast majority of the frescoes this modelling is considerably flattened through the loss of the top layers of paint.

UNKNOWN SAINT. Fresco on the north-east pillar support-ing the dome. 1043–6.   19

State of preservation bad, except for the face. The red in the cheeks has blackened. In comparison with the other frescoes of the central cross, this head is distinctive for its completely different style of painting; it is bold and expressive.

THE CENTURION CORNELIUS, from 'The Apostle Peter with the Centurion Cornelius'. Detail of the fresco in the prothesis. 1046–61/7.   45

The state of preservation of all the frescoes in the apse of the prothesis is very bad. Here scenes from the life of Peter were presented. By chance, one head has survived from a com-position otherwise almost completely lost. D. V. Ainalov classified the composition as *The Apostle Peter with the Cen-turion Cornelius*, but such an interpretation still needs further confirmation. The colours in the face have preserved all their original freshness—bright-red outlines of nose and mouth, thick green shading, and red on the cheeks, which has grown darker only in one place. The bold style of painting is very similar to that of the head of the saint shown in *19*.

UNKNOWN VIRGIN MARTYR. Detail of fresco in the northern nave. 1046–61/7.   20

Fig. 18. Unknown Saint.
Fresco, 1043–6. Kiev, S. Sophia.

Fig. 19. Unknown Saint.
Fresco, 1043–6. Kiev, S. Sophia.

Fig. 20. Unknown Virgin Martyr.
Fresco, 1046–61/7. Kiev, S. Sophia.

Fig. 21. Unknown Bishop.
Fresco, 1043–6. Kiev, S. Sophia.

Fig. 22. Unknown Prophet.
Fresco, 1046–61/7. Kiev, S. Sophia.

Fig. 23. Unknown Bishop.
Fresco, 1046–61/7. Kiev, S. Sophia.

State of preservation satisfactory. Considerable loss of paint. At the lower left-hand corner there is a new addition. There is some thin restoration in oils.

THE PROPHET ELIJAH. Detail of fresco in the northern nave. 1046–61/7. 39

State of preservation relatively good. The greatest loss to the surface of the paint is in the background and in the nimbus. The red in the cheeks has blackened. During the overpainting in oils, this figure was turned into John the Baptist. In fact it is the prophet Elijah who is depicted here; in his left hand he holds an open scroll (cf. the portrait of the prophet Elijah in the Church of Daphni).

UNKNOWN PROPHET. Detail of fresco in the northern exterior nave. 1046–61/7. 22

State of preservation relatively good. The greatest loss to the paint surface is in the nimbus and in the background. The red in the cheeks has blackened. In his left hand the prophet holds an open scroll. Judging from his features, he is probably the prophet Isaiah (cf. the mosaic in the Church of Daphni).

UNKNOWN BISHOP. Detail of fresco in the northern exterior nave. 1046–61/7. 23

State of preservation relatively good. There is some damage and loss to the upper layer of paint. In the top right-hand corner the mid nineteenth-century oil-paint restoration has been left untouched.

SERAPH. Detail of fresco in the southern nave. 1046–61/7. 49

State of preservation relatively good. There is some thin touching up in oils.

Figs. 24 and 25. Archangels. Frescoes, 1043–61/7. Kiev, S. Sophia.

ARCHANGELS. Frescoes in the cupolas of the southern nave and in the southern part of the gallery. 1046–61/7.

44, *24, 25*

State of preservation good. There are only some slight losses in the top layer of paint. A fragment of mid nineteenth-century oil-paint restoration has been left untouched in one of the frescoes. It is noteworthy that the artists have succeeded in portraying different types of faces though still following the established style for depicting archangels. This they achieved by scarcely noticeable alterations to the oval of the

faces, the cut of the eyes, and the position of the pupils. The portraits of the archangels which, by chance, are better preserved than the rest of the frescoes, are proof of the high quality of the original paintings in the cathedral.

GROUP PORTRAIT OF YAROSLAV'S FAMILY. Fresco in the central nave. About 1045.   30, 36, *26, 27*

State of preservation bad. The top layer of paint is badly damaged and the faces have suffered from several restorations. In places where the picture has disappeared completely, it has been thinly touched up in oils. The numerous members of Yaroslav's family were seen converging from both sides on the portrait of Christ on the demolished west wall. From the left comes the Grand-princess with her five daughters, from the right the Grand-prince, holding a model of the church in his hands, and his five sons (see diagram, *26*). In this unique royal portrait, two of the sons and four of the daughters, on the north and south walls respectively, have fortunately, in part, survived. It is impossible to identify the persons depicted with any certainty. The daughters wear white kerchiefs on their heads, and their garments, cut from expensive foreign cloth (silk and velvet), are richly decorated. The older daughters hold candles in their left hands. The best preserved part is the face of the second figure from the left.

SCENES FROM THE HIPPODROME OF CONSTANTINOPLE. Frescoes in the south-west tower. 1113–25.   40, 41 *28*

Of all the paintings in the south-west tower that of the Palace of Kathisma is the best preserved; but even here, particularly on the right side, much of the top layer of paint is missing. There has been an insignificant amount of touching up in oils. The red of the cheeks has blackened with age. The fundamental researches of R. Guilland, devoted to the reconstruction of the Hippodrome of Constantinople, allow us to confirm a series of details in the paintings in the south-west tower. Guilland's article on the Palace of Kathisma is particularly important (R. Guilland, 'Le Palais du Kathisma.'

Fig. 26. Schema of the Frescoes on the West wall of the central nave. Kiev, S. Sophia.

Τὸ Παλάτιον τοῦ Καθίσματος, Études sur l'hippodrome de Byzance', *Byzantinoslavica*, 1957, XVIII, pp. 39–76). His conclusions amount, in short, to this: the Palace of Kathisma was built by Constantine the Great, and was still in use at the beginning of the thirteenth century. It was located on the eastern side of the hippodrome and its west façade, which was between 80 and 90 metres long, faced the arena. Boxes and galleries for the emperor and his courtiers ran along this west façade on the level of the first and second floors, while the ground floor was occupied by the state judicial archives. The imperial box consisted of two compartments. One was situated on the second-floor level. This was the emperor's private box (κλούσιον, παρακυπτικὸν κλούσιον), from which he supervised the preparations for the games. After eventually making his official appearance before the people, the emperor descended into the second compartment, a large suite on the first floor. Here were a rest room and dressing-room, two reception halls and a vestibule. Below the level of the ground floor were rows for the spectators. The eastern façade overlooked the court of Daphne and faced the Great Palace, which was reached by a special staircase (ὁ μυστικὸς κοχλίας). The Palace of Kathisma ended in a wide terrace (ἡλιακόν) decorated with statues, among them one of Diocletian. Specifying the position of the palace in relation to the arena, Guilland establishes that it was in fact from the Kathisma that the starting signal for the chariot race was given.

The conclusions of Guilland, though strangely omitting any mention of the Kiev frescoes, are nevertheless very important for correct interpretation of the latter. N. P. Kondakov had already recognized that the fresco showing a building with galleries and boxes for spectators was the Palace of Kathisma (N. Kondakov, 'O freskakh lestnits Kievo-Sofiyskogo sobora'—On the staircase frescoes of S. Sophia Cathedral in Kiev—*Zapiski Imp. Arkheologicheskogo Obshchestva*, 1888, III, pp. 298–300). But all his subsequent arguments about the Kathisma are incorrect and, since the appearance of Guilland's article, need radical revision.

The fresco shows plainly that the Palace of Kathisma has three floors; a large ground floor and two floors with a gallery on each one for spectators. It also has two boxes, one of which is on a lower level than the other. This is the principal box and it is here that the emperor sits, attended by two courtiers. In the upper box and in the lower gallery the spectators have taken their places. The ground floor, built of massive blocks, has round, barred windows and square windows with heavy shutters; bodyguards (?) look out of these windows. Beneath the royal box, a man is shown with his right arm raised and with a group of people before him. N. P. Kondakov (op. cit., p. 300) thought that here were represented the leaders of the factions with the silentiarius, who announced either the start of the games or the choice of teams by lots. The contours of two quadrigas have recently been discovered and have been preserved. The lower part of the wall was no doubt set aside for a representation of the arena and the competing chariots. It is quite possible that the artists who worked in the south-west tower drew upon the advice of the mother of Vladimir Monomakh, who was the daughter of Constantine X,

Fig. 27. Yaroslav's Daughters. Fresco, about 1045. Kiev, S. Sophia.

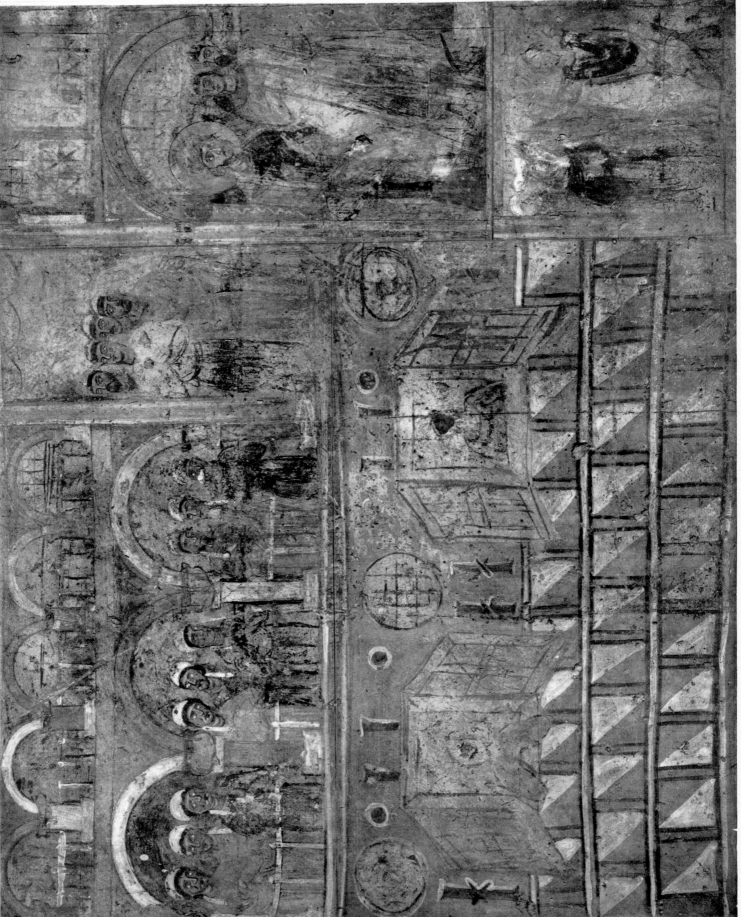

Fig. 28. The Palace of Kathisma with the Imperial Box and Galleries for the Spectators. Fresco, 1113–25. Kiev, S. Sophia.

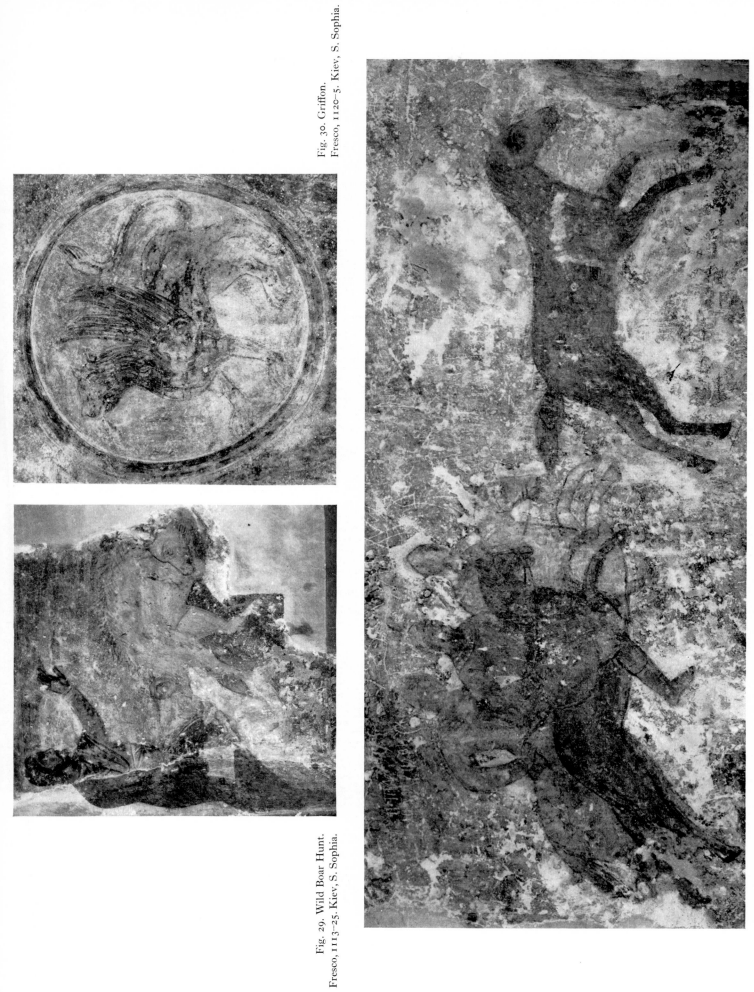

Fig. 30. Griffon.
Fresco, 1120–5. Kiev, S. Sophia.

Fig. 29. Wild Boar Hunt.
Fresco, 1113–25. Kiev, S. Sophia.

Fig. 31. Wild Horse Hunt. Fresco, 1113–25. Kiev, S. Sophia.

Fig. 32. Griffon. Fresco, 1113–25. Kiev, S. Sophia.

Emperor of Byzantium. She would have undoubtedly known what the Palace of Kathisma looked like both from outside and in. As for the artists, they had nothing in common with Constantinople; this is evident from their extremely primitive manner of painting, particularly in the treatment of the faces of the spectators. Apart from the fact that these faces do not possess Greek or Slav characteristics, they are painted with particular harshness and garishness. One cannot help feeling that here we have a group of eastern nomads rather than the higher ranks of the court of Byzantium. In any case it is in the paintings of the south-west tower that the barbaric strain makes itself most strongly felt.

GRIFFONS. Frescoes in the south-west tower. 1113–25.

50, 32

The Standing Griffon is one of the best preserved frescoes in the south-west tower. The top layer of paint, including the light white lines and dots, has suffered practically no damage at all. The type of griffon is close to similar designs on Byzantine silks, such as those found on silk material of the eighth century in the Museum of Fine Arts in Boston. The painting of the griffon crouching on its front paws has suffered greatly from time; the upper layers of paint are almost completely lost.

HUNTING SCENES. Frescoes in the south-west tower. 1113–25.

29, 31

In the scene of the wild-boar hunt the best preserved figures are that of the hunter, whose entire left side is lost, and that of the boar.

The scene showing a wild horse being hunted with a lasso has suffered from time to such an extent that it has been necessary to leave much of the oil-paint restoration intact.

One cannot regard the hunting scenes as compositional parts

of the hippodrome theme. They form an independent and parallel cycle; moreover, the various episodes are scattered across the walls and vaults of the tower in the most arbitrary fashion and are purely decorative. The bearded hunter following the boar has a Slavonic type of face.

WARRIOR FIGHTING A MASKED MAN. Fresco in the north-west tower. About 1120–5.

43

Nearly all the upper layers of paint are lost. Thin oil-paint restoration has been preserved in places. Traces can be seen of a double circular groove in the plaster, surrounding the figures.

N. P. Kondakov and A. N. Veselovsky consider that this is a representation of one of the episodes from the so-called 'Games of the Goths' (N. P. Kondakov, *O freskakh lestnits Kievo-Sofiyskogo sobora*, pp. 293–4 and A. N. Veselovsky, 'Razyskaniya v oblasti russkogo dukhovnogo stikha. XIV, Genvarskii rusalii i gotskiye igry v Vizantii'—Researches into the field of the Russian religious poem. XIV. The January rusalii and the games of Goths in Byzantium—in *Sbornik otdeleniya russkogo yazyka i slovesnosti Imp. Akademii Nauk*, 1889 (XLVI), No. 6, pp. 282–3.) These Games took place at the time of the royal feast, on the 3rd of January, and were described in detail by Constantine Porphyrogenitus (*De cerim. aulae Byzantinae*, ed. Bonn, vol. I, 1. I, 83). Constantine Porphyrogenitus speaks of four people, disguised as Goths, who appear in animal skins or in furs turned inside out. In the fresco only the single combat of the warrior and the masked man is depicted, and there is no indication of the fur coat. This scene may therefore be considered to represent one of the entertainments of the prince of Kiev.

MOUNTED WARRIOR FIGHTING A BEAR. Fresco in the north-west tower. 1120–5.

9, 42

The upper layers of paint are almost entirely lost. This scene, belonging to the hunt cycle, without a doubt reflects Kievan life and cannot have any relation to the hippodrome theme, as do many other hunting scenes in the south-west and north-west towers.

EMPEROR WITH TWO BODYGUARDS. Fresco in the north-west tower. About 1120–5.

33

Very bad state of preservation. Almost all the upper layers of paint have worn away. Among the frescoes in the north-west tower are scenes from the court life of Byzantium. Various fragments of the frescoes have survived, showing the figures of the emperor and empress with their train against a background of rather complicated architectural settings, and also showing the figure of the emperor on horseback. N. P. Kondakov is probably incorrect in suggesting that these episodes are connected with the life of the private hippodrome of the palace (op. cit., pp. 295–8.).

CAMEL WITH DRIVER, MUSICIAN, GRIFFON. Frescoes in the north-west tower. About 1120–5.

47, 48, 30

The worst preserved of these is the griffon, where much of the upper layer of paint is missing. The other two frescoes are in a relatively good state of preservation. All three are derived from eastern sources. The face of the musician playing a stringed instrument, which appears in one of the medallions of the vault, is distinctly oriental in type.

Fig. 33. Emperor with two Bodyguards. Fresco, 1120–5. Kiev, S. Sophia.

Figs. 34 and 35. SS. Domnus and Philippol. Frescoes, first half of the twelfth century. Kiev, S. Sophia.

241

Fig. 36. Unknown Martyr.
Fresco, first half of the twelfth century.
Kiev, S. Sophia.

Fig. 37. S. Adrian.
Fresco, twelfth century.
Kiev, S. Sophia.

Fig. 38. S. Nataliya.
Fresco, twelfth century.
Kiev, S. Sophia.

SS. DOMNUS AND PHILIPPOL. Frescoes in the west arch of the south outer gallery. First half of the twelfth century.

34, 35

State of preservation relatively good. There is some physical damage to the paint surface and there are some patches where the paint has rubbed off.

Both frescoes were discovered by Prakhov in 1881. In 1889, according to the newspapers, it was still possible to read the inscription Philippol, but by 1897 this inscription had completely disappeared. A. N. Grabar (A. Grabar, 'Freski Apostol'skogo pridela Kievo-Sofiyskogo sobora'—Frescoes of the Apostles' chapel of the Kievan S. Sophia Cathedral—in *Zapiski otdeleniya russkoy i slavyanskoy arkheologii Russkogo Arkheologicheskogo Obshchestva*, 1918, XII, pp. 98–106), who was the first to publish both frescoes, mentions one of the inscriptions (ΔOMNOC), but this inscription has since then become illegible. The late N. V. Malitsky (*Seminarium Kondakovianum*, 1928, II p. 94) doubted whether it was possible to identify the characters depicted here correctly, but he regarded them as presbyters rather than martyrs. The priestly robes do not exclude the possibility that these are in fact portraits of SS. Domnus and Philippol of Thessalonica. If one compares them to the paintings produced between 1040 and 1050 one is struck by the much flatter treatment of the face, and by a more abstract rhythm of line.

UNKNOWN MARTYR. Fresco on the flying buttress of the western outer gallery. First half of the twelfth century.

36

State of preservation relatively good. The coat of paint is entirely lost on the right hand and on the clothing next to it. The traces of grooves in the plaster, encircling the borders of the medallion, can clearly be seen. Stylistically this half-length figure is very close to the portraits of SS. Domnus and Philippol.

SS. ADRIAN AND NATALIYA. Frescoes on an arch of the north outer gallery. Twelfth century.   *37, 38*

State of preservation relatively good. There are losses to the top coat of paint. Contemporary inscriptions in Slavonic, painted beside each figure and giving their names, have survived. Not only the inscriptions, but also the style of painting, indicate the work of a local master. (See V. Myasoyedov, 'Freski severnogo pritvora Sofiyskogo sobora v Kieve'—Frescoes of the north chapel of the Sophia Cathedral in Kiev—in *Zapiski otdeleniya russkoy i slavyanskoy arkheologii Russkogo Arkheologicheskogo Obshchestva*, 1918 [XII], pp. 1–7). Myasoyedov incorrectly attributes the frescoes to the middle of the eleventh century.

BAPTISM. Fresco in the conch of the baptistry. Second half of the twelfth century.   *39*

State of preservation satisfactory. Much loss of and physical damage to the paint surface. The baptistry was built no earlier than the second quarter of the twelfth century. In spite of the remains of a Greek inscription, the fresco reveals the hand of a local artist. The thick features of the faces, outlined with heavy strokes, find a parallel in the paintings of Nereditsa. Above the conch of the apse is the half-length figure of Basil the Great and in the apse itself, under the *Baptism*, are the figures of bishops, which have almost disappeared. The pillars flanking the apse still carry portraits of two martyrs, though they are scarcely recognizable. N. L. Okunev thought, not without good cause, that they represented SS. Boris and Gleb. All the other paintings in the baptistry, including the figures of bishops and the large composition *The Forty Martyrs of Sebaste*, are of an earlier period, and probably date from the beginning of the twelfth century.

See N. Okunev, 'Kreshchal'nya Sofiyskogo sobora v Kieve'—Baptistry of the Sophia Cathedral in Kiev—in *Zapiski otdeleniya russkoy i slavyanskoy arkheologii Imp. Russkogo Arkheologicheskogo Obshchestva*, 1915 (X), pp. 113–37.

Cathedral of the Transfiguration (Spas-Preobrazheniye), Chernigov

S. THECLA. Fragment of a fresco. About 1040. *40*

State of preservation mediocre. There is much damage and some loss to the paint surface.

The face of S. Thecla with its noble, classically proportioned lines, is stylistically close to the portrait of S. Paraskeva in one of the miniatures of the Paris Codex of Gregory of Nazianzus (gr. 510, fol. 285). The greenish shadows are arranged with delicate artistic forethought, showing a high degree of skill on the part of the painter.

Church of the Archangel Michael, Kiev

COMMUNION OF THE APOSTLES. Mosaic. About 1108.

51-54, 57

State of preservation good. The central portion, which represented the right side of the Royal Doors and the ciborium rising behind the altar, is missing. There are also two blank patches at the feet of Peter and Paul. The horizontal and vertical lines seen on the gold background are traces of sawmarks in the mosaic, made when it was taken from the wall of the church before the latter was pulled down in 1935. Before the mosaic was removed it had two vertical seams passing between the figures of Christ and the apostles Peter and Paul and also a long horizontal seam at the level of the calves of all twelve apostles; even now these lines are clearly visible. They indicate the junction of consecutive sections of the work, though these sections are not necessarily the work of one day. It is very striking that below the long horizontal seam the lower parts of all the garments of the apostles and their feet are done in a clumsy way; the design is loose and lacks rhythm, and the folds are stylized and flattened. Probably the artist in charge ordered one of his assistants to lay the lower part of the mosaic.

The figures of Christ and especially that of the angel to the right, whose delicate and inspired face was long hidden under subsequent oil painting, are certainly the finest of the figures. Those on the extreme right are much weaker in design and look rather flat. They were probably done by the least skilled mosaicist.

HEAD OF ARCHDEACON STEPHEN. Detail of mosaic. About 1108. 55

The head is well preserved. Certain areas in the lower part of the figures and in the golden background are lost. Stephen is shown in diaconal dress. In his right hand he holds a censer, in his left a martyr's crown, and on both sides of his head are Greek inscriptions indicating his name. This mosaic was placed on the inner side of the chancel arch. This detail of the head gives a good idea of the style used for laying the mosaic, where large tesserae predominate.

S. DEMETRIUS OF THESSALONICA. Mosaic. About 1108.

56, Colour plate

The mosaic is in a good state of preservation. Certain parts are missing in the lower half of the figure and in the ground. On either side of the head is a Greek inscription giving the name of the saint. This mosaic decorated the inner side of the chancel arch, and after being taken from the wall, it was transferred to the Tretyakov Gallery. From the point of view of colours the mosaic of S. Demetrius is one of the most sophisticated.

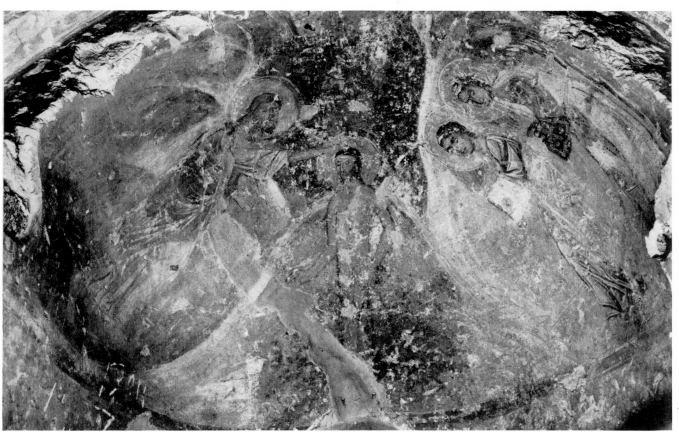

Fig. 39. Baptism. Fresco, second half of twelfth century. Kiev, S. Sophia.

Fig. 40. S. Thecla. Fresco, about 1040.
Chernigov, Cathedral of the Transfiguration.

Fig. 41. Stylite. Fresco, about 1108.
Kiev, Church of the Archangel Michael.

STYLITE. Fresco. About 1108.   *41*

Bad state of preservation. Much of the fresco is lost and the colours are faded.

In the Church of the Archangel Michael, as in S. Sophia in Kiev, mosaic was combined with fresco. Fragments preserved after the church was demolished are kept in one of the upper chapels of S. Sophia. The manner of painting suggests that the fresco was painted by local artists.

Cathedral of the Dormition, Vladimir

FIGURE OF PROPHET AND ORNAMENTS.
Wall painting on the north wall. About 1161.   *59*

Bad state of preservation. The layers of paint have suffered severe loss. The lower part of the figure of the prophet facing to the right has been completed with oil-paint.

SS. ARTEMIUS AND AVRAAMY. Frescoes. About 1189.

58, 42

Bad state of preservation. Very great loss to the top layer of paint, and much damage to the surface. Portraits of the saints Artemius and Avraamy are very rare in early wall paintings. S. Artemius was Commander-in-Chief of the Egyptian army and witnessed the legendary appearance of the cross in the sky to Constantine the Great. After this he left the army and became a Christian. He was executed by the Emperor Julian

in 363 for his vigorous fight against paganism. The cult of Artemius was practised in Constantinople as early as the fifth century, and a church in his honour was built in Constantinople by Emperor Anastasius (491–518). As for the second portrait, it is not clear which Avraamy is represented here. It could be either Avraamy of Rostov, whose relics were discovered at the time of Vsevolod, or Avraamy of Edessa (fourth century), whose cult was established in Constantinople. Should it be the second, we have further proof of Vsevolod's leanings towards Constantinople.

Cathedral of S. Demetrius, Vladimir

THE LAST JUDGEMENT. Details of frescoes in the large and small vaults of the Cathedral. About 1195.

60–68, 70

The state of preservation is, on the whole, good. Less well preserved are the figures of angels in the left part of the south side of the big vault and the representation of *Paradise* on the south side of the small vault. The original colouring was far brighter. Just how bright the colours must have been may be assessed by examining the fragments of frescoes in the window opening of the drum, discovered in 1952, which show remnants of the ornamentation and of the figure of a bird. See N. Sychyov, 'K istorii rospisi Dmitriyevskogo sobora vo Vladimire'—On the history of decoration of the

Dmitriyevsky Cathedral of Vladimir—in *Pamyatniki Kul'tury*, I, Moscow, 1959, pp. 145–8, figs. 2–4.

N. P. Sychyov (ibid., p. 154, fig. 6), who has closely studied the painting in the large vault, discovered clear traces of lines, scratched on the wet ground, which served the painter as points of reference for the construction of his composition. One horizontal line passes beneath the feet of the apostles, another above the thrones. The latter is divided into twelve equal parts, in order to determine the position of the backs of the thrones and of the poles between them. The haloes of the six apostles were also traced in the same way. Only after this did the artist start to paint figures, using no more incised lines: this gave him greater freedom in his brush-work.

N. P. Sychyov (ibid., pp. 156–61) does not agree with me about the authorship of the painting in the large vault. In his opinion three masters worked on it: the first painted the figures of the apostles Thomas, Philip, John, Bartholomew, Paul, Peter and Luke; the second, the figures of Simon and Matthew; the third, the figures of Andrew, James and Mark, and also the figures of Isaac, Jacob, Peter and Mary of Egypt in the small vault. These attributions curiously ignore the figures of the angels, though it is precisely they who show the stylistic differences most clearly. Sychyov's argument finds no support either in the methods used by medieval fresco-painters, who were not in the habit of dividing the prepared surface into such small sections. For this reason I hold to my opinion that all the figures of the apostles were painted by one (i.e., the principal) master.

Nor is Sychyov's proposition (ibid., pp. 170–7) that the frescoes of the Cathedral of S. Demetrius were made by masters from Thessalonica any more tenable. There is no stylistic similarity between the frescoes in the Cathedral of S. Demetrius and the wall paintings of Thessalonica or those of Macedonia. But the frescoes here have a lot in common with the works of the masters of Constantinople, such as the mosaics in the Church of the Archangel Michael in Kiev, the mosaics of Cefalù, the portable mosaic of S. Demetrius in Xenophontos at Athos, etc. For a similar treatment of the folds of the dresses of the apostles, see the mosaic of the end of the twelfth century at Grottaferrata (*Descent of the Holy Ghost*).

Cathedral of the Birth of the Virgin, Suzdal'

UNKNOWN SAINT. Detail of the fresco in the diaconicon. 1233. 69

The state of preservation is good. On the dress one can see traces of lines cut into the damp plaster, which marked the portion of the folds. This procedure was not often used in ancient Russian frescoes where the delineation of folds was usually indicated by means of brush-work.

Cathedral of S. Sophia, Novgorod

HEAD OF S. HELENA. Detail of painting in the south gallery. Second half of the eleventh century. 71

Good state of preservation with some damage to the colour surface. The figures of Constantine and Helena are painted on the pinkish-white ground, applied in a very thin layer to the uneven surface of the pilaster. This technique partially explains the light character of the painting, which resembles watercolour.

Although V. Suslov gave the date of the figures of Constantine and Helena quite rightly as the eleventh century (*Arkheologicheskiye Izvestiya i Zametki*, 1898 [VI], N 5–6,

Fig. 42. S. Avraamy. Fresco, about 1189. Vladimir, Cathedral of the Dormition.

p. 194), V. K. Myasoyedov definitely dated it 1144 ('Fragmenty freskovoy rospisi svyatoy Sofii Novgorodskoy'—Fragments of the fresco decoration of the S. Sophia at Novgorod—*Zapiski otdeleniya russkoy i slavyanskoy arkheologii Russkogo Arkheologicheskogo Obshchestva*, 1915 [X], pp. 15–34).

This fragment is also mentioned in my book *Iskusstvo Novgoroda* (Moscow–Leningrad, 1947, p. 26, plate 3 b), where it is also attributed to this wrong date. As a result of the research done by Yu. N. Dmitriyev (*Zametki po tekhnike russkikh stennykh rospisey X–XII vekov*, pp. 271–6) it can be considered conclusively proved that the fragment dates from the eleventh century.

M. K. Karger (*Novgorod Velikiy*, Moscow, 1946, pp. 22–3) states that when the painting was cleaned in the 1890's, the inscription Olena in Old Slavonic script was discovered above the head of Helena. This inscription disappeared later, but the fact that it once existed, further suggests, taking into account its linguistic peculiarities, that the fragment was painted by a local artist; and this conjecture is also supported by the unique manner of painting.

PROPHETS DANIEL AND SOLOMON. Frescoes in the drum of the dome. 1108.   72, 73

The dome was hit by two shells during the Second World War and the fresco was almost completely destroyed. The destroyed part depicted the Pantocrator. The figures of four archangels in the dome and of eight prophets in the drum were also damaged by shrapnel. The figure of the prophet Daniel was completely ruined. The surviving seven prophets were

Fig. 43. Unknown Saint. Fresco, 1125. Antoniyev Monastery, Cathedral of the Birth of the Virgin.

restored in the years 1944–5 and 1963–4. The photographs of the paintings reproduced in No. 72, 73 were made after the last restoration, when the faces were carefully washed and repaired.

Nikolo-Dvorishchensky Cathedral, Novgorod

HEAD OF THE WIFE OF JOB FROM 'JOB ON THE DUNGHILL'.

Detail of fresco in the lower part of the Nikolo-Dvorishchensky cathedral in Novgorod. Shortly after 1113.   74

The state of preservation is good apart from the bullet-holes made by the Nazis, during their retreat from Novgorod. Job's wife stands in front of her husband, who sits on the ground. He holds a stick from which a pot of food is suspended. The confident manner of painting reveals the hand of an experienced artist.

Cathedral of the Birth of the Virgin in the Antoniyev Monastery, Novgorod

UNKNOWN SAINTS AND YOUTH FROM 'THE DISCOVERY OF THE HEAD OF JOHN THE BAPTIST'. Details of frescoes in the chancel of the cathedral. 1125.   75, 76, *43, 44*

The state of preservation is good apart from the chipped surface of the frescoes. The cleaned frescoes are single, unconnected fragments, and this makes it difficult to reconstruct the system of painting in the cathedral.

Fig. 44. Unknown Saint. Fresco, 1125. Antoniyev Monastery, Cathedral of the Birth of the Virgin.

As the old inscriptions have been lost, it is not possible to determine the names of the saints, particularly as there are also many monks and anchorites. Very characteristic are the squat proportions of the heads, outlined by what are practically perfect circles. The faces of the bearded saints closely resemble those in the frescoes at Santa Croce in Jerusalemme in Rome (1144) and the faces of the young saints are very similar to those in Cod. 9428 in the Bibliothèque Royale at Brussels (School of Reichenau, eleventh century), in the Liber Florum by Theophrid of Echternach (end of the eleventh century) and in Cod. clm. 14159 in the Staatsbibliothek in Munich (about 1170–85).

Further discoveries are possible in the cathedral of the Antoniyev Monastery because by no means all of the wall surface has been carefully examined.

Fig. 45. Christ before Annas and Caiaphas.
Fresco, middle of twelfth century. Mirozhsky Monastery,
Cathedral of the Transfiguration.

Cathedral of the Transfiguration (Spaso-Preobrazhensky Cathedral), Mirozhsky Monastery, Pskov

FRESCOES. Middle of the twelfth century, but before 1156.
8, 77–83, 45, 46

The cleaning of the frescoes in the Spaso-Preobrazhensky Cathedral was begun in 1926, but later this work was stopped, so it is possible that further important discoveries will one day be made there. The majority of the cleaned paintings are in a reasonably good state of preservation, but several figures and heads show traces of repairs done in the sixteenth century, when the frescoes were restored for the first time. Traces of such repairs are visible in the scene of the *Dormition* [46], *Christ before Annas and Caiaphas* [45] (the whole of the left group of figures, including Christ), and others. In *The Miraculous Draught of Fishes* [79] the left part of the composition is new.

Unfortunately during the eighteenth century or at the beginning of the nineteenth all the frescoes were partially

Fig. 46. The Dormition. Fresco, middle of the twelfth century. Mirozhsky Monastery, Cathedral of the Transfiguration.

247

Fig. 47. Mother of God, Apostles, Angels from 'The Last Judgement'. Fresco, about 1167. Staraya Ladoga, S. George.

Fig. 48. S. John, Apostles and Angels from 'The Last Judgement'. Fresco, about 1167. Staraya Ladoga, S. George.

Fig. 49. Christ and S. John. Fresco, about 1189. Arkhazi, Church of the Annunciation.

Fig. 50. Presentation of the Head of S. John to Herod. Fresco, about 1189. Arkhazi, Church of the Annunciation.

covered with plaster and whitewashed. After the whitewash had been removed in 1889, they were carelessly over-painted in 1897 by icon painters from Suzdal, who were specially recruited for this task. All this has naturally had a bad effect on the state of preservation of the frescoes. Moreover, many of the frescoes have suffered from crystal-lization of salts, especially in the lower parts.

The late N. V. Malitsky and M. I. Artamonov attributed the paintings of Mirozh to the beginning of the thirteenth century ('Odin iz stiley monumental'noy zhivopisi XII–XIII vekov'—One of the styles of monumental painting in the twelfth to thirteenth centuries—in the book *Sbornik I aspirantov Akademii Istorii Material'noy kul'tury*, Leningrad, 1929, pp. 52–4, 57–8). But both the history of the building of the cathedral and the style of the paintings are evidence against such a late date. Of great importance in establishing the date the cathedral was built are the inscriptions on a cup which Niphont gave to the cathedral in the year of his death. In the bottom of the cup there is the inscription 'In the year 6664 (1156) on April 8th to the Spaso-Mirozhsky Monastery', and a silver band round the rim of the cup has another inscription and the date 1701. This inscription tells us that Niphont, together with Vsevolod, the orthodox prince of Pskov, founded several monasteries and churches when he was bishop, and, after Prince Vsevolod's death, came to Pskov and built the Church of the Transfiguration of the Lord between the Velikaya and Merezha rivers. As Vsevolod died in the year 1137–8, the cathedral must have been built sometime between 1138 and 1156. N. Serebryansky reached the same conclusions on the strength of his research into different sixteenth-century manuscripts of the life of Niphont, where it is stated that the Mirozhsky Monastery was founded before 1153, and possibly even before 1148, and that by 1156 everything was complete including the paintings (*Ocherki po istorii monasheskoy zhizni v Pskovskoy zemle*—Studies on the history of monastic life in the Pskov lands, Moscow, 1908, pp. 215–16). In several sixteenth-century manuscripts Niphont is referred to as the builder of the Mirozhsky Monastery. For a commentary on the inscriptions on the cup see: I. Vasil'yev, *Khronologichesky Ukazatel' pskovskikh pamyatnikov, sokhranivshikhsya v pskovskoy gubernii* (The chronological list of the monuments preserved in the Pskov Guberniya), tetrad' 1, Pskov, 1878, pp. 3–4; N. Pokrovsky, 'Zametki o pamyatnikakh pskovskoy tserkov-noy stariny' (Notes on the ancient ecclesiastical monuments of Pskov), *Svetil'nik*, 1914, no. 5–6, pp. 39–40.

This dating of the frescoes is confirmed by their style of paint-ing. They are very similar to those in the Church of S. Pantaleon in Nerezi (1164), but they are not of the same quality.

Church of S. George, Staraya Ladoga

FRESCOES. About 1167.   10, 84–91, *47, 48, 51, 52*

On the whole the state of preservation is good. The white efflorescence seen on many of the fragments is caused by the crystallization of the salts of sodium sulphate and calcium sulphate, a process known as yamchuga. This condition exists because when the building was restored in 1904, the outer walls and parts of the inner walls were plastered with cement. To save the surviving fragmentary frescoes from yamchuga they should be removed from the walls without delay. Because the paintings have been covered for such a long time by the layer of new plaster and whitewash, the colours have faded and lost their original freshness.

Fig. 51. Anna, from 'The Refusal of Joachim's Offering'. Fresco, about 1167. Staraya Ladoga, S. George.

The architectural restoration of the Church of S. George was carried out in 1926–7 and again in 1951. Later additions were pulled down, the roofs of the vaults were restored, old windows were unblocked and windows added at a later date were blocked in, and as a result the church now looks as it did originally. The frescoes were restored in 1927 and 1933, when the plaster was strengthened and the yamchuga, mould, dirt and dust was removed. Most of the inscriptions, which were still to be seen by research workers in the nineteenth century, have since disappeared.

The identification of the figure of the warrior as the martyr Prince Gleb, though hypothetical, is probably correct. See V. Lazarev, *Freski Staroy Ladogi*—Frescoes of Staraya Ladoga, Moscow, 1960, pp. 40–2.

Most of the fragments of the surviving frescoes reveal the hand of the chief master. To his assistant can be ascribed the group of pious women, sinners and angels from the *Last Judgement*, the medallion showing S. Agaton, the medallions in the apse, and the four angels in the northern and western parts of the dome, an area which was frequently entrusted to an assistant as the dome was very far from the spectator.

The degree of linear stylization in the highlights of the faces approaches that of frescoes such as are found in Mirozh (about 1156), Nerezi (1164) and Ras (about 1168). The earliest fragment of fresco in this style is the head of the apostle in the Church of San Pietro *alli marmi* at Eboli (1156). See V. Lazarev, *Freski Staroy Ladogi*—Frescoes of Staraya Ladoga, pp. 88–90.

Fig. 52. S. Gleb. Fresco, about 1167. Staraya Ladoga, S. George.

Church of the Annunciation, near Arkazhi

FRESCOES. About 1189.   92, 93, *49, 50, 53*

The state of preservation of the frescoes is mediocre. There is much damage to the paint surface, and in most cases the colours have blurred and lost their original freshness. Best preserved are two scenes from the cycle of the Virgin (*Betrothal of the Virgin* and *Joseph leading Mary into his House*) and the portraits of saints in the arches between the central and side apses [92]. The restoration and cleaning of the frescoes took place in the years 1930, 1936, 1944 and 1946–8.

The cycle of scenes from the life of John the Baptist in the diaconicon includes the following episodes: *The Beheading, Presentation of the Head to Herodias* [50], *The Feast of Herod* and *Dance of Salome, The Entombment of S. John, The Story of the Baptist's Relics,* and *The Appearance of Christ to S. John.* Above was represented the figure of Elizabeth (?), of which only the lower part has survived. When the Church of the Annunciation was used as a barracks by the Nazis, they drove beams into the walls of the diaconicon to support a wooden canopy. As a result the *Head of a Youth carrying a basket* [93, *53*] has disappeared. During the German occupation all

the frescoes cleaned before the war were made so dirty by smoke that it was necessary to clean them again.

From the cycle of the Holy Virgin, which decorates the prothesis, the following scenes have been preserved: *Caressing of the Virgin Mary, The Blessing of Mary, The Suitors kneeling before the altar on which their wands are deposited, Betrothal of the Virgin, Joseph leading Mary into his House, The Visitation, The Annunciation at the Well, Joseph's anxiety.* Above the window stands the Virgin in the *Orans* attitude. On the western wall above the saints, is a large painting *The Seven sleeping youths of Ephesus* the upper part of which is missing. This subject was very popular in Rus' and is often found on amulets. The frescoes of Arkazhi occupy, both chronologically and stylistically, an intermediate place between the wall paintings in the Church of S. George at Staraya Ladoga (about 1167) and those in the Church of Spas-on-Nereditsa (1199). The assertion of O. Demus (*The Mosaics of Norman Sicily*, London, 1950, p. 425) that Greek artists took part in the painting of these frescoes is completely without foundation.

Fig. 53. Youth from 'The Story of the Baptist's Relics'. Fresco, about 1189. Arkhazi, Church of the Annunciation.

Cathedral of S. Sophia, Novgorod

THE APOSTLE PETER FROM THE DEESIS. Detail of painting in the Martiriyevskaya Parvis. Late twelfth century.   *54*

The state of preservation is good, though there is some damage to the surface.

The face of S. Peter, painted in a bold style, shows a distinct stylistic similarity to the frescoes of the late twelfth century, e.g., Arkazhi, Nereditsa.

Church of the Saviour, Nereditsa (Spas-on-Nereditsa) near Novgorod

FRESCOES. 1199.   13, 94–108, *55–61*

The Church of Spas was demolished by Nazi artillery in the early days of the German invasion of Novgorod. When the building collapsed nearly all the frescoes were destroyed. Only fragments in the eastern part survived (in the central apse the lower parts of six figures from the upper row on the southern side; parts of three figures from the lower row on the northern side and all the figures on the southern side; above the entrance to the diaconicon—the image of S. Ignatius in a medallion; to the right of the entrance into the diaconicon—the lower part of the figure of the Archdeacon Aviva and the figure of S. Eudocia; in the arcosolium on the southern side of the central apse—the head of the prophet Elijah; in the arcosolium on the northern side of the apse—a fairly well-preserved half-length figure of Peter of Alexandria; in the prothesis—a portrait of S. James Minor; in the diaconicon—badly damaged figures of female saints (relatively well preserved, however, is that of Fevroniya on the northern side), in the arch between the prothesis and the diaconicon—portraits of S. Catherine and S. Nicolas). On the southern wall, where there was once a *Baptism*, there remain only a few unimportant fragments: a group of people undressing and part of a landscape with trees in the lower right corner; the hand of one of the angels on the left; and part of the figure of the last angel on the right. There also remain some fragments from the *Last Judgement* on the western and northern walls (an angel, rolling back the scroll of heaven, the fornicatrix, the serpent of Satan, some figures of the Elect and small fragments from scenes of the torments of the Damned). In the arcosolium of the northern wall the figure of S. Thecla has survived. Of the exceptionally interesting portrait fresco only the lower part of the figure of Christ remains, as well as an unimportant fragment of the figure of the prince, and the last word of the inscription (Amen). All the fragments are battered and scratched, and the paint surface is badly rubbed away. The Church of Spas has now been rebuilt and the fragments of frescoes which did survive are preserved there.

The wall-paintings of Nereditsa were in an excellent state of preservation until they were destroyed and only in a few places were they damaged by yamchuga (e.g., 106). All the photographs published here were taken before the Second World War.

The arrangement of gospel scenes on the vaults and walls of Nereditsa was so arbitrary that it would be futile to attempt to work out their chronological sequence. The *Nativity* decorated the western wall, above the *Last Judgement*, early evangelical episodes, such as the *Presentation of the Virgin*, *Presentation in the Temple* and the *Baptism*, were placed in the lower register, and the later events (*Transfiguration*, *Entry into Jerusalem*, *The Bearing of the Cross*, *The Agony in the Garden*, *Crucifixion*, *Descent from the Cross*, *The Appearance*

Fig. 54. The Apostle Peter from the 'Deesis'. Fresco, Late twelfth century. Novgorod, S. Sophia, Martiriyevskaya Parvis.

of Christ to the Holy Women) in the upper register. There was no strict order in the sections of the upper register, and even less in the paintings on the vaults. Here the *Raising of Lazarus* was next to the *Last Supper;* the *Appearance of Christ to Cleopas* and *Christ finding the Apostles sleeping in the Garden of Gethsemane* was the next to *The Kiss of Judas* and the *Smiting off of Malchus' Ear;* and *Descent into Hell* was next to scenes of the Passion of Christ. We are forced to the conclusion that the painters who worked at Nereditsa were in a great hurry to complete the task. For this reason they intentionally avoided making an elaborate plan which would have taken a long time. They merely decided how many evangelical scenes to paint and where to paint them, without giving any special thought to the development of the Gospel story in its proper historical sequence. They were not concerned that the visitor to the church should be able to 'read' the Gospel story by following the walls in one direction as in the Cathedral of S. Sophia at Kiev.

From eight to ten artists worked at Nereditsa, a fact established by V. K. Myasoyedov (*Freski Spasa-Nereditsy*—Frescoes of Spas-on-Nereditsa, Leningrad, 1925, p. 16) and M. I. Artamonov ('Mastera Nereditsy'—Masters of Nereditsa —*Novgorodsky Istoricheskiy Sbornik*, fascicle 5, Novgorod, 1939, pp. 33–47). One of the masters painted the southern part of the composition in the dome, the figures of the prophets Aaron [*61*], Elijah and Jonah in the drum, the Holy Face above the western arch, S. Mark the Evangelist, the archangel Raphael in the southern lunette, probably also the southern part of the Communion of Apostles in the apse, the bishops on the same side [94, 95, 99], *Elijah fed by Ravens by the brook* [97], *The Crucifixion* [103] and *Descent from the Cross* on the northern wall. His manner of painting is very free and bold, and he makes use of bright highlights changing into deep shadows. According to V. K. Myasoyedov (and I am in agreement with him) this manner of painting is very similar to the technique used for the late encaustic icons. The second master painted the great composition of the *Last Judgement*, done in five stages (in that part of it which is placed on the western wall and also the *Baptism* [102] *Nativity*, *Presentation of the Virgin* [101], *Presentation in the Temple* [101] and many of the single figures. He paints easily,

Fig. 55. Christ the Priest, from the 'Deesis'.
Fresco, 1199. Nereditsa, Church of the Saviour.

Fig. 56. Holy Face
Fresco, 1199. Nereditsa, Church of the Saviour.

Fig. 57. Prince Yaroslav Vsevolodovich offering a model of the Church to Christ. Fresco, about 1246. Nereditsa, Church of the Saviour.

Fig. 58. S. Phocas. Fresco, 1199.
Nereditsa, Church of the Saviour.

Fig. 59. S. Luke. Fresco, 1199.
Nereditsa, Church of the Saviour.

Fig. 60. SS. Dometian, Amphilocius and Blaise. Fresco, 1199. Nereditsa, Church of the Saviour.

Fig. 61. Aaron. Fresco, 1199. Nereditsa, Church of the Saviour.

yet his faces, with their strong aquiline noses and large, slightly protruding eyes are rather stereotyped. He applies his colours thinly and likes to use deep rich tones. His bold skilful style was apparently much to the taste of Novgorod. The third master was responsible for the figure of Peter of Alexandria, the evangelist John [106], Luke, the apostles Paul, John, James and Simon, Christ the Priest [55], John the Baptist from the *Deesis*, and the first row of bishops on the north side of the apse as far as the window and the second row, ending with the figure of John Chrysostom. He works in a more graphic, one might even say more ornamental, manner. He paints the highlights with thin whitish streaks, which form a netlike pattern on the cheekbones, the cheeks, and the forehead. His figures have rather elegant proportions and relatively small heads; he pays great attention to hands, which are always very carefully drawn. Of the artists who worked at Nereditsa, he is most like those who worked on the church of S. George at Staraya Ladoga and on the Church of the Annunciation near Arkazhi. In addition to these three basic styles of painting in Nereditsa several others can be found, but they are less clearly defined.

Cathedral of the Birth of the Virgin at the Monastery of Snetogorsk

FRESCOES. 1313.   109–114, *62*

The state of preservation is mediocre, and there is much damage to the colour surface. The original colours have faded and lost their freshness because after 1581 the paintings were whitewashed, and in places plastered over. Originally the range of colours consisted of the three basic colours of the spectrum—blue for the background, orange-red for faces and frames, and yellow for haloes and clothes. This bright, contrasting mixture of colours was completed by white for the dresses and highlights on the faces, olive-grey for the light areas and violet. In their present state the frescoes look more monochrome than they did when they were first painted.

Fragments of the original frescoes were discovered as far back as 1910, and in 1928–9 the task of systematically cleaning them was begun. This work was resumed in 1948 and is still not finished, so that new discoveries may yet be made.

The frescoes which have been cleaned were the work of three masters, the most gifted of whom was the one who painted the *Descent of the Holy Ghost* [109], *Jesus among the Doctors* [*62*], the figures of saints on the east wall of the north transept, *Descent from the Cross*, and the archangel Gabriel from the scene of the *Annunciation*. The faces of his compositions are particularly expressive. He makes use of bright highlights, which give the figures a decisive and strong-willed expression [111, 112]. Of all the painters who worked here, he comes closest to the masters of the fourteenth century. The author of the *Dormition*, who is still strongly influenced by the artistic traditions of the twelfth century is more conventional. His manner of painting is bolder and more static, he exaggerates features and avoids sharp transitions between light and shadow. Even more archaic is the creator of the *Last Judgement*. His images are full of simple-mindedness and naïve spontaneity. His manner of painting is broad and free but more restrained than that of the author of the *Descent of the Holy Ghost*. Two scenes from the *Last Judgement*, in particular, give a good idea of his artistic approach. Below the figures of beasts personifying four kingdoms, Earth is represented. She is seated on a terrible monster which is vomiting parts of a human body.

Fig. 62. Jesus among the Doctors. Fresco, 1313.
Snetogorsky Monastery, Cathedral of the Birth of the Virgin.

Her head is surrounded by a diamond-shaped nimbus, and in her raised right hand she holds a vessel with a serpent stretching towards it. The serpent's coiled body is shaped like the first letter of the word *zemlya*, which is the Russian for Earth. To the right of the monster are shown six half-length figures in shrouds emerging from their coffins. Sea is represented as an old man, seated on a fantastic fish with the muzzle of a beast and a tail like a fan. On his head, surrounded by a diamond-shaped nimbus, is a crown; in his raised right hand he holds a small ship with a sail, and fish swim around him. Here we can clearly see to what an extent themes from popular fables are incorporated into the frescoes of religious buildings and how, in this instance, they bring an element of lightheartedness into the scene of the *Last Judgement* thus helping the simple spectator to comprehend this otherwise purely ecclesiastical composition. In the same way the treatment of the parable of Lazarus, Abraham and the Rich Man is very characteristic [113]. The weighty figure of the Rich Man is humorously contrasted with the nimble figure of a devil. The Rich Man is asking Abraham to send to him the beggar Lazarus, sojourning in Paradise, so that Lazarus might relieve his infernal suffering, and dipping his finger in water, cool his tongue (Luke xvi, 19–25). To the right of the Rich Man the artist has placed a crown symbolizing Svyatopolk and the figure of Satan, seated on a white serpent. The serpent has two heads, one at the front and one at the back; their toothed mouths are open and breathe fire. Satan has a broad face, framed by a thick white beard and white hair, which radiates like needle-shaped rays; another interesting detail is his long white moustache. In his left hand he holds a small figure of the traitor Judas, and in this figure too there are many mythical elements, doubtless borrowed from folklore sources, which the third master used particularly extensively.

The artists who worked at the Cathedral of the Snetogorsky

Fig. 63. Obadiah. Fresco, about 1360. Skovorodsky Monastery, Church of the Archangel Michael.

style to his frescoes (e.g., the *Deesis* on a red background with archangels and with the apostles Peter and Paul, and also the icon of the apostle Thomas in the Russian Museum at Leningrad).

Yu. A. Olsuf'yev attributed the paintings in the Skovorodsky Monastery to the end of the fourteenth century ('Vnov' raskrytyye freski v Novgorode'—Recently discovered frescoes at Novgorod, *Arkhitekturnaya Gazeta* of 12th October 1937). He based his argument firstly on the stylistic similarity between the facial highlights found in the Skovorodsky frescoes and those of the Church of the Nativity at the Cemetery, and secondly on the palaeographic characteristics of the inscriptions. As far as the first argument is concerned, it is of too general a nature to be considered decisive. Moreover it is hard to establish any stylistic similarity between the two cycles of frescoes. Nor does the second argument stand up to examination, because letters of the same type can be found in the scrolls of the Fathers of the Church in the early paintings of Volotovo, dating from 1363. The only argument which can be used in support of the late date proposed by Yu. A. Olsuf'yev is the relatively uninspired treatment of the faces, especially those painted by the chief master. But this style is very different from that of the Novgorod icons of the turn of the fifteenth century; in these the techniques of easel-painting were used in conjunction with standardized icon types with small hooked noses, small round eyes, and round heads. In the Skovorodsky frescoes many traces of the free picturesque style of the fourteenth century still exist, especially in the work of the second and third masters; and for this

Monastery were citizens of Pskov, which is proved by the many stylistic similarities between their frescoes and the thirteenth century icons of Pskov (e.g., the *Prophet Elijah*, *Our Lady's Assembly* in the Tret'yakov Gallery, *Descent into Limbo* in the Russian Museum).

Church of the Archangel Michael in the Skovorodsky Monastery near Novgorod

FRESCOES. About 1360.   117–120, *63, 64*

The Skovorodsky Monastery, built in the water-meadows on the right bank of the Volkhov, four kilometres south of Novgorod, was completely destroyed in the Second World War. The frescoes had been restored in 1928 and 1937 when they were cleaned of whitewash and overpainting. The state of preservation of the cleaned frescoes was good, except for some damage to the paint surface. All the inscriptions were in Slavonic.

Among the artists who worked there it is possible to recognize the hands of three masters. The chief master painted most of the Gospel scenes and such figures as the prophets David [*64*], Obadiah [*63*] and Zacharias [118]. He drew on the tradition of easel-painting, and applied many of its devices to his fresco work. This included the use of intensive local colour, a graphic manner of painting, and emphasis on the silhouette-like character of the figures. The Novgorod icons of the middle of the fourteenth century are very similar in

Fig. 64. King David and the Virgin of the Annunciation. Fresco, about 1360. Skovorodsky Monastery, Church of the Archangel Michael.

Figs. 65 and 66. The Healing of the Blind Men and the Procession to Calvary.
Frescoes, end of 1370's to 1380's. Novgorod, Church of Theodore Stratelates.

257

reason they cannot be dated as late as the end of the century. The final argument against a late date is the complete absence of any influence of the art of Theophanes the Greek, who, as is well known, appeared at Novgorod during the second half of the 'seventies.

Church of the Transfiguration (Spas Preobrazheniye), Novgorod

FRESCOES by Theophanes the Greek. 1378.

121–129, 152

These frescoes were for a long time hidden under whitewash and plaster. Their chance discovery by amateurs in 1910–13 was followed by methodical restoration in 1918, 1920–1, 1935 and 1944. The cleaned frescoes were in a good state of preservation, apart from some damage to the surface and the usual change in the blue colour of the backgrounds, which had lost its former brightness. During the Second World War the Nazis set up an observation post in the dome and the frescoes in dome and drum were so blackened with smoke that in spite of all attempts to clean them, it was not possible to restore their original freshness of colour. As a result of an explosion small cracks appeared on several frescoes in the chapel in the west corner.

The frescoes were not done by Theophanes alone. He must have had assistants, otherwise the great differences in quality between the figures would be inexplicable. The frescoes in the west corner-chapel were painted by Theophanes alone, but in the church itself he only did the basic parts of the frescoes. In painting the *Communion of the Apostles* the master

was undoubtedly helped by an assistant; an assistant also collaborated with him in the dome. It is possible that Theophanes brought an assistant with him from Constantinople, but it is more probable that he took on local painters in Novgorod to help him. Should this be the case, it would be the beginning of the Russification of Theophanes' style. This Russian influence was further developed in the wall-paintings of the Church of Theodore Stratelates and the Church of the Dormition in the field of Volotovo.

Church of Theodore Stratelates, Novgorod

FRESCOES. End of seventies to eighties of the fourteenth century.

130–131, *65, 66*

The frescoes have come down to us in a very damaged state. In the 1870's they were whitewashed and in 1910 they were freed from whitewash and from overpainting. But the lime had so eaten into the surface of the frescoes that the whole of the top layer of colour was damaged. For this reason the frescoes now look as if they had been half washed away. Originally the colours were much brighter, and one must also bear in mind that since 1910 they have faded even more.

A. I. Anisimov ('La peinture russe de XIVe siècle', *Gazette des Beaux-Arts*, 1930, p. 173) considered the frescoes from Theodore Stratelates to be the earliest work of Theophanes the Greek. Should we accept this hypothesis, it would be necessary to reconcile the incredible fact that Theophanes could work in the Novgorod style as early as the 'sixties (i.e., immediately after his arrival from Constantinople) with the evidence that in 1378, after eighteen years in Novgorod, he worked in a purely Greek style. Additional argument

Fig. 67. Prophets. Fresco, 1380's. Volotovo, Church of the Dormition.

Fig. 68. S. John. Fresco, 1380's. Volotovo, Church of the Dormition.

Figs. 69 and 70. The Apostles from 'The Eucharist'. Frescoes, 1380's. Volotovo, Church of the Dormition.

against this view is the fact that if Theophanes had arrived in Novgorod as early as the 'sixties, his arrival would certainly have been recorded by the chronicle in which the activities of the famous artist were fully reported.

D. V. Ainalov (*Geschichte der russischen Monumentalkunst der vormoskovitischen Zeit*, Berlin und Leipzig, 1932, p. 59) recognized the great stylistic similarity between the frescoes in the Church of the Transfiguration and those in the Church of Theodore Stratelates, considering the latter, however, as a preparatory step towards the style of the Theophanes. In this way he made the greater artistic phenomenon depend on the lesser, an obvious contradiction to the elementary logic of the artistic process.

Since the cleaning of the icons of the Deesis tier, painted by Theophanes in the year 1405 for the Cathedral of the Annunciation in Moscow, it is no longer possible to ascribe the frescoes of Theodore Stratelates and of Volotovo to Theophanes, because there is no way in which they can be included in a systematic chronology of the artist's development leading from the frescoes of Spas Preobrazheniye to the icons of the Cathedral of the Annunciation.

Church of the Dormition in the field of Volotovo near Novgorod

FRESCOES. Eighties of the fourteenth century.

132–146, *67–73*

Before they perished, the frescoes of Volotovo were one of the best preserved groups of paintings in Novgorod. They had never been whitewashed or overpainted, and, with the exception of some damage to the surface layer, they were without defects. About 1910 they were cleaned of soot and dust and washed with a special liquid which formed a thin dark film, and in places caused the colours to shrink and thus to flake off. The best preserved frescoes were those of the west chapel (*Resurrection of Christ* and two figures of angels), skilfully cleaned in the 1930's.

As the Church of Volotovo was consecrated to the Holy Virgin and was a monastic church, this largely determined the choice of subjects. Among the saints, for example, were represented the founders of monastic life and ascetics: John Climax, Euthymius, Barlaam and Joasaph, Zosimus giving the Eucharist to Mary of Egypt, Pachomius receiving from an angel the rule of monastic life. In the system of wall-paintings at Volotovo the most important place was given to scenes from the life of the Virgin, beginning with the *Presentation in the Temple* and ending with the *Dormition*. The Virgin painted on the conch was glorified by Cosmas of Mayuma and John of Damascus represented on the inner sides of the chancel arch. Connected with the glorification of the Virgin are rich compositions in the chapel such as *Wisdom creates a Temple to itself* and *Jacob's Ladder* (the ladder was treated in the middle ages as a prototype of Mary).

Proof that the master of Volotovo was acquainted with the work of Theophanes the Greek is provided by the figures of Abraham, Adam, Melchisedek, Aaron, Theodore the Studite and John Climax, undoubtedly inspired by Theophanes' portraits of old men. The archangel Michael with the sphere is very similar to angels from the Trinity by Theophanes. The treatment of folds, zigzag lines like lightning, thin white threads and acute triangles, reminds us of the flowing garments painted by Theophanes for his saints. The reddish-brown tone of the flesh tint with its rich white dabs is very close to that of the frescoes in the Church of the Transfiguration. Also the decorative frieze found in the Volotovo frescoes, imitating diagonally laid bricks is derived from the Church of the Transfiguration. For these reasons we are justified in stating that the master of Volotovo was familiar with the works of Theophanes the Greek, and in fact made a careful study of these works the basis of his artistic development. Among south Slavonic wall paintings those in the rock church near the village of Ivanovo in Bulgaria (so called Tsarkvata) are nearest in style to the frescoes of Volotovo. In principle, Novgorod and Ivanovo show the same radical Slavonic changes in the forms that were typical of the Palaeologue age: there is more expression and greater realism.

The master of Volotovo was such a strong personality that he overshadows his assistants. Of all the Novgorod paintings of the fourteenth century those in the Church of the Dormition were the most monolithic in style, and this makes it extremely difficult to differentiate the work of the various artists.

259

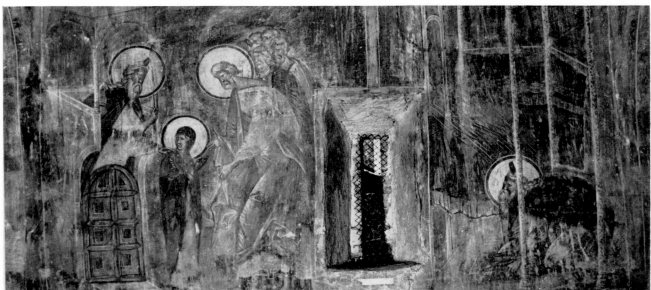

Figs. 71, 72 and 73. The Meeting at the Golden Gate; The Betrothal; The Presentation in the Temple. Frescoes, 1380's. Volotovo, Church of the Dormition.

Fig. 74. Frescoes on the North wall, including 'The Queen of Heaven standing at Thy Right Hand', 1380. Kovalyovo, Church of the Saviour.

Fig. 75. Head of an Angel. Fresco, 1380. Kovalyovo, Church of the Saviour.

Church of the Saviour (Spas), Kovalyovo near Novgorod

FRESCOES. 1380.   147, 148, *74–78*

Before the destruction of the church, the frescoes were in a relatively good state of preservation. They were freed of whitewash in 1910–12 and 1921.

At least three masters worked at this church. The first master, who painted the hermits [*76*], John the Baptist and the old men, and also the composition *Jesus among the Doctors*, worked in a fairly picturesque manner. He undoubtedly knew the frescoes of Theophanes the Greek in the Church of Spas Preobrazheniye and tried to imitate him. He used a very wide range of colours including light, translucent tones, and bright highlights, and he avoided sharp lines. His whole style is marked by great delicacy of touch. Very similar in style is the second master, who painted the dome and the drum [*75, 77*]. It is possible that he collaborated here with the first master, since one of the prophets is very like one of the hermits. He too has a picturesque manner of painting but adds highlights not only in dabs but also arranged in short parallel lines or in a fan-shaped pattern, examples of the tendency to make use of linear-graphic principles [*75*]. Undoubtedly we must attribute the frescoes in the prothesis to him, that is the composition *Do not mourn for me, Mother* and also the figures of Constantine and Helena. The third master painted the warriors [*78*], the scenes from the Gospels [147, *74*] and the composition of *The Queen of Heaven standing at Thy Right Hand* [*74*]. This artist, working in a different style, is much more closely connected with the tradition of icon-painting. His treatment is drier and more

detailed, and the highlights have the character of linear markings. In everything he stresses the use of line. He liked to elaborate form with ornamentation and was very fond of highlighting the flesh, a device much loved by the icon-painters; his dense colour lacks translucence, and in the features of his faces we find a sharpness unknown in the work of the first and second masters. Though he paints figures in violent movement (as for example in the *Transfiguration* [147]), they nevertheless lack an inner dynamism. One has the impression that he did not himself share the feelings of his figures, but merely repeated the dynamic movement borrowed in its entirety from the models which he used. Of all the artists who worked in the Church of Kovalyovo the third master is most alien to the school of thought which found its purest expression on Novgorod soil in the work of Theophanes the Greek.

Church of the Nativity of Christ at the Cemetery, Novgorod

HEADS OF APOSTLES FROM THE 'DORMITION'. Detail of fresco on the northern wall. Late fourteenth century.

149

The frescoes were whitewashed in 1827. They were cleaned in several stages in 1912, 1936–7 and 1946–8. Their state of preservation is mediocre, with much loss and damage to the picture surface and considerable change in colour values, especially in the backgrounds.

According to the third Novgorod Chronicle the church was founded in 1381. The frescoes, however, may have been painted later, possibly in the last decade of the fourteenth century. Such a late date is suggested by their style, which is similar to that of the Novgorod school of icon painting at the turn of the fifteenth century (cf. the icon *Dormition* from the village of Kuritskoye near Novgorod).

Fig. 76. Hermit. Fresco, 1380. Kovalyovo, Church of the Saviour.

Fig. 77. Moses. Fresco, 1380.
Kovalyovo, Church of the Saviour.

Fig. 78. Warrior. Fresco, 1380. Kovalyovo,
Church of the Saviour.

Church of S. Nicolas in the Gostinopol'sky Monastery near Novgorod

FRESCOES. About 1475–80.   *79, 80*

The cleaned fragments show that before the destruction of the church the frescoes were well preserved. Without any supporting evidence A. I. Nekrasov states that the frescoes were begun in 1483 (*Drevnerusskoye iskusstvo*—Ancient Russian art, Moscow 1937, p. 160). As the bell on the bell-tower of the monastery is dated 1475, it seems reasonable to attribute the same date to the destroyed wall-paintings and the partially surviving iconostasis from the church.

Cathedral of the Dormition on Gorodok, Zvenigorod

FRESCOES on the south-east and north-east pillars. End of the fourteenth to the beginning of the fifteenth century.   151, *83*

The frescoes on the east pillars were hidden for a long time behind the wooden iconostasis. They were discovered in 1918, and were then cleaned and strengthened. Fortunately the frescoes have never been whitewashed, and thanks to this they have preserved their original freshness of colour to a considerable extent. But those that decorate the lower part of the pillars have suffered greatly from damage to their colour surface.

Fig. 79. S. Nicolas. Fresco, about 1475–80.
Gostinopol'sky Monastery, S. Nicolas.

Fig. 80. S. Laurus (?). Fresco, about 1475–80.
Gostinopol'sky Monastery, S. Nicolas.

I. E. Grabar' was the first to recognize the hand of Rublyov in the portraits of Florus and Laurus (*Andrey Rublev*, pp. 92–5). He also correctly ascribed the frescoes on the lower part of the pillars to another master, whom he identifies, wrongly in our opinion, with Daniil Chyorny (Daniel the Black).

According to the ingenious hypotheses of N. D. Protasov the scene of the *Appearance of an Angel to S. Pachomius* hints at one of the principal episodes in the biography of Prince Yury of Zvenigorod, the builder of the cathedral ('Freski na altarnykh stolpakh Uspenskogo sobora v Zvenigorode'—Frescoes on the pillars of the altar in the Cathedral of the Dormition at Zvenigorod, *Svetil'nik*, 1915, No. 9–12, pp. 47–8). The Egyptian hermit Pachomius, at the suggestion of an angel, exchanged his lonely existence in a cave for the communal life of a monastery. Like Pachomius, Savva, who was the beloved disciple of Sergius of Radonezh and who died on the 3rd of December 1406, left his modest lodgings at the Monastery of S. Trinity in 1399 for the princely residence, where, on the initiative of Prince Yury, he founded a new monastery—the Savvin Storozhevsky Monastery.

Cathedral of the Dormition, Vladimir

FRESCOES. 1408.   Frontispiece, 150, 153–161, *81, 82, 84*

All that has been preserved of the murals in the cathedral from the time of Rublyov are isolated parts of the great composition, *The Last Judgement*, and a few figures of saints. The surviving frescoes were restored with complete lack of knowledge in the years 1768–74: the frescoes of the central

nave were overpainted in oil, the rest was whitewashed. New restoration was undertaken in the 'eighties by N. M. Safonov, an icon-painter from Palekh. He overpainted all the frescoes with tempera, partly over the original paintings, partly over the new oil colours, and partly directly on whitewash. In 1918, under the direction of I. E. Grabar', all overpainting was removed and it became clear that much had been lost: the layer of colours was frayed, there was damage to the colour surface, a change in the blue colour of the background, etc. Best preserved are the frescoes of the southern nave, which had never been covered by oils but only whitewashed. In classifying these wall-paintings I follow the basic conclusions of I. E. Grabar', though correcting many points. For instance I ascribe the figures of Anthony the Great and Onuphrius not to Daniil Chyorny but to Andrey Rublyov. See I. Grabar', *Andrey Rublev*, pp. 26–33, 66–7, 71–2, 97, 109. It is not difficult to relate Rublyov's wall-paintings in Vladimir to his famous icon of the Trinity and to the best icons of the Feasts in the Cathedral of the Annunciation in Moscow. (Compare, for instance, the angels standing beyond Peter and Paul [*81, 82*] with angels from the icon of the Trinity and angels from the *Baptism* in the Cathedral of the Annunciation). Certain similarities also exist between the icons of the much later iconostasis in the Cathedral of the Trinity (compare King David in the medallion [150], with the parallel figure on the icon *Descent into Limbo*). It is very interesting to note that the apostle Peter is undoubtedly inspired by a similar figure from the *Deesis* in the Cathedral of the Annunciation. This indicates once again how much attention Rublyov paid to the art of Theophanes and his closest collaborators.

Figs. 81 and 82. SS. Peter and Paul, with Angels. Frescoes, 1408. Vladimir. Cathedral of the Dormition.

Fig. 83. Angel appearing to S. Pachomius. Fresco, end of fourteenth to early fifteenth century. Zvenigorod, Cathedral of the Dormition.

Fig. 84. S. Onuphrius. Fresco, 1408. Vladimir, Cathedral of the Dormition.

Fig. 85. The Acathistus of the Virgin. Fresco, 1500–2. Ferapontov Monastery, Church of the Birth of the Virgin.

Fig. 86. The Last Judgement. Fresco, 150c–2. Ferapontov Monastery, Church of the Birth of the Virgin.

Fig. 87. The Return of the Prodigal Son. Fresco, 1500–2. Ferapontov Monastery, Church of the Birth of the Virgin.

Cathedral of the Dormition, Moscow: Pokhval'skiy Chapel

THE ADORATION OF THE MAGI. Wall-painting. About 1479.
164

The plaster covering the frescoes in the Pokhval'skiy Chapel was removed in 1913 by the restorer E. I. Bryagin. The state of preservation of the frescoes is fairly good; there is only some unimportant damage caused by the fraying of the upper layer of colour.

The Adoration of the Magi is the upper part of the fresco *Our Lady's Assembly* (*Sobor Bogomateri*); the lower part is lost. It is a theme which became popular in early Russian painting from the fourteenth century onwards (compare the well-known icon from Pskov in the Tret'yakov Gallery at Moscow), expressing the glorification of the Holy Virgin and the Infant Christ, to whom gifts are brought from everywhere,

at His appearance in the world. The composition as a whole is a Christmas hymn, glorifying the Holy Virgin and the Infant.

P. P. Muratov has wrongly dated this wall-painting 1459, i.e. the year of the foundation of the chapel, suggesting that this chapel was still part of the old Cathedral of the Dormition and was later included in the new building by Aristotele Fieravanti ('Dva otkrytiya'—Two Discoveries, *Sofia*, 1914, No. 2, pp. 5–11). In fact the Pokhaval'skiy Chapel is contemporary with the Fieravanti building. The most probable date of the painting in the chapel is about 1479, when the cathedral built by Fieravanti was consecrated (Iosafovskaya Chronicle under the year 1479). The cleaning of the frescoes of the Petro-pavlovskiy Pridel and of the prothesis in the Cathedral of the Dormition in 1961 proved beyond any doubt that these frescoes, similar in style to the wall-painting in the Pokhval'skiy Chapel, have very much in common with the work of Dionisy and his school.

Church of the Birth of the Virgin in the Ferapontov Monastery

FRESCOES. 1500–2.   162, 163, 165–175, *85–88*

The frescoes are on the whole well preserved. Restoration in 1738 was done fairly cautiously, and the frescoes were not totally overpainted, as was the usual practice in the eighteenth century; they were touched up with tempera only in those places where the paintings had greatly suffered from time. Unfortunately there is some rubbing away and damage to the upper layer of colour. For more details about the state of preservation see N. Chernyshyov, *Iskusstvo freski v Drevney Rusi—Art of fresco in Ancient Rus'*, pp. 82–4.

At least four stylistic groups can be identified among the wall-paintings in the Ferapontov Monastery. Undoubtedly the greatest of these artists was the one who painted the wall surrounding the west door [165–169]. His compositions are the most rhythmic, his slender figures are remarkably graceful, yet they show no mannerism, his colours are particularly mellow and harmonious, and he was still influenced by the traditions of the fifteenth century. It is very likely he who painted the saints in the apse, and the half-length figure of Nicolas Thaumaturgus in the diaconicon. Probably this master was Dionisy himself, who in 1500 must have been about 60 years old. The artist responsible for the majority of the Gospel scenes also belongs to the older generation of painters. But his work has not nearly the quality of the frescoes on the west wall. He was, no doubt, a very different personality, less gifted and more primitive in outlook.

Besides these the largest group of wall paintings is that which includes the principal episodes from the cycle of the Virgin (*The Virgin of Mercy (Pokrov)*, *In Thee Rejoiceth* [163], *Praise of Our Lady*, *Annunciation*, *Visitation* and the majority of the illustrations to the Acathistus [*85*], the *Parable of the Unprofitable Servant* [172], *The Wedding at Cana* [173] the best parts of the *Last Judgement* [175, *86*], and the *Œcumenical Councils* [170]. The style of these paintings is extremely refined and approaches that of the sixteenth century in its use of thin, delicate figures, exaggerated proportions, a light tread, detailed elaboration of form, and abundance of decoration. These frescoes were painted by a younger man. One is tempted to identify him with Feodosy, who was one of Dionisy's sons. It is probable that since Dionisy was by now an old man, he assigned the larger share of the work to his sons, although he still played a leading role. The weakest master was the author of a series of scenes from the life of Nicolas Thaumaturgus (which suffered from the restoration of 1738) and of the conversations of three bishops. His rigid compositions lack rhythm and are rather spiritless and stereotyped.

The paintings in the dome, drum, and transverse arches also show the hand of someone who was not a great artist. It is not clear though, whether these are the work of a fifth master or of one of those already mentioned. If the latter should be the case, the paintings could only have been done by the second or fourth master, that is to say, either the author of the Gospel scenes or the author of the life of Nicolas Thaumaturgus.

Dionisy, who was the head of the team and in charge of all the work, had probably acted in the following way: he himself took on the paintings which were to be in the most conspicuous

Fig. 88. S. Nicolas. Fresco, 1500–2. Ferapontov Monastery, Church of the Birth of the Virgin.

places in the church (the west wall, the apse and the conch in the diaconicon). He assigned to his more gifted son the principal and most important part of the total work (the frescoes on the walls and pillars). To his other son (incomparably less gifted than the first) and to his assistants he entrusted the paintings in the prothesis, diaconicon, vaults, transverse arches, drum and dome, rightly calculating that the spectator would have difficulty in seeing them clearly. This stylistic classification is only preliminary: it needs further research and has to be formulated more exactly. But even so it can serve as a starting-point for solving one of the complex problems in the history of early Russian painting.

S. S. Churakov recently attempted to recognize in the scene of the *Last Judgement* portraits of the well-known Italian architects who participated in the building of the Kremlin, Aristotele Fieravanti and Pietro Antonio Solari ('Portrety vo freskakh Ferapontova monastyrya'—Portraits in the frescoes of the Ferapontov Monastery—*Sovetskaya Arkheologiya*, 1959, No. 3, pp. 99–113). This hypothesis is, in my opinion, not very convincing especially as the faces in these supposed portraits are not at all individual. Another conjecture put forward by S. S. Churakov seems to me to be more probable. It is that the fresco which illustrated the eleventh hymn of the Acathistus of the Virgin (*Every Song is Vanquished*) is a family portrait of Dionisy, his wife and his two sons. It is necessary to stress, however, that here also the faces do not seem to have the character of portraits.

The Archangel Michael. Fresco, 1380's.
Volotovo, Church of the Dormition

BIBLIOGRAPHY

General Works

I. Tolstoy and N. Kondakov, *Russkiye drevnosti v pamyatnikakh iskusstva* (Russian antiquities in the monuments of art), fascicles 4 and 6, St. Petersburg, 1899.

N. Pokrovsky, *Ocherki pamyatnikov khristianskogo iskusstva i ikonografii* (Essays on the monuments of Christian art and iconography), 3rd edition, St. Petersburg, 1910.

I. Grabar', *Istoriya russkogo iskusstva* (History of Russian Art), vol. VI, Moscow, 1915, pp. 5–285 (Text by P. P. Muratov).

L. Réau, *L'art russe des origines à Pierre le Grand*, Paris, 1921.

V. Nikol'sky, *Istoriya russkogo iskusstva* (History of Russian Art), Berlin, 1923.

V. Shchavinsky, *Ocherki po istorii tekhniki zhivopisi i tekhnologii krasok v drevney Rusi* (Essays on the history of the technique of painting and the technology of colours in Ancient Rus'), Moscow–Leningrad, 1925.

G. Zhidkov, *Moskovskaya zhivopis' serediny XIV veka* (Moscow painting of the mid-14th century), Moscow, 1928.

Ph. Schweinfurth, *Geschichte der russischen Malerei im Mittelalter*, Haag, 1930.

M. Alpatov and N. Brunov, *Geschichte der altrussischen Kunst*, Augsburg, 1932.

D. Ainalov, *Geschichte der russischen Monumentalkunst der vormoskovitischen Zeit*, Berlin–Leipzig, 1932.

D. Ainalov, *Geschichte der russischen Monumentalkunst zur Zeit des Grossfürstentums Moskau*, Berlin–Leipzig, 1933.

A. Nekrasov, *Drevnerussoye izobrazitel'noye iskusstvo* (Ancient Russian figurative art), Moscow, 1937.

V. Mikhaylovsky and B. Purishev, *Ocherki istorii drevnerusskoy monumental'noy zhivopisi so vtoroy poloviny XIV veka do nachala XVIII* (Essays in the history of ancient Russian monumental painting from the second half of the 14th century to the beginning of the 18th century), Moscow–Leningrad, 1941.

V. Lazarev, *Iskusstvo Novgoroda* (The art of Novgorod), Moscow–Leningrad, 1947.

N. N. Voronin and M. K. Karger (editors), *Istoriya russkoy kul'tury* (History of the culture of ancient Rus'), vol. II, Moscow–Leningrad, 1951.

I. E. Grabar', V. S. Kemenov and V. N. Lazarev (editors), *Istoriya russkogo iskusstva* (History of Russian Art), vols. I, II, III (the chapters on painting by V. Lazarev), Moscow, 1952–5 (there is a German translation).

N. Chernyshyov, *Iskusstvo freski v Drevney Rusi* (The art of fresco in ancient Rus'), Moscow, 1954.

G. H. Hamilton, *The Art and Architecture of Russia* (The Pelican History of Art), Harmondsworth, Middx., 1954.

Yu. Dmitriyev, 'Zametki po tekhnike russkikh stennykh rospisey X–XII vv.: Zhivopis' i mozaika' (Notes on the technique of Russian wall-paintings of the 10th–12th centuries: Paintings and Mosaics), in *Ezhegodnik Instituta Istorii Iskusstv Akademii Nauk S.S.S.R.*, 1954, pp. 238–78.

M. Alpatov, *Vseobshchaya istoriya iskusstva* (A general history of the arts), vol. III, Moscow, 1955 (a popular work).

J. Blankoff, *L'art de la Russie ancienne*, Brussels, 1963.

T. Talbot Rice, *A Concise History of Russian Art*, London, 1963.

M. Karger, *Drevnerusskaja monumental'naya zhivopis'* (Ancient Russian monumental painting), Moscow-Leningrad, 1964 (album).

Fragment of the Desyatinnaya Church

N. Sychyov, 'Drevneyshiy fragment russko-vizantiyskoy zhivopisi' (The oldest fragment of Russian-Byzantine painting), in *Seminarium Kondakovianum*, 1928 (II), pp. 91–104.

N. Sychyov, *Iskusstvo srednevekovoy Rusi* (The art of medieval Rus'), pp. 183–4, in 'History of the art of all times and peoples', fascicle 4, Leningrad, 1929.

M. Karger, *Drevniy Kiev* (Ancient Kiev), II, Moscow–Leningrad, 1961, p. 56, pl. XI–XII.

The Mosaics of the Cathedral of S. Sophia in Kiev

Drevnosti Rossiyskogo Gosudarstva, Kievskiy Sofiyskiy sobor (Antiquities of the Russian State, the Cathedral of S. Sophia in Kiev), fascicles I–IV, St. Petersburg, 1871–87.

A. Prakhov, 'Kievskiye pamyatniki vizantiysko-russkogo iskusstva' (Monuments of Russian and Byzantine art in Kiev), in *Drevnosti, trudy Moskovskogo Arkheologicheskogo Obshchestva*, vol. IX, fascicle 3, 1887, pp. 7–8.

D. Ainalov and E. Redin, 'Kievo-Sofiyskiy sobor' (The Cathedral of S. Sophia in Kiev), in *Zapiski Russkogo Arkheologicheskogo Obshchestva*, new series, 1890 (IV), pp. 231–381.

N. Tolstoy and N. Kondakov, *Russkiye drevnosti v pamyatnikakh iskusstva*, fascicle 4, pp. 115–60.

F. Shmit, 'Sofiyskiy Sobor v Kieve' (The Cathedral of S. Sophia in Kiev), in *Svetil'nik*, 1913, No. 8.

F. Shmit, 'Zametki o pozdnevizantiyskikh khramovykh rospisyakh' (Notes on late Byzantine decoration of religious buildings), in *Vyzantiyskiy Vremennik*, 1915–16 (XXII), pp. 118–24.

K. Sherotsky, *Kiev* (Kiev, a guidebook), Kiev, 1917, pp. 37–47.

F. Shmit, *Iskusstvo Drevney Rusi Ukrainy* (The art of ancient Rus' and the Ukraine), Kharkov, 1919, pp. 44–70.

D. Ainalov, 'Novyy ikonograficheskiy obraz Khrista' (A new iconographic image of Christ), in *Seminarium Kondakovianum*, 1928 (II), pp. 19–23.

N. Sychyov, *Iskusstvo srednevekovoy Rusi*, pp. 190–6.

V. Lazarev, *Istoriya vizantiyskoy zhivopisi* (History of Byzantine painting), Moscow–Leningrad, 1947–8, vol. I, pp. 92–4, 306–7; vol. II, plates 112–19.

Akademiya Arkhitektury U.S.S.R. Gos. arkhitekturno-istoricheskiy zapovednik 'Sofiyskiy Muzey'. Ornamenty Sofii Kievskoy (Akademy of Architecture of the U.S.S.R., State Architectural and Historical Preserve—the 'Sophia Museum'. Ornaments of S. Sophia at Kiev), Text by Yu. Aseyev, Kiev, 1949.

A. Radchenko, *Putevoditel' po Gos. arkhitekturno-istoricheskomu zapovedniku 'Sofiyskiy Muzey'* (Guide to the State Architectural and Historical Preserve—the 'Sophia Museum'), Kiev, 1950, pp. 27ff.

O. Powstenko, *The Cathedral of S. Sophia of Kiev*, New York, 1954, pp. 111–22.

V. Lazarev, 'Novyye dannyye o mozaikakh i freskakh Sofii Kievskoy' (New facts on the mosaics and frescoes of S. Sophia of Kiev), in *Vizantiyskiy Vremennik*, 1956 (X), pp. 161–77.

N. Kresal'nyy, *Sofiya Kievskaya* (S. Sophia of Kiev), Moscow, 1958, pp. 23–8.

V. Levitskaya, 'O nekotorykh voprosakh proizvodstva nabora Mozaik Sofii Kievskoy' (On some questions of the mosaic setting in S. Sophia at Kiev), in *Vizantiyskiy Vremennik*, 1959 (XV), pp. 170–183.

N. Kresal'nyy, *Sofiyskiy zapovednik v Kieve* (The Preserve of Sophia in Kiev), Kiev, 1960.

V. Lazarev, *Mozaiki Sofii Kievskoy* (Mosaics of S. Sophia of Kiev), Moscow, 1960.

V. Lasareff, 'Constantinopoli e le scuole nazionali alla luce di nuove scoperte', in *Arte Veneta*, 1959–60 (XIII–XIV), pp. 7–24.

V. Levitskaya, 'Materialy issledovaniy palitry mozaik Sofii Kievskoy' (Materials of the researches of the mosaic palette in S. Sophia at Kiev), in *Vizantiyskiy Vremennik*, 1963 (XXIII), pp. 105-157.

Frescoes of the S. Sophia in Kiev

N. Kondakov, 'O freskakh lestnits Kievo-Sofiyskogo sobora' (On the frescoes of the staircases in the Cathedral of S. Sophia at Kiev), in *Zapiski Imp. Russkogo Arkheologicheskogo Obshchestva*, 1888 (III), pp. 288–306.

N. Okunev, 'Kreshchal'nya Sofiyskogo sobora v Kieve' (Baptistry of the Cathedral of S. Sophia in Kiev), in *Zapiski otdeleniya russkoy i slavyanskoy arkheologii Imp. Russkogo Arkheologicheskogo Obshchestva*, 1915 (X), pp. 113–37.

K. Sherotsky, *Kiev* (Kiev, a guidebook), Kiev, 1917, pp. 52–60.

A. Grabar, 'Freski Apostol'skogo pridela Kievo-Sofiyskogo sobora' (Frescoes of the Apostles' Chapel of the Kievan S. Sophia Cathedral), in *Zapiski otdeleniya russkoy i slavyanskoy arkheologii Imp. Russkogo Arkheologicheskogo Obshchestva*, 1918 (XII), pp. 98–106.

V. Myasoyedov, 'Freski severnogo pritvora Sofiyskogo sobora v Kieve' (Frescoes of the northern chapel of the Sophia Cathedral in Kiev), in *Zapiski otdeleniya russkoy i slavyanskoy arkheologii Imp. Russkogo Arkheologicheskogo Obshchestva*, 1918 (XII), pp. 1–7.

I. Skulenko, 'Restavratsiya Sofiyskogo sobora v Kieve' (Restoration of the Cathedral of S. Sophia at Kiev), in *Sovetskiy Muzey*, 1936, No. 1, pp. 55–9.

V. Lasareff, 'A Great Rediscovery of 11th Century Byzantine Art', in *Illustrated London News*, 17 July, 1937, pp. 127–9.

A. Grabar, 'Les fresques des escaliers à Sainte-Sophia de Kiev et l'iconographie impériale byzantine', in *Seminarium Kondakovianum*, 1935 (VII), pp. 103–17.

O. Powstenko, *The Cathedral of S. Sophia of Kiev*, New York, 1954, pp. 123–41.

M. Karger, 'Portrety Yaroslava Mudrogo i yego sem'i v Kievskoy Sofii' (Portraits of Yaroslav the Wise and of his family in the Sophia of Kiev), in *Uchyonyye Zapiski Leningradskogo Gos. Universiteta*, 1954, No. 160, seriya istoricheskikh nauk, fascicle 20, pp. 143–80.

V. Lazarev, 'Novyye dannyye o mozaikakh i freskakh Sofii Kievskoy' (New facts on the mosaics and frescoes of S. Sophia at Kiev), in *Vizantiyskiy Vremennik*, 1956, (X), pp. 161–77.

N. Kresal'ny, *Sofia Kievskaya* (S. Sophia of Kiev), Moscow, 1958, pp. 28–34.

V. Lazarev, 'Novyye dannyye o mozaikakh i freskakh Sofii Kievskoy. Gruppovoy portret semeystva Yaroslava' (New facts on the mosaics and frescoes of S. Sophia at Kiev. A group-portrait of the family of Yaroslav), in *Vizantiyskiy Vremennik*, 1959 (X), pp. 148–69.

N. Kresal'ny, *Sofiyskiy Zapovednik v Kieve* (The Sophia Preserve at Kiev), Kiev, 1960.

V. Lazarev, *Mozaiki Sofii Kievskoy* (Mosaics of S. Sophia of Kiev), Moscow, 1960, pp. 38–59, 60–76.

Fresco of Chernigov with Image of S. Thecla

M. Makarenko, 'Naydavnisha stinopis' knyazhoi Ukraini' (The oldest wall-painting of princely Ukraine), in *Ukraina*, 1927, book 1, pp. 7–13.

Mosaics and Frescoes in the Church of Archangel Michael at Kiev

A. Prakhov, Kievskiye pamyatniki vizantiysko-russkogo iskustva (Kievan monuments of Byzantine-Russian art), in *Drevnosti, trudy Moskovskogo Arkheologicheskogo Obshchestva*, vol. XI, fascicle 3, 1887, p. 9.

I. Tolstoy and N. Kondakov, *Russkiye drevnosti v pamyatnikakh iskusstva*, fascicle 4, pp. 162–3.

N. Petrov, *Istoriko-topograficheskiye ocherki drevnego Kieva* (Historical-topographical essays on ancient Kiev), Kiev, 1897, pp. 153–4.

F. Shmit, 'Zametki o pozdne vizantiyskikh khramovykh rospisyakh' (Notes on late Byzantine decorations of religious buildings), in *Vizantiyskiy Vremennik*, 1915–16 (XII), pp. 62–126.

F. Shmit, *Iskusstvo drevney Rusi Ukrainy*, pp. 81–5.

N. Sychyov, *Iskusstvo srednevekovoy Rusi*, pp. 203–5.

V. Lazarev, *Istoriya vizantiyskoy zhivopisi*, I, pp. 119–20, 321–2; II, Plates 169–76.

M. Karger, 'K voprosu ob ubranstve inter'yera v russkom zodchestve domongol'skogo perioda' (On the question of pre-Mongolian interior decoration in Russian architecture), in *Trudi Vserossiyskoy Akademii Khudozhestv*, 1947 (I), p. 28.

D. Ainalov 'Die Mosaiken des Michaelklosters in Kiev', *Belvedere*, 1926 (9–10), October, pp. 201, 216.

S. Cross, 'The Mosaic Eucharist in St. Michael's (Kiev)' *American Slavic and East European Review*, 1947 (VI), Nos. 16–17, pp. 55–61.

R. Salvini, *Mosaici medievali in Sicilia*, Firenze, 1949, pp. 17, 62–63.

O. Demus, *The Mosaics of Norman Sicily*, London, 1950, pp. 371, 374, 387–388.

G. Galassi, 'Mosaici di Kiew a San Michele arte russa', in *Felix Ravenna*, 1956, fasc. 19, pp. 5–30.

M. Karger, *Drevniy Kiev*, II, Kiev, 1961, pp. 261–82.

Decorations in the Cathedral of the Dormition at Vladimir

I. Grabar', 'Andrey Rublev' (Andrey Rublyov), in *Voprosy Restavratsii*, *1926* (I), pp. 25–6.

N. Sychyov, 'K istorii rospisi Dmitriyevskogo sobora vo Vladimire' (On the history of the decoration of the Dmitriyevskiy Cathedral at Vladimir), in *Pamyatniki kul'tury*, Moscow, 1959 (I), pp. 164–8.

Decorations in the Dmitriyevskiy Cathedral in Vladimir

I. Grabar', 'Rospisi Dmitriyevskogo sobora vo Vladimire' (Decorations of Dmitriyevskiy Cathedral at Vladimir), in *Russkoye Iskusstvo*, 1923, No. 3, pp. 41–7.

A. Anisimov, 'Domongol'skiy period drevnerusskoy zhivopisi' (The pre-Mongolian period of ancient Russian painting), in *Voprosy Restavratsii*, 1928, (II), pp. 111–19.

M. Artamonov, 'Odin iz stiley monumental'noy zhivopisi XII–XIII vekov' (One of the styles of monumental painting in the 12th–13th centuries), in *Sbornik I aspirantov Gos. Akademii Istorii Material'noy Kul'tury*, Leningrad, 1929, pp. 56–7.

V. Lazarev, *Istoriya vizantiyskoy zhivopisi*, vol. I, pp. 123–4, vol. II, plates 188–94.

I. Grabar', *Die Freskomalerei der Dimitrij Kathedrale in Wladimir*, Berlin, 1926.

L. Réau, 'Les fresques de la cathédrale Saint Dmitrij à Vladimir', in *Recueil Uspenskij*, II, Paris, 1932, pp. 68–76.

V. Lasareff, 'La méthode de la collaboration des maîtres byzantins et russes', in *Classica et Mediaevalia, revue danoise de philologie et d'histoire*, 1956 (XVII), pp. 82–90.

N. Sychyov, 'K istorii rospisi Dmitriyevskogo sobora vo Vladimire' (On the history of the decoration of the Dmitriyevsky Cathedral at Vladimir), in *Pamyatniki Kul'tury*, I, Moscow, 1959, pp. 143–76.

Frescoes in the Cathedral at Suzdal'

A. Varganov, 'Freski XI–XIII vekov v Suzdal'skom sobore' (Frescoes of the 11th–13th centuries in the Cathedral at Suzdal'), in *Kratkiye soobshcheniya o dokladakh i polevykh issledovaniyakh Instituta Istorii Material'noy Kul'tury Akademii Nauk S.S.S.R.*, 1940, fascicle 5, pp. 39–40.

Decorations in S. Sophia at Novgorod

V. Suslov, 'Kratkoye izlozheniye issledovaniya novgorodskogo Sofiyskogo sobora' (Summary of research on the Cathedral of Sophia at Novgorod), in *Zodchiy*, 1894 (XXII), pp. 86–8.

'Obsuzhdeniye proyekta stennoy rospisi novgorodskogo Sofiyskogo sobora' (Conference on the project of wall decoration of the Cathedral of Sophia at Novgorod), in *Materialy po arkheologii Rossii, izdavayemyye Arkheologicheskoy Komissiyey*, No. 21, St. Petersburg, 1897, figs. 4, 5, 9–11, 13, 14, 16.

V. Myasoyedov, 'Fragmenty freskovoy rospisi svyatoy Sofii Novgorodskoy' (Fragments of fresco decoration of the Cathedral of S. Sophia at Novgorod), in *Zapiski otdeleniya russkoy i slavyanskoy arkheologii Russkogo Arkheologicheskogo Obshchestva*, 1915 (X), pp. 15–34.

Yu. Dmitriyev, 'Stennyye rospisi Novgoroda, ikh restavratsiya i issledovanniye' (Wall-paintings of Novgorod, their restoration and research-works undertaken in the years

1945–8), in *Praktika restavratsionnykh rabot*, I, Moscow, 1950, pp. 133–46.

Yu. Dmitriyev, *Zametki po tekhnike russkikh stennykh rospisey*, pp. 271–6.

Frescoes in Nikolo-Dvorishchensky Cathedral

N. Sychyov, 'Zabytyye fragmenty novgorodskikh fresok XII veka' (Forgotten fragments of Novgorod frescoes of the 12th century), in *Zapiski otdeleniya russkoy i slavyanskoy arkheologii Russkcgo Arkheologicheskogo Obshchestva*, 1918 (XII), pp. 116–31.

Decorations of the Cathedral of the Birth of the Virgin at the Antoniyev Monastery

A. Anisimov, 'Domongol'skiy period drevnerusskoy zhivopisi' (The pre-Mongolian period of ancient Russian painting), in *Voprosy Restavratsii*, 1928 (II), p. 179.

A. Strokov and V. Bogusevich, *Novgorod Velikiy* (Novgorod the Great), Leningrad, 1939, p. 61.

A. Vinner, 'Freski Novgoroda' (Frescoes of Novgorod), in *Arkhitektura S.S.S.R.*, fascicle 10, Moscow, 1945, pp. 22–8.

Decorations of the Spaso-Mirozhsky Monastery in Pskov

A. Pavlinov, 'Spaso-Mirozhsky monastyr' v g. Pskove' (Spaso-Mirozhsky Monastery at the town of Pskov), in *Drevnosti, trudy Moskovskogo Arkheologicheskogo Obshchestva*, 1889 (XIII), part 1, pp. 154–62.

I. Tolstoy and N. Kondakov, *Russkiye drevnosti v pamyatnikakh iskusstva*, fascicle 6, pp. 177–85.

O. Parli, *Freski khrama Preobrazheniya Gospodnya v pskovskom Spaso-Mirozhskom monastyre* (Frescoes of the Church of the Transfiguration of Our Lord at Spaso-Mirozhsky Monastery at Pskov), Album of Photos, 1903.

A. Uspensky, 'Freski tserkvi Preobrazheniya Gospodnya Spaso-Mirozhskogo monastyrya' (Frescoes of the Church of the Transfiguration of our Lord at the Spaso-Mirozhsky Monastery), in *Zapiski Moskovskogo Arkheologicheskogo Instituta*, 1910 (VII), pp. 1–12.

N. Pokrovsky, *Ocherki pamyatnikov khristianskogo iskusstva i ikonografii*, pp. 253–60.

A. Nekrasov, *Drevniy Pskov* (Ancient Pskov), Moscow, 1923, pp. 28–30.

M. Artamonov, 'Odin iz stiley monumental'noy zhivopisi XII–XIII vv.' (One of the styles of monumental painting in the 12th–13th centuries), in *Sbornik I aspirantov Gos. Akademii Istorii Material'noy Kul'tury*, Leningrad, 1929, pp. 52–4, 57–8.

M. Millet, *Recherches sur l'iconographie de l'évangile aux XIVe et XVIe siècles*, Paris, 1916, pp. 48, 176, 177, 183, 573–4.

A. Anisimov, *Les fresques de Pskov*, Cahiers d'Art, 1930, pp. 7–10.

L. Nadejena, 'The Pskov School of Painting', in *Art Bulletin*, 1939 (XXI), pp. 183–8.

Frescoes of the Church of S. George at Staraya Ladoga

V. Prokhorov, 'Stennaya ikonopis' (freski) XII veka v tserkvi Sv. Georgiya v Staroy Ladoge' (Wall icon-painting of the 12th century in the Church of S. George at Staraya Ladoga), in *Khristianskiye Drevnosti*, book I, St. Petersburg, 1871.

N. Brandenburg, *Staraya Ladoga* (Staraya Ladoga), St. Petersburg, 1896, plates LXV–XC.

N. Repnikov, 'O freskakh tserkvi sv. Georgiya v Staroy Ladoge' (On the frescoes of the Church of S. George in Staraya Ladoga), in *Izvestiya Komiteta izucheniya drevnerusskoy zhivopisi*, fascicle 1, Petrograd, 1921, pp. 1–4.

N. Repnikov, 'Predvaritel'noye soobshcheniye o raskrytii pamyatnikov drevney zhivopisi v Staroy Ladoge' (Preliminary report on the uncovering of monuments of ancient painting in Staraya Ladoga), in *Voprosy Restavratsii*, 1928 (II), pp. 183–4.

M. Artamonov, *Odin iz stiley monumental'noy zhivopisi XII–XIII vekov*, pp. 54–6, 61–4.

V. Lazarev, *Freski Staroy Ladogi* (Frescoes of Staraya Ladoga), Moscow, 1960.

Decorations in the Church near Arkazhi

A. Strokov and V. Bogusevich, *Novgorod Velikiy*, p. 71.

Yu. Dmitriyev, *Stennyye rospisi Novgoroda*, pp. 158–61.

Decorations in the South Gallery of the Cathedral of S. Sophia at Novgorod

A. Mongait, 'Raskopki v Martir'yevskoy paperti Sofiyskogo sobora v Novgorode' (Excavation of the Martir'yevskaya parvis of the Cathedral of Sophia at Novgorod), in *Kratkiye Soobshcheniya Instituta Istorii Material'noy Kul'tury*, fascicle XXIV, 1949, pp. 95–6.

Yu. Dmitriyev, *Stennyye rospisi Novgoroda*, pp. 146–54.

Decorations in the Church Spas-on-Nereditsa

I. Tolstoy and N. Kondakov, *Russkiye drevnosti v pamyatnikakh iskusstva*, fascicle 6, pp. 129–46, 165.

J. Ebersolt, 'Fresques byzantines de Néréditsi d'après les acquarelles de M. Braylovsky', in *Monuments et mémoires Piot*, 1906, (XIII), pp. 33–5.

V. Suslov, 'Tserkov' Spasa-Nereditsy bliz Novgoroda' (Church of Spas-on-Nereditsa near Novgorod), in *Pamyatniki drevnerusskogo iskusstva*, fascicle 1, St. Petersburg, 1908, pp. 1–10; fascicle 2, St. Petersburg, 1909, pp. 1–2; fascicle 3, St. Petersburg, 1910, pp. 1–10.

N. Kondakov, 'Zametki o nekotorykh syuzhetakh i kharaktere Spaso-Nereditskoy rospisi' (Notes on some subjects and the character of the decorations of Spas-on-Nereditsa), in *Pamyatniki drevnerusskogo iskusstva*, fascicle 2, St. Petersburg, 1909, pp. 3–5.

A. Uspensky, 'Freski tserkvi Spasa-Nereditsy' (Frescoes of the Church of Spas-on-Nereditsa), in *Zapiski Moskovskogo Arkheologicheskogo Instituta*, 1910 (VI), pp. 1–24.

V. Myasoyedov, *Freski Spasa-Nereditsy* (Frescoes of Spas-on-Nereditsa), Leningrad, 1925.

Ch. Amiranachvili, 'Quelques remarques sur l'origine des procédés dans les fresques de Neredicy', in *Recueil Uspenskij*, II, Paris, 1932, pp. 102–28.

N. Syčev, 'Sur l'histoire de l'église du Sauveur à Neredicy près de Novgorod', in *Recueil Uspenskij*, II, Paris, 1932, pp. 77–108.

Yu. Dmitriyev, 'Izobrazheniye ottsa Aleksandra Nevskogo na Nereditskoy freske XIII veka' (Image of the father of Alexander Nevsky on a Nereditsa fresco of the 13th century), in *Novgorodskiy istoricheskiy sbornik*, fascicles 3–4, Novgorod, 1938, pp. 39–57.

M. Artamonov, 'Mastera Nereditsy' (Masters of Nereditsa), in *Novgorodskiy istoricheskiy sbornik*, fascicle 5, Novgorod, 1939, pp. 34–47.

Yu. Dmitriyev, *Stennyye rospisi Novgoroda*, pp. 154–8.

A. Frolov, 'Sainte Marthe ou la Mère de Dieu', in *Bulletin of the Byzantine Institute*, 1946, pp. 79–82.

Ph. Schweinfurth, *Die Fresken der Erlöserkirche von Neredica bei Novgorod. Ihre Stellung in der Kunstgeschichte Russlands*, München, 1953.

Frescoes of Snetogorsk

L. Matsulevich, 'Fragmenty stenopisi v sobore Snetogorskogo monastyrya' (Fragments of wall paintings in the Cathedral of the Monastery of Snetogorsk), in *Zapiski otdeleniya russkoy i slavyanskoy arkheologii Russkogo Arkheologicheskogo Obshchestva*, 1915 (X), pp. 35–7.

A. Nekrasov, *Drevniy Pskov* (Ancient Pskov), Moscow, 1923, pp. 30–3.

A. Anissimoff, 'Les fresques de Pskov', in *Cahier d'Art*, 1930, pp. 10–12.

L. Nadejena, 'The Pskov School of Painting', in *Art Bulletin*, 1939 (XXI), pp. 188–91.

N. Chernyshyov, *Iskusstvo freski v drevney Rusi*, pp. 31–60.

V. Lazarev, 'Snetogorskii rospisi' (Wall paintings of Snetogorsk), in *Soobshcheniya Instituta Istorii Iskusstv Akademii Nauk S.S.S.R.*, fascicle 8, 1957, pp. 78–112.

Decorations in the Church of S. Michael in the Skovorodsky Monastery

V. Bogusevich, 'Vnov' otkrytyye freski russkikh masterov XIV veka' (Rediscovered frescoes of Russian masters of the 14th century), in *Novgorodskiy istoricheskiy sbornik*, fascicles 3–4, Novgorod, 1938, pp. 216–18.

V. Lazarev, 'Rospisi Skovorodskogo monastyrya v Novgorode' (Wall paintings of the Skovorodsky Monastery at Novgorod), in *Pamyatniki iskusstva, razrushennyye nemetskimi zakhvatchikami*, Moscow–Leningrad, 1948, pp. 77–101.

Decorations of the Church of Spas-Preobrazheniye at Novgorod

A. Anisimov, 'Novootkrytyye freski Novgoroda' (The rediscovered frescoes of Novgorod), in *Staryye Gody*, December, 1913, pp. 53–5.

I. Grabar', *Feofan Grek* (Theophanes the Greek), Kazan', 1922.

M. Alpatov, 'Kratkiy otchyot o poyezdke na Vostok' (Short report of a journey to the Orient), in *Vizantiyskiy Vremennik*, 1923–6 (XXIV), pp. 58–9.

P. Mouratov, *Les icones russes*, Paris, pp. 119–47.

N. Porfiridov, 'Novyye otkrytiya v oblasti drevney zhivopisi v Novgorode' (New discoveries in the field of ancient painting in Novgorod: 1918–28), in *Sbornik Novgorodskogo Obshchestva lyubiteley drevnosti*, Novgorod, 1928 (IX), pp. 4–5.

A. Anissimov, 'La peinture russe du XIVe siècle (Theophane le Grec)', in *Gazette des Beaux-Arts*, 1930, pp. 158–77.

A. Strokov and V. Bogusevich, *Novgorod Velikiy*, pp. 107–10.

B. Mikhaylovsky and B. Purishev, *Ocherki istorii drevnerusskoy monumental'noy zhivopisi*, pp. 15–16, 26–33, 157–64.

D. Likhachyov, *Novgorod Velikiy* (Novgorod the Great), Leningrad, 1945, pp. 53–4.

V. Lazarev, *Istoriya vizantiyskoy zhivopisi*, vol. I, pp. 218–20, vol. II, plates 291–300.

V. Lazarev, 'Etyudy o Feofane Greke' (Studies on Theophanes the Greek), in *Vizantiyskiy Vremennik*, 1953 (VII), pp. 250–8.

K. Onasch, 'Gross-Novgorod und Feofan der Grieche', in *Ostkirchliche Studien*, 1954 (III), pp. 287–306.

V. Lazarev, *Feofan Grek i yego shkola* (Theophanes the Greek and his school), Moscow, 1961, pp. 35–45.

Decorations of the Church of S. Theodore Stratelates

N. Okunev, 'Vnov' otkrytaya rospis' tserkvi sv. Feodora Stratilata' (Rediscovered wall-paintings of the Church of S. Theodore Stratelates at Novgorod), in *Izvestiya Arkheologicheskoy Komissii*, fascicle 39, 1911, pp. 81–101.

A. Anisimov, 'Restavratsiya tserkvi Feodora Stratilata v Novgorode' (Restoration of the Church of S. Theodore Stratelates in Novgorod), in *Staryye Gody*, February 1911, pp. 43–50.

D. Gordeyev, 'O Novgorodskikh fedorovskikh freskakh' (On the Novgorod frescoes of the Church of S. Theodore), in *Vyzantiyskiy Vremennik*, 1917 (XXII), pp. 281–96.

I. Grabar', *Feofan Grek*, p. 15.

A. Anissimov, 'La peinture russe du XIVe siècle', *Gazette des Beaux-Arts*, 1930, pp. 173–4.

Yu. Dmitriyev, *Stennyye rospisi Novgoroda*, pp. 167–8.

V. Lazarev, *Feofan Grek i yego shkola*, pp. 46–52.

Decorations of the Church of the Dormition in Volotovo

L. Matsulevich, 'Tserkov' Uspeniya Presvyatoy Bogoroditsy v Volotove' (Church of the Dormition at Volotovo), in the series *Pamyatniki drevnerusskogo iskusstva*, fascicle 4, St. Petersburg, 1912.

D. Ainalov, *Vizantiyskaya zhivopis' XIV stoletiya* (Byzantine painting of the 14th century), Petrograd, 1917, pp. 124–56.

I. Grabar', *Feofan Grek*, p. 15.

A. Anissimov, 'La peinture russe du XIVe siècle', in *Gazette des Beaux-Arts*, 1930, p. 171.

M. Porfiridov, 'Zhivopis' Volotova' (Paintings of Volotovo), in *Novgorodskiy istoricheskiy sbornik*, fascicle 7, Novgorod, 1940, pp. 55–65.

N. Alpatov, 'Freski khrama Uspeniya na Volotovom pole' (Frescoes of the Church of the Dormition on the field of Volotovo), in *Pamyatniki iskusstva razrushenyye nemetskimi zakhvatchikami v S.S.S.R.*, Moscow–Leningrad, 1948, pp. 103–48.

V. Lazarev, *Feofan Grek i yego shkola*, pp. 52–63.

Decorations of the Church of Kovalyovo

Makary the Archmandrite, *Arkheologicheskoye opisaniye tserkovnykh drevnostey v Novgorode i yego okrestnostyakh*, (Archeological description of the ecclesiastical antiquities of Novgorod and its surroundings), part I, Moscow, 1860, pp. 578–85.

M. Porfiridov, 'Novyye otkrytiya v oblasti drevney russkoy zhivopisi v Novgorode' (New discoveries in the field of ancient Russian painting in Novgorod), in *Sbornik Novgorodskogo Obshchestva lyubiteley drevnosti*, Novgorod, 1928 (IX), p. 61.

A. Strokov and V. Bogusevich, *Novgorod Velikiy*, pp. 88–92.

V. Lazarev, 'Kovalyovskaya rospis' i problema yuzhnoslavyanskikh svyazey v russkoy zhivopisi XIV veka' (Wall paintings of Kovalyovo and the problem of South Slavonic connexions with Russian painting of the 14th century), in *Ezhegodnik Instituta Istorii Iskusstv Akademii Nauk S.S.S.R.*, 1957, pp. 233–78.

Frescoes in the Church of the Nativity at the Cemetery

A. Anisimov, 'Novootkrytyye freski Novgoroda' (Rediscovered frescoes of Novgorod), in *Staryye Gody*, December 1913, pp. 51–2.

P. Muratov, 'Russkaya zhivopis' do serediny XVII veka' (Russian painting to the middle of the 17th century), in I. Grabar', *Istoriya russkogo iskusstva*, vol. VI, pp. 51–2.

Yu. Dmitriyev, *Stennyye rospisi Novgoroda*, pp. 168–70.

M. Karger, *Novgorod Velikiy* (Novgorod the Great), Leningrad–Moscow, 1961, pp. 216–22.

Decorations of the Monastery of Gostinopol'ye

V. Peredol'sky, 'Zapiska o sostoyanii velikonovgorodskoy stariny' (Memorandum on the state of preservation of the antiquities of Novgorod the Great), in *Sbornik Novgorodskogo Obshchestva lyubiteley drevnosti*, Novgorod, 1910 (III), p. 8.

N. Repnikov, 'Pamyatniki ikonografii uprazdnyennogo Gostinopol'skogo monastyrya' (Monuments of iconography of the abolished monastery of Gostinopol'ye), in *Izvestiya Komiteta izucheniya drevnerusskoy zhivopisi*, fascicle 1, Petrograd, 1921, pp. 13–20.

Decorations of the Cathedral of the Dormition on Gorodok in Zvenigorod

N. Protasov, 'Freski na altarnykh stolpakh Uspenskogo sobora v Zvenigorode' (Frescoes on the pillars of the altar in the Cathedral of the Dormition in Zvenigorod), in *Svetil'nik*, 1915, Nos. 9–12, pp. 26–48.

I. Grabar', 'Andrey Rublyov', in *Voprosy restavratsii*, 1926 (I), pp. 91–5.

Frescoes of the Cathedral of the Dormition at Vladimir

I. Grabar', *Andrey Rublyov*, pp. 22–33.

N. Dyomina, 'Freski Andreya Rublyova vo Vladimire' (The frescoes of Andrey Rublyov in Vladimir), in *Dekorativnoye Iskusstvo*, 1960, No. 8, pp. 5–9.

M. Alpatov, *Andrey Rublyov*, Moscow, 1959, pp. 15–20.

J. Lebedewa, *Andrei Rubljow*, Dresden, 1962, pp. 50–65.

S. Churakov, 'Andrey Rublyov i Daniil Chyornyy' (Andrey Rublyov and Daniil Chyornyy), in *Iskusstvo*, 1964, No. 9, pp. 61–69.

Frescoes of the Pokhval'skiy Pridel in the Cathedral of the Dormition in Moscow

P. Muratov, 'Dva Otkrytiya' (Two Discoveries), in *Sophia*, 1914, No. 2, pp. 5–11.

S. V., Pokloneniye volkhvov—freska, nedavno otkrytaya na stene moskovskogo Bol'shogo Uspenskogo sobora (Adoration of the Magi, fresco recently discovered on the wall of the great Cathedral of the Dormition in Moscow), in *Svetil'nik*, 1914, No. 2, pp. 3–4.

Khudozhestvennyye pamyatniki Moskovskogo Kremlya (The monuments and works of art of the Kremlin in Moscow), Moscow, 1956, p. 28.

Frescoes of the Church of the Birth of the Virgin in the Ferapontov Monastery

V. Georgiyevsky, *Freski Ferapontova monastyrya* (Frescoes of the Ferapontov monastery), St. Petersburg, 1911.

E. Georgievskaja-Družinina, 'Les fresques du monastère de Théraphon. Études de deux thèmes iconographiques', in *Recueil Uspenskij*, II, Paris, 1932, pp. 121–34.

B. Mikhailovsky and B. Purishev, *Ocherki istorii drevnerusskoy monumental'noy zhivopisi*, pp. 32–52.

N. Chernyshyov, *Iskusstvo freski v drevney Rusi*, pp. 61–96.

S. Churakov, Portrety vo freskakh Ferapontova monastyrya (Portraits in the frescoes of the Ferapontov Monastery), in *Sovetskaya Arkheologiya*, 1959, No. 3, pp. 99–113.

I. Danilova, 'Ikonograficheskiy sostav fresok Rozhdestvenskoy tserkvi Ferapontova monastyrya' (Iconographical content of the frescoes in the Church of the Birth of the Virgin in the Ferapontov Monastery), in *Iz istorii russkogo i zapadnoyevropeyskogo iskusstva*, Moscow, 1960, pp. 118–29.

N. Tret'yakov, Freski Dionisiya (The frescoes of Dionisy), in *Tvorchestvo*, 1962 (9), pp. 13–16.

GLOSSARY

ACATHISTUS: (Greek); a liturgical hymn in honour of the Virgin; it is sung standing.

AL FRESCO: (Italian); term used by mural painters to describe the practice of painting on to plaster while it is still wet.

AMBO: a pulpit.

ANCHORITE: a devout and ascetic hermit.

ARCOSOLIUM: a niche for a tomb.

ARRICIO: (Italian); term used by mural painters to describe the first layer of plaster applied to the wall, which was roughened to provide a key for the subsequent layer.

ARTEL: (Russian); an association of artists working together; a 'workshop' or 'atelier.'

BASILEUS: (Greek); king or emperor.

BEMA: the area between the *Prothesis* and the *Diaconicon* in a Byzantine church; the equivalent to the chancel in a western church.

BOYAR: (Russian); a land-owning nobleman.

CHASUBLE: a sleeveless vestment worn by the celebrant when celebrating the Eucharist.

CONCH: the curved semi-dome surmounting the apse of a church.

DIACONICON: (Greek); a chamber south of the sanctuary in a Byzantine church, entered by a door in the *Iconostasis*.

DEESIS: a representation of Christ between the Virgin and St. John the Baptist, who intercede.

DOME: a circular vault, with a hemispherical surface on the inside.

DRUM: a hollow cylinder on which the *Dome* rests.

DRUZHINA: (Russian); a loose association of artists similar to an *Artel*.

ETIMASIA: (Greek); 'preparation', an empty throne symbolic of Christ in glory after the Resurrection.

EXEMPLUM: (Latin); a model or pattern from which a medieval artist worked.

GRAFFITO: writing on a wall done not at the time of the completion of the decoration, but subsequently.

GRAFYA: (Russian); lines scratched on damp plaster to guide the fresco painter.

HISTORIATED INITIAL: an initial in a manuscript, with figural decoration.

ICONOSTASIS: (Greek); a screen dividing the Eastern end of a Byzantine Church from the main area; it has entrances in it to the sanctuary, *Prothesis* and *Diaconicon* and is richly decorated with icons.

INTONACO: (Italian); term used by mural painters to describe the second layer of plaster applied over the *Arricio*.

KEYSTONE: the stone in the centre of the top of an arch which locks the whole structure when the scaffolding is removed.

LUNETTE: a flat segmental or semi-circular area produced by filling in the upper part of an arch.

MEDIATRIX: one who acts as a mediator.

MENOLOGY: Church's calendar arranged to commemorate the saints and martyrs.

METROPOLITAN: a bishop having authority over the bishops of a province, ranking in the Orthodox Church above an archbishop and below a patriarch.

NARTHEX: an antechamber to the main body of a church.

NIMBUS: a disk or aureole depicted behind the heads of figures of saints and members of the imperial family.

PANTOCRATOR: (Greek); a representation of Christ as the 'All-powerful'.

PARECCLESION: a side chapel.

PENDENTIVE: a curved triangular structure that enables a dome to be supported over a square or polygonal space.

PROTHESIS: (Greek); a chamber to the north of the sanctuary in a Byzantine church, opposite to the *Diaconicon*, in which the solemn preparation of the Eucharistic gifts takes place.

PROTO-EVANGELIUM: an apocryphal gospel.

ROTULUS: (Latin); a continuous strip, which can be rolled up, on which narrative scenes or writing can be depicted.

SILENTARIUS: a Byzantine court official.

SLAKED LIME: quicklime to which water has been added, to form calcium hydroxide.

STARETS: (Russian); a monk.

STYLITE: an ascetic hermit who lived on top of a column.

SYNOD: an ecclesiastical council.

TESSERA (*pl.* TESSERAE): small coloured glass cubes from which mosaics are formed.

TYMPANUM: the space between the lintel and the arch above a doorway.

VIRGIN ODIGETRIA: (Greek); 'showing the way'; a type of representation of the Virgin in which she points at the infant Christ.

VIRGIN ORANS: (Latin); a representation of the Virgin in which she has her hands raised in prayer.

ICONOGRAPHICAL INDEX

GENERAL INDEX

287

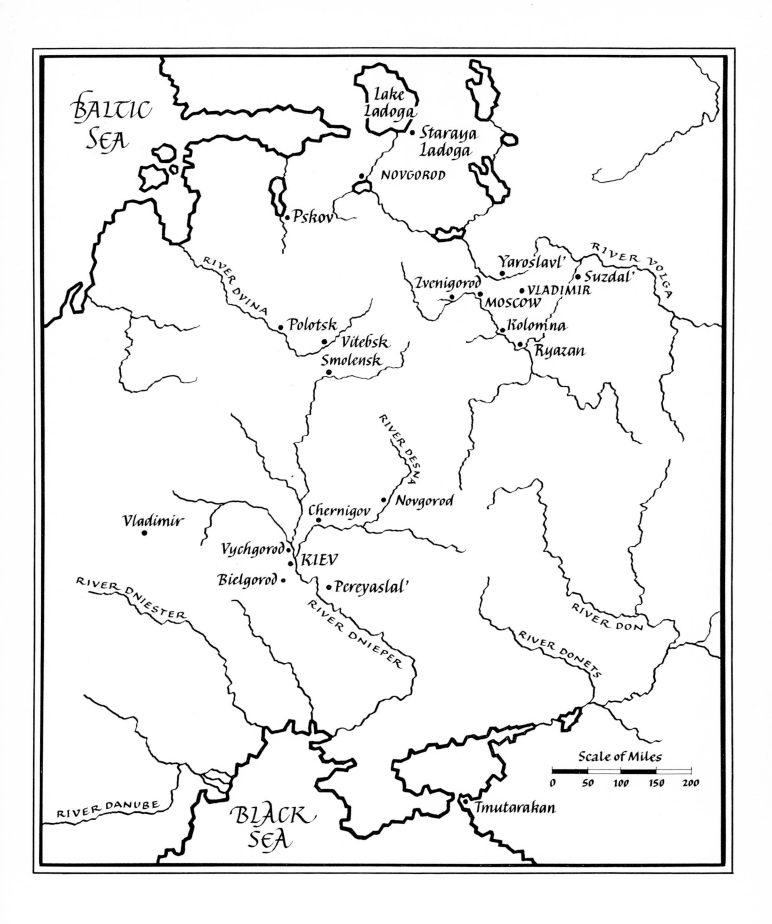